The
BAKER'S TRADE

The BAKER'S TRADE

A Recipe For Creating The Successful Small Bakery

Zachary Y. Schat

Acton Circle
Ukiah, California

The Baker's Trade: A Recipe for Creating the Successful Small Bakery

Published by: Acton Circle Publishing Company
                   P. O. Box 1564
                   Ukiah, California 95482
                   (707) 462-2103

Cover design by Jeanne H. Koelle, Koelle & Gillette. Illustrations by Irene Stein. Back cover photograph by Evan Johnson; cover photograph by Tom Anderson. Chapter opener illustration: *Bright wheat*, from *The Herbal, or General History of Plants,* by John Gerard, 1633.

Trademarked names are used throughout this book. Rather than put a trademark symbol at every occurrence of a trademarked name, we state that we are using the names in an editorial fashion and to the benefit of the trademark owner with no intention to infringe the trademark. No such use of any trademark or trade name is intended to connote an endorsement or other affiliation with the book.

Disclaimer

This book provides information about the subject matter covered. It is sold with the understanding that the publisher and author are not engaged in giving legal, accounting, or other professional services or advice in the book. A reader who requires legal or other expert assistance should seek the services of the appropriate competent professional.

---

10   9   8   7   6   5   4   3

Library of Congress Cataloging-in-Publication Data

Schat, Zachary Y., 1968-
     The baker's trade : a recipe for creating the successful small bakery / Zachary Y. Schat.
          p.   cm.
     Includes bibliographical references and index.
     ISBN 0-9639371-6-2
     1. Baked products industry—United States—Management.   2. Bakers and bakeries—United States.   I. Title.
HD9057.U59S365 1997
664'.752'068—dc21   97-19409
                                                                  CIP

IN APPRECIATION

This book was the joint effort of a lot of people whose assistance, kindness, and guidance I can hardly repay; but those I am happy to have this opportunity to thank are:

Carole Hester, Lila Lee, and Judy Pruden for their help in fixing the location of Laura Scudder's one-time restaurant here in Ukiah—

Dennis Wilson, publisher of *The Ukiah Daily Journal*, for letting us reprint Carole Hester's profile of Sunny Poeng's donut shop—

Everyone who was generous enough to take time out and tell about his or her bakery business: Mike Bielenberg of Mrs. Denson's Cookies, Muriel Glave of the Landmark Bakery, Bruce Hering and his daughter Ellen Hering of Bruce Bread, Chris Kump and Tim Bottom of Cafe Beaujolais and its Brickery, Jacquie Lee of the Garden Bakery, Paul Levitan of the Cheesecake Lady, Ken Moore of Moore's Flour Mill, Bakery & Deli, and Don Pittman for his account of the curriculum at the California Culinary Academy—

Evan Johnson who got us all to sit still for our picture longer than we thought we could, Jean Koelle for her cover design and graphic arts assistance, Irene Stein for her drawings, and Tom Anderson for editing the book—

The people who kindly reviewed my manuscript: Terry De Blasio of Main Street Wine and Cheese in Ukiah, Don Pittman at the Courthouse Bakery and Café, and Kathy Wallis in Napa—

My father Jack who taught me what an honest day's work meant, my mother Nancy Sue who by her example as much as anything taught me her skills of tact and diplomacy, my brother Brian for his patience in teaching me how to bake, and my sister Valerie Ketner just for being a sister to me, and—

Finally, I am grateful to the tireless staff at our downtown and home-improvement center shops, without whose steady support and irrepressible good humor this book, not to say the bakeries, would not have been possible.

CONTENTS

MANAGEMENT AND OPERATIONS

MONEY MATTERS

FOLLOWING THROUGH

INTRODUCTION

I'm a fifth-generation baker. I have a picture of my great-great-grandfather's bakery in Utrecht, Holland, which he started in 1846. It has always been passed on through the children—not necessarily the oldest or youngest, but somebody has always taken it. The building is still there, but the shop has grown into a huge corporate enterprise, Do Schat's Bakeries.

My dad moved here from Holland in 1950. After serving in the U.S. Army in Korea and Germany, he worked at a cousin's dairy in Orange County, California, until he got a job as a baker. He has owned and operated bakeries and restaurants—22 in all—since he was 27. Sometimes he had two or three of them at once, mostly on the Central California coast. Only one of them ever failed. That was when he first got successful and over-extended himself with an excess of vans and fancy equipment. Once he had the formula, though, he did very well at the business from then on.

Three months before I graduated from studies in communications and business economics at U.C. Santa Barbara he telephoned me. "I have an opportunity for you," he said. "I'll let you take over this bakery. Pay me as you go." For me that was a dream come true, something I had always wanted to do. I had grown up in bakeries and restaurants, and paid my way through college by working in one way or another at food service. You might say it's in the genes: I couldn't not be a baker. I was 22 years old and had $5,000 in the bank. I gave it to my dad and agreed to pay him the other $80,000 in installments. Then after I graduated I worked with him for three months, learning what I could about baking. It wasn't completely foreign to me, but suddenly becoming a baker, even after a lifelong exposure, is a bigger step than you might think. My older brother Brian was running an in-store bakery for a large supermarket in Washington state at the time, so I invited him down to be a partner. It wasn't until then that I really began to learn to bake. As the shop got busier I worked with him more and asked questions whenever I got the chance. Brian was a good baker and a good teacher, and it's important to learn from someone who is both a baker and a teacher. After two years I finally got to where I could consider myself a baker, too.

You never stop learning how to bake or run a bakery, even with several generations of the craft behind you. The Courthouse Bakery has not only taught me about baking but has provided a good living in the six years since we started it. This book is my chance to share with other bakers and prospective bakers what I've learned not only from the bakery but from 150 years of family experience.

—Z.Y.S

A First Glance

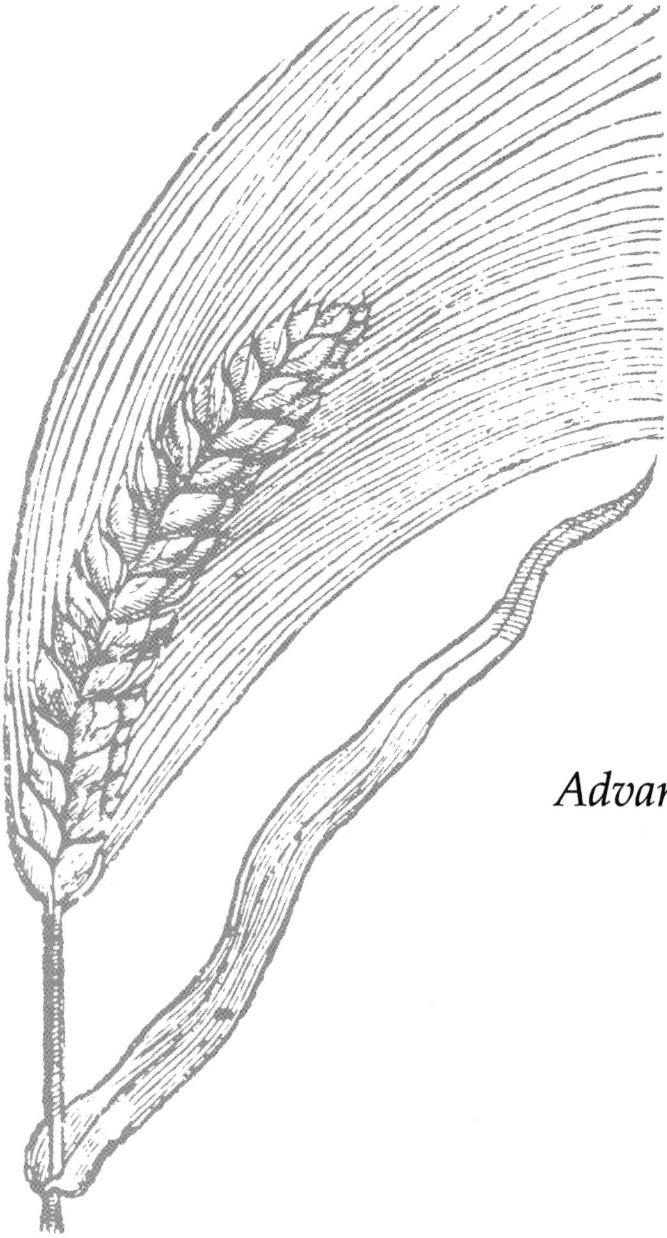

1

THE BAKER AND THE BAKERY

THE COURTHOUSE BAKERY is a snug little brick place built in 1898 on a side street across from the Mendocino County Courthouse in Ukiah, California. The bakery is old and far from ideal, but it has a prime location. My dad bought it in 1989 to set up a family member in the business. He had just retired and moved to Fort Bragg on the coast, 60 miles west of Ukiah. His last bakery, at Bishop, California, in the Sierras, was a corporate plant that wholesaled 25,000 loaves a day. He intended, after a successful career involving some 20 bakeries, to return to his roots and reacquaint himself with his passion for baking. His plan for the family member didn't fly, however, so he ended up driving to Ukiah at 2:30 every morning to run the bakery, then going back to Fort Bragg at 10 or 11.

I showed up as the bakery's new owner just before midnight on the 10th of January 1990 and went to work at 4 a.m. on the 11th, with no idea of what I was getting into. I had never laid eyes on the town or on this business that I just committed $85,000 to buy from my dad. Dad had been swinging it by himself for 12 months but he had to turn it over to a manager and counter help after he left every morning. It had acquired a small customer base but had not really taken off. With both of us there all the time and turning out a good product, business increased steadily that first year. It was a four-person shop. My dad's wife Chris was in charge of the books, personnel, and management in general. She gave me the one-week short course on payroll, daily receipts, and quarterlies, then said, "There you go"—I said, "No, you're kidding!"—and she was gone.

I got my older brother Brian, an accomplished baker up in Washington state, to join me, telling him that this was an opportunity and that we could pay Dad as we went. At first business was slow enough for Brian alone to bake. But soon we had a steady clientele of lawyers, bailiffs, judges, and county employees coming over for breakfast, coffee breaks, and lunch. Word got around, and our customer base began to grow. People would come for coffee, then stay for coffee and a roll, and keep coming back. Before long I was pitching in to help Brian and, after two years of working with him, managed to become a baker myself. We decided eventually, however, that we couldn't run a business together, and so we parted company.

There has always been a bakery on the site.* It was the "City Bakery" from 1899 until 1927 when a man named Herman Mattern built a wood-fired brick oven for it. Then it was the "Model Bakery" through two generations until 1980. The brick oven has long since disappeared, and after 1980 the shop changed hands several times. But the site of the old City and Model bakeries went into a decline and it didn't get going again until we acquired the building with its equipment for the Courthouse Bakery.

Sometimes when you walk into a business you can tell if it is doing well or poorly. You may have noticed it yourself. You go to a shop and everyone gives off an air of dejection or indifference and you sense that things will start to go wrong. There is no reason for that to happen in a bakery. The rules for running one can be learned, and you don't have to be a genius to do it well. You do have to know how to bake good products, market them well, and manage the business. And you have to like, or at least reconcile yourself to, hard work. If you don't like to work, don't go into the bakery business. It can be hard physical labor and it takes a lot out of you, but there are rewards for that hard work.

RETAIL BAKERIES TODAY

The *New York Times* reported in 1995 that just before World War One the United States had about 263 retail bakeries per million people. Then, as large commercial bakeries began to capture market share with the doughy white loaf that most Americans have grown up on, the number of small retail bakeries steadily declined. By the early 1990s there were only about 80 shops per million people. That trend appears to be reversing. *The Economist*, also reporting in 1995, noted that there were some 25,000 retail bakeries in the United States. It predicted, however, that by year's end 1,600 to 1,700 new bakeries would have opened. Many of them would be selling mostly bagels or other specialty baked goods. Recent growth has also come

---

* In 1915 Laura Scudder—a Philadelphian who arrived via Seattle and San Francisco—opened a restaurant next door to the bakery. There she cooked great chips and read her customers' law books for three years. In April 1918 she passed the California State Bar Exam and then moved with Mr. Scudder to Los Angeles where she went on to make culinary and corporate history.

from new chains, such as the Saint Louis Bread Company, Great Harvest Bread, and Baker's Place, which set up convenience outlets to sell fresh-baked sourdough, pumpernickel, and variety breads. Saint Louis Bread mixes and shapes its loaves by hand in central facilities for delivery to its stores. The stores bake them almost hourly.

Real bread—bread with good texture, plenty of flavor, and no preservatives—is gaining a new popularity and status. And although New Yorkers, San Franciscans, and the lucky inhabitants of a few other cities may take fresh bread from a good bakery for granted, people in most communities across the nation still lack access to the real thing. It's a luxury—one that most Americans haven't had in their diets for years. Better yet, it's a luxury that sells for well under $5.00.

A neighborhood shop's product, while not out of the oven hourly, is made on premises for its own market, and it can benefit from people's growing awareness that they can buy better baked goods than appear on supermarket shelves. The new chains with big advertising budgets and national name recognition may become formidable competition, but they will also do for bread and other bakery products what Starbuck's did for coffee. They'll stimulate a national appetite for and appreciation of quality baked goods. A small neighborhood shop will be able emulate or outdo the best of the chains. It can respond more quickly to the local market, and it can draw on centuries of baking traditions.

ADVANTAGES AND DISADVANTAGES

The chief attraction of the business is not monetary, although a well-run bakery can provide a very good living. It's the positive feeling you get when people come in and say, "That was the best loaf of bread I've ever had." It feels great, and it's why you keep putting out new products and trying to make them better. The second advantage is that you can write your own ticket. If you do a good job, there is money to be made and a potential for expansion. Finally, you are in charge. Your accomplishments and failures flow from your own drive and desire to succeed, and nobody else's.

The main disadvantage is how much more time and commitment owning and operating a bakery takes than a 9-to-5 job. The commonest complaint I hear from one baker after another is the lack of time to spend with family. Running a bakery solo would be an impossibility for a single parent who lacked a very close and strong family to take up the parenting slack or couldn't make other arrangements. You can't call in sick, either. Your employees will call in sick, and as often as not you'll have to fill in. Sometimes you will get exhausted with the work.

If you accept the responsibility of your own business, you have to keep up that responsibility every day. It's a responsibility not only for yourself but for the people you employ and the customers you serve. I don't consider responsibility a disadvantage, but it is something to think about. If you're not responsible in your job or can't pay your own bills on time, you can't expect to go into business and suddenly have things change.

Finally, the hallmark of the bakery business—I don't consider this a disadvantage either—is that you get up early. In fact, moving to a small town works out perfectly. One piece of good advice for a prospective baker is don't live where there are too many late-night distractions. For example, as luck would have it, I went from Santa Barbara, where I was up until 3:00 a.m. to Ukiah, where I get up at 3:00 a.m. It's a perfect environment for a baker because it offers plenty of afternoon and evening activities like going to the woods or boating. Then you can be in bed by eight or nine and not miss much. By 3:30 a.m. you're wide awake and the day is going. And that's great, because from 3:30 till noon, the hours move fast. Most people will only have had their first coffee break when a baker's shift is done. A bakery owner's day doesn't necessarily end at noon, but usually the baking does.

QUALITY CONTROL

As a baker you are a manufacturer as well as a retailer, or possibly a wholesaler or both, and you need a wide range of skills. Typically, small bakeries that produce mainly by hand with limited space and equipment will have very few wholesale accounts. If you can't produce in volume for wholesale accounts, you put out an excess of effort for very little return. To broaden your opportunities, however, you could select wholesale accounts that you know will represent your product well. One of ours is Angelo's Restaurant here in town. Angelo comes in every day to buy 15 loaves of bread, slices them, and presents the product as fresh bread. You'll want to be very careful to avoid retailers that may buy bread once a week and tell customers it's your bread when it's a week old.

Small bakeries make money selling retail. The retail market can provide a good living even though it means a heavy investment in labor and high-quality ingredients. Good ingredients are expensive, but a bakery's success has to be built on a clientele that appreciates good fresh food. Unless you want to court a fast-food crowd, you'll find that the principal joy of owning and operating a bakery is to have loyal customers who know good quality and will stand in line for it.

High quality also means that you won't be competing with the large commercial bakeries and supermarket shops. If their product has been in your pantry for two weeks and it doesn't mould, you have to wonder what's going into it. That's where the commercial product is inferior and no competition at all. In-store bakeries are called bake-off shops. They get most of their products frozen and have an immediate market because they're convenient and do a nice

The biggest problem is people are afraid to take a risk. If you're afraid to take risks you will always be working for somebody. That's the way it is. You have to say, Okay, I'm gonna do it; I'll take the risk. . . . You can lose everything, but you've gotta get away from that attitude of dependency that you are taught all the way through school. They don't teach independence. My dad always worked two jobs. So when it was time for me to do things like this, I was comfortable with it. Otherwise it's going to be tough. You can still do it but you'll have to deal with that horrible feeling of, Wow, what have I done?
—KEN MOORE
MOORE'S FLOUR MILL, BAKERY & DELI

job of presentation. Their product looks good; it looks appetizing. But when you bite into it you find the quality's not there.

Large commercial bakeries add conditioners to their dough to make it move faster. That way they can mix it, divide it, round it, and bake it after a very short proof (rising) time. But what makes bread good is time—time to let the yeast work and give it character and flavor and texture. That doesn't happen in an hour, so for a good product or a special event, people will continue go to a real bakery.

Your competition will be other small "scratch" bakeries. Since we've been here a few bakeries have come to town; so we saw the competition move to us, rather than the other way around. The first was a croissant shop on the other side of the courthouse. The owners were willing, hardworking, and enthusiastic, but were unprepared for the demands of running a bakery and had to close. Their location was equally as good as ours. They had the desire to succeed and an attractive shop, but they didn't make their goods from scratch. Lacking a mixer, they got frozen products from a reasonably good commercial bakery to put in their freezer, then thaw out, proof, and bake. In my experience you've got to complement your location. You can have a great location and a good potential market, but, if you can't respond with best products your market demands, your bakery will have to struggle against overwhelming odds.

Two years ago a new bakery opened around the corner. The owner is a fine, skilled baker, and she's going to succeed by putting out an excellent product for which she commands a good price. As you will see throughout this book there is an infinite variety of bakeries. Starting with a simple donut or cookie place, to a full-range shop, or an upscale boutique, you will find niches for different bakers in almost all markets. For example, one of my favorite books right now is *Bread Alone* by Daniel Leader and Judith Blahnik. It's about neither the craft nor the business of baking. It's about the *art* of baking. It describes getting the best brick-oven builder in Paris to build an old-world wood-fired oven, and then using the purest water, stone ground organic flours, and fine imported wild yeast cultures to bake original old peasant loaves that people will travel miles to get in wintry weather. It is a master text of the art.

Any good baker with experience, however, can do just fine. You learn as you go. My dad is a master baker. He's been doing it for 48 years, since he was 14, so my six or seven years can't even compare. He's faster and good at experimenting. But I can turn out a product that's equally as good as his. I've been fortunate enough to help pass the family knowledge on to somebody else. Much of baking is still self-taught or passed on from master to apprentice. In the end how you bake depends on the philosophy you bring to it. A baker can bake the most artful bread in four states, or make the best products possible in a full-scale shop, or find a comfortable life in a do-

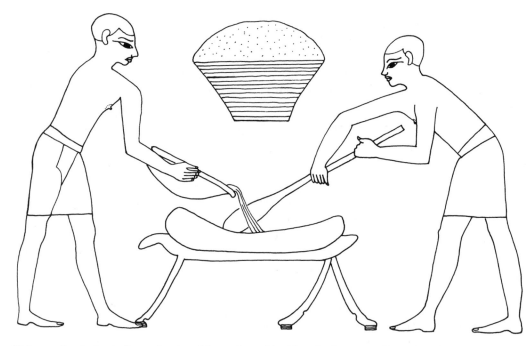

This earliest depiction of raised bread and baking is from an Egyptian tomb painting.

nut shop. You can "stack the product high and watch 'em buy," or you can put a fine scone here and a fine torte there and have people lined up outside the door. There are a few fundamentals that apply to all bakeries. We've touched on one or two. We will cover the rest as we go.

SKILL REQUIREMENTS

As with any new business, you have to think about rates of failure. Most people cite the Dun & Bradstreet figure that only one in five businesses survives its first five years. The Small Business Administration (SBA) is a little more optimistic. It notes that 77 percent survive the first three years and about a third get through the first five. More to the point, the National Restaurant Association estimates that there are close to half a million eating and drinking establishments in the country, and that 10 to 15 percent of them close their doors every year. Another survey estimates restaurant failure rates of 27 percent in the first year, 50 percent after three years, 60 percent after five, and the survival of only about 30 percent after ten years. The rate for bakeries may be lower because costs and prices are lower than for restaurants, and break-even is lower.

Even so, opening a bakery is not something to rush into without thinking it through and getting enough experience. The SBA report gave inexperience as the cause of most failures. Some people may make a good pie and decide they want to open a bakery. It's not that easy. Making the transition involves acquiring a wide range of new skills. There are, of course, exceptions even to this rule. Debbi Fields was a housewife who made delicious cookies, opened one

BREAD'S BEGINNINGS

People's teeth and stomachs were never made for a steady diet of grass seeds. Making them the staff of life took major steps: winnowing, grinding, and mixing with water, then baking to dry the wet, mealy seed-pies. Grain agriculture began in the Middle East where wild grass seeds fit for domestication and improvement—chiefly barley and wheat—grew best. The first ovens appeared in the Middle East at around 7000 B.C. Archaeologists have unearthed ovens from 5600 b.c. next to grain bins and grinding slabs both in Jericho and at Hacilar in Turkey

Wild yeast spores, a plentiful fungus in dusty air, will contaminate and sour a wet dough by fermenting it. Wheat dough's gluten is viscous enough to trap the fermentation's gas bubbles, which raise or leaven the dough. The original batch of raised bread was probably an accident. Somebody forgot about the dough; it went sour and puffy but into the oven anyway, and it made a nice surprise. It's been with us ever since. The essential step, however, was learning to use the sour dough from one batch to leaven the next.

By about 2600 B.C. ancient Egyptians, the world's first regular bread leaveners, were keeping stocks of sourdough starters to "inoculate" fresh doughs. As leavened bread became popular, wheat displaced barley as the main grain crop. A Metropolitan Museum of Art expedition of 1936 discovered several loaves of bread 35 centuries old in a tomb in the Asasif Valley, the site of the Ramesside temples. Some of the loaves resembled modern rye bread. One was like present-day honey bread, and another resembled plum pudding. Egyptian bakers developed over 50 kinds of bread, varying in shape and flavored with things such as poppy seeds, sesame seeds—even camphor. Egyptian royalty's bread was of finely sifted flour, but commoners ate rough flour with grit from the millstones that wore down their teeth.

Since Egyptians did not mint money until the Iron Age, the old kingdoms paid workers and officials in grain, bread, and beer. Money is still sometimes called "bread," just as "dough" and "breadwinner" are fairly common money terms.

shop, worked very hard at it, and built up a hugely successful business. She's written a book about it, *One Smart Cookie*, which we list in the appendix. Mrs. Fields Cookies gives first-rate customer service, and its single product won't break anybody's bank. Anyone can go through a mall and spend a dollar or two on cookies.

This exception has a qualification. If you plan to market one or two items, you have to sell wholesale or to a retail market big enough to let you specialize. Even then, the most important factor is still a strong grounding in both baking and business skills. If you start small like Mrs. Fields, with a good and appealing product already developed, you may be able to get enough business experience as you go. If you want to step into a full-scale bakery or anything like it, you had better get the experience first. Then, if you're good and you fill a market niche, you'll stay in business. Everybody has to eat, nobody likes to eat at home all the time, and anyone can afford a cup of coffee and a roll; so you don't have to be a bread baker to get by. You can buy donut dough from one of the large bakery suppliers. This is a town of about 15,000 people, and it supports three or four donut shops; so we don't even bother with donuts.

Usually you learn by working for someone. I employ a young man, Chris Pittman, who is my head baker now. He started at the Courthouse Bakery as a dish washer when he was 19 years old. He was one of those people who you know will be around for awhile. He's a company man, and that's a compliment, because he will do anything for the shop. He concentrates on what he's doing and he cares about the business. He was good with customers; so he went from washing dishes to working at the counter. Then we got so busy there was too much for just my brother and me to bake. We got him to help mix muffins, doughs, and the rest of the product. While he was mixing our doughs we would explain what the processes meant. What yeast does to dough. What salt does. What happens when you don't put salt in the dough. You make your share of mistakes when you first start as a baker's apprentice. There are so many distractions in a bakery—people yelling your name, noise and clatter—that you're always looking around as you're following the formula for what goes in the dough. If you skip one line—just one line—it can ruin the entire batch. We've had to throw two- and three-hundred-pound doughs away; those are major costs. We all still make mistakes, but any bakery worth the name will refuse to market a product one day that isn't as good as the day before's.

Chris worked his way up. After a while he was not just mixing, he was rolling doughs on the bench. Then he was baking. When my brother and I decided we couldn't continue to work together, I sent Chris to work at my dad's bakery in Fort Bragg for three months. My dad is a drill sergeant when it comes to working. You don't talk or anything; you work and you concentrate—hard. Chris came back with a new appreciation of the work and he's my head baker now. He's 22 years old and he's every bit as accomplished as I am.

Just recently the bakery was lucky enough to acquire a baker from the California Culinary Academy in San Francisco, one of the country's foremost cooking schools. Don Pittman, Chris's dad, was 48 years old when his employer, the local Blue Shield office, closed down. The county job-retraining agency agreed to sponsor him at CCA's pastry-chef course. Since his return we've been able to watch over his shoulder and get an idea of some pretty high-class baking.

Regardless of the style of baking, you need hands-on experience. You need to work or have worked in a bakery and have a good grasp of production. And you have to give more than you will get in immediate return. It means staying after hours, if necessary, to learn all the jobs and it means being a good company man or woman. This is an old-fashioned trade in many ways, and bakers work a long time to learn the craft. Their recipes—like ours, which have been in the family for generations—are not the kind of trade secrets they give away.* Even today, with excellent baking schools available both here and abroad, there is nothing to prepare you like baking in a commercial environment. And then the gap between being an employee and running your own shop can be pretty intimidating. It's a gap we hope to help bridge.

The other requirement is to get the financing you need to start the business. You have to take a hard look at your plans and consider how much you will risk, not only of your own money but other people's, too. Chances are you won't have enough to start up on your own; so you have to find sources of financing and analyze your venture's risks and potential return. If you're experienced and research the market, you can greatly improve your chances of success. Start-up tasks and costs mount quickly, and you have to be the kind of person who can cope with the burdens of opening then operating the bakery.

PERSONAL REQUIREMENTS

First, you need to be decisive and able to deal with the fall-out from every decision you make. In a way that's the best part of decision-making, because once you've made a decision you only have to react to the consequences. That's true for big decisions and little ones, like whether to put caramel in something or not. Things like that are so minor that they may seem insignificant but they are not, and you have to be decisive, always.

Most beginners balk at making decisions. I had that problem, so did Chris. We are afraid at first to change the formula or process. You have to make decisions continually as you're baking. For example, bagel dough has to be really cold. If it's too warm in the mixing process, it won't get a good kick or spring in the oven—that final big rise before the heat stops the yeast activity. You have to decide when to cool the dough by putting ice in the water and then do it. That's the line between learning and being a baker. Our bagels had been coming out small for three or four days. Having been through the same school, I mentioned the small bagels to Chris. Then I took him aside, as I had been, and said of the bakery—the production area—"This is our house. The product that goes out of here is ours. Whether you I or make it, it's our responsibility, because we're the only people to answer for a batch and we have to make the decisions." He's a first rate baker now and he makes those decisions, but how's that for harsh and old fashioned? Well, a baker just cannot afford to praise the staff for anything except succeeding, because a bakery with a product that's only a "nice try" won't stay in business long.

---

* You'll find a few of our recipes in this book, but the editor had a tough time prying them loose.

You also need flexibility because every day will present a challenge. That's the greatest thing about being in business for yourself, it's never the same twice. There are bad days, too, days when you just want to sell it. I've put the bakery up for sale three times in six years. I've listed it twice, mainly because of problems with my brother. It could happen to anybody: You just say, I am not going to deal with this anymore. And there is always plenty to deal with. It could be a bad storm, that puts your electricity out while you have $400 of product in your oven, or your antiquated equipment fails. You learn to scramble and make the best of it. In a recent winter's storm we had taken the product out of the oven just when the electricity went out. We brewed coffee campfire-style on the gas stove. We put candles on our tables in front, and, when the electricity came on two hours later, were one of the few shops that got it. Business was fantastic. We stuck it out, gave it an effort, and our big crisis turned into an opportunity. It doesn't always, but you have to learn to roll with whatever comes along.

You have to be flexible also because when you run your own shop you do everything. For example, you become a real estate operator. Every business has to be somewhere. You can't avoid being in real estate; so you should make the most of it. You also have to do all of the ordering, all of the pricing, and be a bookkeeper in the sense that, if you're a small business operator, you are the only one who should handle the money. Your daily reports will probably go to a bookkeeper every month in order to get your quarterlies ready, but all the rest will be an on-site job.

As boss you are also next in line for everything else. It's one of the hallmarks of running your own business. When it has to be done and there is no one else to do it, then you're the man, or the woman. When the dish washer doesn't show up and you can't find anyone else to cover, you don't take someone from his or her position and say, "You aren't a salesperson or cook anymore today; you're the dish washer and I'll be doing your job." *You* are the dish washer that day. So you wear a score of different coats. And this is just a brief list of all you have to do. What it comes to again is being the decision maker. You've got to make the decision about every aspect of every question that comes to your table—and there is no shortage of them.

If you serve the public, you must have a positive personality. You can't dislike your job, and you can't have help that doesn't like their job. Everybody in customer service gets burned out waiting on people, but you have to greet customers with a smile. If you like people and like to talk to them about your mutual interests, you will get over the tough days just by being yourself and enjoying what your customers have to offer.

My daughter Ellen has been in contact with Café Beaujolais quite a bit. I did a lot of work on the whole grain bread, but Ellen has developed a French bread, and all these new kinds of breads we have. We have a fougasse, an olive bread, a blue cheese—that was her invention. Our output has changed in 10 years. It used to be all whole-grain, but we've found now that French bread is more than 50 percent of our business. I'm not sure if tastes are changing or if we're just reaching more people.
—BRUCE HERING
BRUCE BREAD

You get to know people. We have a manager up front named Fred Mendez, who seems to know everybody in town by first name. He's been in retail for 15 years. Everybody knows Freddy and everybody loves him. It's a great attribute to have and it helps create the atmosphere we need. When people come into the bakery it's not our bakery it's their bakery. It's the town's bakery, and if you see it whenever it's crowded you can tell that people just hang out here. They're as comfortable as they are at home. Your customers have to know they can serve themselves and that you'll work with them. That has to flow from your sense of what will make your customers feel comfortable. It's the fresh product. It's the "Hello, how're you doing?" There are little intricacies, things you say or do, that help to create a pleasurable experience.

You also need self-confidence. Once you have the experience, it's easy to be self-confident in your product and in your own environment. You will never worry about a loaf of bread you sell because you'll know it's good. There are so many different tasks you need to do, however, that sometimes you'll find yourself out of your element and the confidence melts away. Recently we got involved in planning for a second shop at the local branch of a regional home-improvement store. Many of the men and women in it were planners, consumer-price-index readers, preoccupied with things a baker doesn't usually deal with. It's hard to stay confident in so different a realm. You can be the expert, however, when it comes to determining what baked items to provide and how to set up the shop. That's the core of experience on which you can build your confidence.

You must be able to administer and delegate. If you use your knowledge of bakeries and your product, and lead by example, it doesn't matter how old you are. If you administer fairly and teach your staff, you'll earn their respect and support, and they will rely on your experience. It helps to think of the job in a team fashion and to try to foster a kind of unity or chemistry. Since retail bakeries usually can't pay much, they must often employ people who are working to get by until something better comes along. It makes for a high employee turnover, and there is constantly a new team. You'll have to make a commitment and be personally involved with your people to keep the team spirit flowing.

You need to be healthy and energetic. This is a very physical job. If you bake by hand, you need a strong back and plenty of stamina. If you want to go into the bakery business after spending your whole career into middle age sitting at a desk, get ready for physical labor. This is not white-collar work. It's blue-collar work. Even if on the outside you project a different image—you're a manager, an organizer, the owner—it's still blue-collar work, and you'll be on your feet all day. If you get a chance to see my dad, you'll see real baker muscles at work. He's 62 and he's still the strongest guy I know. He'll crush my hand, and I have a pretty good grip.

You have to handle limited amounts of sleep. Many bakers are five-hour-, six-hour-a-night people, and do fine with that. Through the holidays it's two hours or three hours a night. There will be a stretch before Christmas when the entire week gets frantic, not only with the increased special orders, but getting ready for the day before Christmas, Christmas Eve. You'll end up working nearly around the clock. You go in at 3:00 in the morning and finish late in the afternoon. Then there are all those other coats an owner wears: paperwork, decision-making, scheduling, and keeping that happy face. Then it's home for dinner, to bed by ten o'clock, and up again by two. By the last couple of days it's home at midnight and up at one. It can be crazy; but it's also the heart of the business and it can be exhilarating.

You won't think of money in the bakery as your money. It's a material you use to buy more product or put into the business. People here seem to appreciate how different the bakery looks from when we first took over. You will constantly make little improvements: a new façade, a bigger product line, more equipment to help add more products. Money is just a commodity. There's never a day when you say, Wow! I'm going to take $10,000 and stick it in my pocket. It constantly rolls over. Today you might be overdrawn $2,000, tomorrow you might be $20,000 ahead. It's never stable. Just like the flour and the salt, it comes and it goes.

WHERE IT TAKES YOU

Many in the business feel that the ideal small bakery today is the bakery-café combination. Sandwiches on fresh-baked bread go together. It's automatic and it seems to do well. We'll stress the bakery and café or deli combination because that's how we operate and it's a natural if you concentrate on baking bread. One drawback is that, like restaurants, the pace is faster and the stress is higher than running a bakery business alone.

As we'll show, bakery's product mix and its approach are limited only by the baker's imagination; and that opens a fair range of possibilities. If you want a slower pace and think that a bakery alone can make it in your market, or, if you want to start off with a bakery and diversify later, you'll find those strategies in the pages that follow.

Personal Inventory - Your Idealized Bakery

Personal inventory and goals
___ You know what you want out of the business
___ You know the kind of baking you do best
___ You are a risk taker
___ You are healthy & energetic
___ You are an organizer
___ You like working with people
___ You can give the business the time it takes to succeed
___ You know good food and can produce it
___ You have or can acquire the other necessary skills
___ You can raise the capital to start the business
___ Money for you is just a means to build the business

Product line and menu
___ Consider the market niche you plan to fill
___ Select which of your products best suit the location
___ Choose a full range or specialized bakery (donuts, cookies, bread)
___ Estimate the potential for future growth

Retail/wholesale
___ Retail
   ___ Take-out
   ___ Café/deli combination
___ Wholesale
   ___ Local specialty stores, cafés, and restaurants
   ___ Regional and national sales

2

THE DAILY BREAD, CAKES, DANISH. . . .

Nowadays the Courthouse Bakery gets going at 2:00 a.m. That's an hour and a half earlier than we used to start, because baking for our new branch requires more production time, and we've stretched our hours. Chris Pittman and I are the main bakers. Chris and I work well enough as a team now to dispense with a third baker—unless by Thursday or Friday we're so weary we want to bring in an apprentice to mix the next day's product. Chris works five, sometimes six, days a week and, as the first baker on, he's there at 2:00. I'm the second on and try to arrive at 3:30. My alarm usually goes off an hour before that, but I'm the snooze king and need a long start. Chris says his alarm starts to go off at 1:10. Most bakers, unless they have the knack of waking up early, seem to be pretty good at snoozing. Getting up that early every day is a great source of baker's humor. When I do get up I take a four-minute shower, put on my whites and I'm at work in five minutes. We're lucky enough to have a climate in which for most of the year our whites consist of a white baking shirt or shop shirt, a pair of white shorts, white socks, white shoes, and that's about it.

A DAY AT THE BAKERY

The first thing we do after going through the front door is walk to the rear of the bakery, turn on the rear lights, and flip on the switch for the oven. The oven dates from 1946 and takes about 45 minutes to an hour to heat up. Our first baking temperature is about 375°. The oven is well insulated and retains quite a bit of heat, and, since we're open consecutively every day but Sunday, it will still be about 150° if it was 375° at the end of the day before.

Those first few hours, from 2:00 to 5:30 a.m., are strictly production time. Chris starts by consulting the master bake sheet. We bake about the same thing every day, with variations, and the master bake sheet tells how many of what we will bake each day. At around closing the day before, we will have collected the day's special orders to add the sheet. For example, the local Masonite factory may want 60 extra danish. So, if we make eight or 10 dozen danish in a normal day, but we have an order for an additional five dozen, we'll make 15 dozen of them. After combining orders, we'll do a quick check of what's left over in the cases up front, so that we don't make a whole new batch of the excess and end up throwing away the day-old products.

After Chris has checked the master bake sheet he'll prep certain items for that day's production by hand rolling bagels or mixing the muffins—fast and easy stuff. But first he'll raid the freezer and get out our frozen bagel, scone, and specialty-bread doughs. We always offer specialty breads but don't make dough for them every day. For example, we sell fresh rye bread every day but we'll mix the dough for 30 to 40 loaves on Monday. We might bake off 12 loaves on Monday and put the other 20 or 30 in the freezer. Freezing doesn't hurt unbaked dough at all. It actually helps to develop the bread by letting it sour a little more. We pull these frozen doughs no later than 4:00 a.m. and put them out to defrost slowly. When they reach room temperature we can separate them a little, then pan and slide them into the proof box.

We have to do everything time-consuming, like the danish and croissant doughs, ahead of time or we'll get buried. We'll often bake off all our birthday cakes or other dessert-case items a day ahead of time. We refrigerate or freeze them partly because they're easier to decorate when they're a little stiff. Occasionally we're tempted to put off prep until the next morning, but then instead of starting at 2:00 Chris has to get there at 1:00, and I have to show up at 2:30. Then it's, Oh man, what am I doing here, why didn't we just prep it yesterday?

After Chris pulls the doughs out of the freezer he'll go to the retarder. A refrigerator is called a "retarder" in the baking industry because it slows down the rising process. He'll take out three pieces of danish dough that we've rolled in with butter and shortening,* and one piece that hasn't been rolled in with anything. We will have made them the day before, then frozen them that morning and put in the refrigerator that night. He'll also take out our defrosted croissant dough. We make a big batch of croissant dough and freeze it about every three days. If we forget to pull the danish or croissant

---

* It isn't always pure butter. Every good baker uses the best ingredients, but the economics of each baker's market determines what "best" is. See Trends and Markets, below.

doughs the night before, we'll have rock-hard lumps that would have to sit out for five or six hours, by which time breakfast will have come and gone.

When I arrive, at 3:30 or 4:00, Chris has finished or almost finished the croissant and danish dough, and is starting to mix the bread doughs. Chris loves to work to country music. I don't; so I go back, and I turn it off and turn on the big stereo up front to a rock and roll station as loud as it'll go. (Sorry, Chris.) That gets me going a little. I turn on the espresso machine first thing because it takes 15 minutes to warm up, and we like to have it going in case we get an early-bird customer. Next I start a pot of coffee because I enjoy an early cup, and it's necessary. We don't turn on the lights over the seating area, because we don't want people to think we're open at 3:30 in the morning. We keep the door locked while we're involved in production and usually unlock it by 4:30 or 4:45. There's a short time, too, when a few reprobates who haven't found their way home from the bar may still be hanging around downtown.

Before I get involved in production I'll go back and take the money out of the safe to count out a till for the register. One of our counter people puts the money in the safe at the end of the day. We use a $250 till every day. Then I'll either help Chris finish up the danish dough, get to work on the muffins, or boil the bagels. Once Chris finishes the danish dough, he mixes the bread doughs for that day.

I take over the oven at that point, too. While Chris concentrates on mixing bread doughs, I make sure that all the danish dough he's been at all morning gets proofed and put in the oven. We don't turn on the proof box until we put in the first items. By this time, 4:30, Chris and I are working at full speed. He's mixing bread doughs, I'm finishing up the danish dough.

Fred Mendez, the counter manager, is scheduled to arrive at 6:00 but he's always there about a half hour early, at 5:30. He'll turn on the lights up front and put out the coffee at the coffee service station. Everything's ready to go at 5:30. We make sure that the tables are straightened out, and that the coffee station has everything our early customers want. With a fresh pot of coffee out, we light up show cases and switch on the soft music.

We hit the open sign when we turn on the lights up front. As soon as the lights go on we unlock the doors. We usually get our first customers between 5:30 and 6:00. It's the same group of guys—contractors and utilities crews—almost every morning. They all buy their own paper and have a cup of coffee. The bakery's a hangout for them. We kid around, tell jokes, roll dice for coffee, and have a pretty good time. Some customers will show up while it's still dark up front. They're locals who know we're there and that coffee's brewing. They may be going out of town or need a cup of coffee at 5:00 a.m.; so if they want to they can come in to help themselves, and we'll ring them in for a dollar. It's a small-town mentality. You don't say, "Hey, we don't open until 6:00—wait outside till we open the doors." We've had people pounding on them at 4:00 or 4:30 with "I need a cup of coffee, man!"

Our early danish is the first out of the oven at 5:45. All the muffins come out by 6:00. We like our cases full and ready to go by 6:30 with our early-morning products, the bagels, the croissants, the danish, maybe the early sourdough breads—a little of everything—so that the morning crowd can get what they want. At 5:30 in the morning it's more likely to be a hot ham-and-cheese croissant or a fresh cinnamon roll than a loaf of sourdough bread.

Our first cook shows up at 5:45. I should say our first "all around person," because our cooks take care of just about everything. Each is our sixth player off the bench when we need one at the counter or nearly anywhere else in the bakery. The second cook shows up at 6:15. When they walk in, all our early morning product is stacked up in racks right in their faces. It surrounds their work area. There will be about five racks of danish, muffins, bagels, croissants, and scones. The cooks' job is to take them off the baking pans, pack the product for our second shop in large brown transit racks, and stock the front area. They put the product in baskets, load the showcases, tilt it forward, merchandise it. They're in charge of all the merchandising up front for that initial rush of items. A few of our morning deliveries are for standing orders. When the cooks come in, they not only pack the orders for our Courthouse shop, the satellite shop, and our regular deliveries, they have to pack and prepare all of our early special orders. They're flying from the time they arrive at 5:45 a.m. until about 6:45 to empty all those racks. Delivering to our other shop by 7:00 a.m. means leaving downtown by 6:45. It's a real crunch time.

We leave all the special order sheets laying on the cooks' bench or taped all the way across the shelf over the bench. We tape up only the orders to be filled from the morning racks, but the cooks are responsible not only for danish, muffin, or croissant orders but also for whatever they fill from their section, like quiche and pizza. They lay out the right size pink boxes next to the special orders. For three dozen danish, they'll use a full-sheet box and put the order inside the box as they clear the racks. They keep laying product in the box until they've filled the order. Then they put on a top, tape the order on it, and send it out front. It's ready to go when customers show up at 6:30 or 7:00 a.m. to pick up their order.

For the rest of the day, the cooks get down to cooking, and the packing falls on our counter personnel, of whom we eventually have three or four. To avoid waste, the first cook, our kitchen manager, will inventory what was left over from the day before. If we served only half of our vegetable soup, it will become vegetable-beef today. That's important in a café. You don't want to serve anything that's

too old, but with a little creativity you can turn a product into a different item every day until you run it out and still keep the quality high, like a good French *pot au feu*.

The cooks always prep their meats and cheeses on a two-day schedule. They'll slice enough cheese on Monday for Monday and Tuesday. On Tuesday they'll slice enough to get them through Wednesday. Slicing the meats and cheeses a day ahead also gives us an idea of how much we'll go through in that time.

Between 7:00 and 10:00 o'clock the next wave of product will be five or six racks of bread. Freddy and our early counter people, who arrive at 7:15 and about 10:00, unload the racks. As they take out each bread variety, they check for orders, and if there are none they split the product between the two shops as the cooks did earlier.

All this time Chris and I are barreling along, baking bread and putting it in racks for somebody to take out front. Usually we have four or five doughs going at once. Depending on the size of the day's production, we'll keep baking breads until about 11:00 or 11:30, and do cookies until 2:00 p.m. There will be racks and racks of bread. If it sits in the rack too long, that's when I yell at the sixth player, "Hey, Julie, can you just get this bread out for me?" My dad had always yelled—and I remember this as a kid—"Hey, I can't sell it back here!" He was right. If it's in the back and people can't see it, you can't sell it. So I have this annoying habit of yelling from my work area, "We can't sell the bread back here!" Instantly that sixth player usually drops the knife and comes over and starts unloading the racks. Or the counter personnel will come get it. They're all at their own jobs, and getting the product out isn't automatic. The bread racks get pushed out of the way and out of mind. Sometimes just for fun I'll see one of the counter people and say, "Gee, look at all this bread around here, do you think we ought to put it on a day-old sale?" And they say, "It's not day-old," and I'll say, "Well, you'd think so, it's been back here so long." It's a little better than growling, "Get the bread out!" They're used to me, anyhow.

I like to be the guy who ices the product, mainly because I can inspect every piece that goes out. If I don't like it—if it's over-baked, if it's too small—I throw it out or put a special on it. Many restaurant managers will be the "expeditor," the person who takes the food from the kitchen and puts it on a tray for the server. That way they inspect all the food. That's a little of my role in the morning too, to see if it's burned or if it's perfect. If it's perfect, I try to tell whoever made it that the product looks great today. People who check the product should compliment the staff when it's good at least as often as criticizing when it is not. For some of us that's hard to learn and easy to forget.

With the arrival of our 7:15 a.m. counter person, there are two cooks and two of us bakers on the job. It's a good time to give everyone the order of march for the day: things to work on, products to push, items to sample out that day, and to decide about running a special if we have too many leftovers. We always sell at a reduced price when products are a day old. We sell nothing two days old. And we always let the public know it's a day old.

If we have a ton of product left, I'll tell everyone we'll run, say, sheepherder bread, one loaf for $1.75 and 99¢ for the second. We have to deal with little fluctuations, but very rarely do we increase a product's price. If the bear claws came out too small that day, we'll knock them down from $1.20 to $1.00 for the day. If the scones are huge today, we may be tempted to charge $1.00 instead of 85¢, but I don't think we ever increased a product's price if we made it too big. If you reduce it 15¢, no one complains because it's cheaper. If it's more expensive, it stands right out, and every customer notices.

If there's a sixth player on the team, there's also a seventh and that's our dish washer/janitor. When the cooks are up to their elbows and the counter is swamped, we'll have the dish washer get the bread out. The dish washer is also responsible for all the trash runs and for loading the truck with our deliveries. So "dish washer" may be the title, but the job is a "go-fer's" and absolutely essential. It's easier to deal with a no-show-counter-person problem than a no-show-dish-washer problem.

The dish washer shows up at 8:30 a.m. for what we would hope was an eight-hour shift, from 8:30 to 4:30. But with our current production, the dish washer puts in nine or nine and a half hours, and we pay overtime for it on a daily basis. When the dish washer arrives not only are there dishes left over from whatever happened after 4:30 or 5:00 the night before, but all the morning cups, plates, and silverware are waiting. And we've used 50 percent of the baking utensils for the day. That includes most of our big mixing bowls, all of our hooks, and all of our muffin pans. The dish washer walks into a six-foot pile of dirty dishes every morning. And there is a list of things to do besides. The most important are, One, to clean the rest room and, Two, to give the whole bakery production area a thorough sweep-down. I usually try to sweep it once or twice before the dish washer arrives, but so much flour accumulates in a bakery that we have to sweep all the time.

By 8:30 the morning crew is about complete. At 9:30 or 10:00 o'clock one more counter person comes in for the rush when the bank and courthouse people have their coffee breaks. The new arrival can help wait on customers and get the bread out. That's our plan, anyway, to get the bread out and set up for lunch.

At 10:00 o'clock we make our second delivery: bread to restaurants, sandwiches to the surgery center, and perhaps cookies and bread to the home-improvement center store. These deliveries take the better part of an hour, because I like to go to the other shop, unload, and check the cases. If we've had a very busy morning down-

I talked to other bakers around northern California and some farther away, for suggestions or advice. Some were very helpful and open. A few of them were very secretive, and I thought that was funny because if you take the same sourdough recipe and bake it in Ukiah or New York it's going to come out differently. . . . I'll qualify that: we do have one recipe, the Austrian Sunflower bread, that we don't give out because we decided we would feel terrible if someone ended up mass-marketing it.

—Christopher Kump
Cafe Beaujolais, The Brickery

town but it's been slow over there, I'll pack up two-dozen danish and bring them back to the courthouse shop. I get back around 11:00. By then Chris has already put in close to nine hours.

Our pastry chef, Don Pittman, comes in at 9:30. He's another all-around employee, not just a pastry chef. He may get involved in packing for the 10:00 o'clock delivery or helping people up front. If I'm out on deliveries, he'll help Chris mix cookies or set up pans for baking cakes.

Everyone here does more than what's in his or her job description. It's a lesson that our new people get in a hurry. Unfortunately, there's no way to ease the workload without adding two or three more employees. But, because we're committed to pay for the new place in two years, our loan payment precludes spending more for help. When the loan is paid, can hire extra people and get everything back to normal. Meanwhile, we all grit our teeth and put in the extra hours and effort. The current schedule would be impossible, of course, without a hardworking and very supportive staff.

Unless Chris has too much work left to handle alone, I'll leave the baking area and go to the lunch line at 11:00 to be sure the cooks are set up. Since they're the sixth players, however, they're always behind. We are seldom ready at 11:00; so the three of us usually do extra prep between 11:00 and noon, while we're also serving lunches. . . . It can get hectic.

At around 11:00 we have six or seven people on the clock in a pretty small area. There's a pile of dishes; there are racks everywhere. It's almost like being in a stockyard, like a bunch of cattle running around. By 11:00 we've emptied all the racks. Our production baking for the day is done, save for the cookies. Any baking after 10:30 or 11:00 is usually for the next day's production, things like mixing bagels or scones. If I'm not helping Chris, I'm on the lunch line. If it's very busy, I'll be there from 11:00 until 1:00 or 1:30.

We also have an 11:00 o'clock counter person who comes in for the lunch rush. Although it's usually less frantic between 11:00 and noon, the extra person can cover everyone for a break, which is very important. A food-service business like this is a tough one in which to take breaks, because peak activity times are hit and miss. Sometimes the peak is at 11:15, sometimes it's at 12:15 or even 1:15. You never know but you have to be there. Whoever is on break when a line forms invariably gets up to help out. It's not like an office job or even many retail jobs where you can get away for a little peace of mind for 10 or 15 minutes. I have never worked in a restaurant or café when there seemed to be a moment when you were definitely on break. You take it and hope you'll get your 10 or 15 minutes, but you're always looking up to see if the shop needs help.

We do lunches until 2:00 p.m. Between 1:30 and 2:30 five people—including Freddy, our early counter people, and the cooks—will come off the clock. The cooks start their clean-up at around 1:30

by packing up the dressings, sealing the lettuces, and making necessary wipe-downs of their equipment so that both of them can leave at around 2:30. All who are left by 2:30 or 3:00 o'clock are the later arriving counter people, Don Pittman decorating cakes and filling the pastry case for both places, and the dish washer. Up front, after the lunch crowd thins out, we concentrate on what we call "marrying the product." Instead of having three pieces of danish on one pan and three on another, we'll fill one pan with six. Our counter staff will do this with all the product to make whatever is left over look more plentiful than it is. Before the early people can clock out they make sure the tables are wiped down and that the product is married, so that the two closing people won't be so overwhelmed with side work that they can't leave on time. We close at 6:00 and want everyone out of there by 6:15 or 6:30 p.m.

A baker's day that begins at 3:00 or 3:30 is usually done at 11:00 or 11:30. And even with our current routine Chris should be able to quit at noon, after 10 hours. Lately, however, because we've been so busy, he doesn't get away until 12:30 or 1:00 p.m. At 1:30 I usually grab something to eat. From 3:30 a.m. till then there are not many sit-down breaks. Sometimes I have a quick bowl of cereal while working at the bench. Chris does about the same. Lately he's been able to go to the office and take up to half an hour's break. Working such long hours, it's the least we can give the guy. When I stop to eat at 1:30, I go to back the office, and start to go through the pile of papers and telephone messages that land on my desk every day. I won't take most phone calls while I'm baking, although I'll answer if it's an order or something of immediate importance. I usually try to answer the rest after 2:00 p.m. That's also when I sit down, grab the daily planner, and note that I have to make the deposits, pay bills, make sure taxes are paid, and perhaps deliver a cake to the other shop by 3:30. Without the list—even with it sometimes—it's impossible to keep up. After making the bank deposit, I go through everything in the checklist. Some things get put off and written in for the next day. While I'm in the office, phone calls are coming in, I'm calling back on messages, and time just flies. The hours from 2:00 to 4:00 can go by without anything on the list getting done. The paperwork on the desk alone can take up the whole two hours.

On Monday, Tuesday, and Wednesday we do most of our ordering for the end of that week and the next week. We don't have a back door for deliveries. Supplies unfortunately come to the front door. That's pretty uncommon; most locations have a back door. It doesn't matter; we do whatever is easiest for the supplier. We aren't sticklers about when the truck shows up. All we ask is that our suppliers try to miss the lunch rush. Fortunately, most of them follow a set schedule. We get produce deliveries Monday, Wednesday, and Friday. That means that we have to place a produce order a day

The Landmark Bakery is a full-range scratch bakery in a busy shopping center that is anchored by a chain supermarket. It has been in that location for about 10 years and enjoys a devoted and growing customer base. Besides drawing customers from supermarket shoppers, the bakery is at a major intersection and attracts an ample drive-by trade. Landmark partner Muriel Glave says of her bakery experience:

"I'm a business accountant. My mother, Geraldine Armond, is my partner. She's had restaurant jobs all her life. I love bookkeeping but I hate taxes. I had done books for this place when the original baker ran it. Two women acquired it from him but only ran it for two years. By then I was very tired of tax season and tired of seeing my mother working all those restaurant jobs with nothing to show for it but wages. When this place came up for sale, I figured it might offer a change for me and an opportunity for her not to work so hard.

"Anyone who wants to buy a business should really look the books over. And you do need a plan before going to the bank. You've got to show where you can change things to make them more profitable, and tell the banker: 'This is what the numbers are; these are my proposed changes.' Since the Landmark had 20 years behind it, and a good reputation with the numbers to show it, that was no problem for the bank. The problem was, what could I possibly know about baking?

**The Landmark Bakery
601 South Main Street
Willits, California**

"The prior owners had agreed to give us 30 days' in-house training. My mother was to be the baker, starting with donut frying. I began with the management and all the prep work for the baker. I was the guy that gets to make all the mixes for the cookies and the muffins, while the baker gets all the glory. When I saw that I decided to become the baker." *Armond preferred customer contact, and, since Glave is busy raising two children, they added an experienced, highly skilled baker to their staff.*

"I've been baking now for two and a half years. It's really crazy because I absolutely hate to cook. If it wasn't for my two boys I would never have food in the house. You create this huge mess and within 10 minutes it's gone. It just doesn't compare to the satisfaction I get in here from making huge quantities of product for all those different people to enjoy. And the compliments I get are beyond price. At home, measuring out a cup of this and a teaspoon of that is dull; but once you get on that scale and start throwing pounds and ounces of ingredients together it's a whole different world."

Glave says one of the first things she did was to increase the bread line dramatically, because part of what a bakery's all about is coming in to get a loaf of bread. Business increased as she diversified production, and the bakery—newly decorated and with more seating—is outgrowing its space. Recently it opened a branch in Laytonville, 25 miles to the north. Location, she emphasized, is very important, whether a bakery is new or established. The new shop is on Highway 101, Laytonville's main street, where you can't miss it.

ahead of time for each of those days. We have a bakery supplies delivery every other Friday at 4:00 a.m., and another on alternate Tuesdays at 5:30 a.m. Two companies delivering in rotation lets us order a minimum from each one each week in order to minimize our storage needs.

Chris will come back at some time around 6:00 o'clock that evening and mix the sourdough for the following day. We bake a sourdough with no commercial yeast in it, and it has to be mixed a good 16 hours before we can bake it. He replenishes the sourdough starter every day. He will also pull the croissant and danish doughs, and everything that we've frozen that day, from the freezer to refrigerate them for the next morning's bake.

Also at 6:00 p.m. Chris or both of us take all the next day's special orders back to the office to make up the next day's master bake sheet. We adjust the normal bake for special orders and unsolds. For example, our normal mix for sheepherder bread is a four-gallon dough. On the average day we make two four-gallon doughs, each gallon yielding about twelve loaves of bread. If one of our restaurant accounts or any customer wants an extra dozen loaves of sheepherder bread, we will make two four-and-a-half-gallon doughs. We integrate all the orders into our baking sheet for the next day. If we have an excess of day-old items, we won't make them the next day; we'll discount the day-old and get rid of them.

These may look like killer hours in print, but the truth is I'm still having fun and enjoying the business. Even with a 12- or 13-hour day, when you walk up in front and see that all the product you made is gone, you feel pretty good. And if there has been a line to the door a couple of times that day, you know you're doing something right. I have also found that there are two things to remember when business gets frantic, when little calamities and stupid errors pile up and nearly wear you out. At end of each day you always have to tell yourself that you did the best you could, and in the morning—when you're awake enough to talk to yourself—you say, This is going to be a great day. . . . More often than not, it is.

PLANT

The major tools and big investment for a bakery are the mixer, the mixing benches, the proof box, the oven, and refrigeration. First off, you can't do it without the big oven—you have to have it. Small bakeries may get away with the smaller convection ovens, in which you can bake eight pans at a time. We have a 24-pan rotating oven, which works very well for us. It's old but it's one of the more popular styles. Nowadays there are "rack ovens." They're as tall as the room. They rotate, and they come with "bun racks," in which you put all your product to proof. Then the entire rack goes right in the oven. The ovens have steam injectors to give bread a nice crust and they give a very consistent result. They're also expensive. The ideal arrangement would be to have a specific oven for every need, like a brick oven for your breads a rotating oven for your cakes, and so on. But as a practical matter you install the best you can afford and go with that.

You need a proof box to keep bread and other yeast doughs at around body temperature—98 to 100 degrees—while they rise. The dough needs to rise in a warm, damp environment. If it rises without enough moisture, a crust that forms before the dough expands will inhibit rising, split, and look ugly. A proof box resembles a closet with one or two doors. With some you can roll an entire rack of bread right inside. They all have a fan and usually a steam generator so the box has moist circulating air.

The mixer is essential. It all starts with the mixer, and they are not cheap. Depending on size, a Hobart mixer—pretty much the industry standard—will run between $12,000 and $15,000 new. Even used they're $5,000 to $7,000. There are different styles of mixer. Floor-model Hobarts are the commonest. Most mixers are measured either in the quart or gallon size or by weight. They come in a 120-quart down to a 10-quart size. Some, like our 80-quart (20-gallon) mixer, come with attachments and an adapter to let you take it down to a 60- or 40-quart machine. At going rates, mixers are definitely items to buy used—if you can.

You can't get away without a refrigerator. It's an absolute necessity. You might be able to skip a freezer if, for example, you choose to offer fewer items and bake them every day. And you must have a commercial refrigerator, preferably one that lets you slide full bun pans in and out. A consumer model wouldn't work, except for a few dairy products and pre-made muffin mixes, or perhaps for a small place that bakes a few items every day. You will also use refrigeration to retard your dough when it's moving too fast. If you've made a dough in the morning but your oven is too hot, you can retard it in the refrigerator. When the oven is ready you can pull it out and continue the proofing and baking.

Like many bakeries, we use all sorts of tools, the names of which are lost to memory. Most have just been handed down. We have what we call a bear-claw cutter, a wheel with little blades across its rim. Rolling the danish dough over the almond paste you get a smooth seal. In order to get the bear claw effect, you run this wheel across the seal; it cuts it at every quarter inch, and bending the pastry back opens it for the bear claw look. It beats whacking the dough with a knife.

You need a good, heavy wood rolling pin. My 18-inch model weighs 12 pounds and cost $75, but well-maintained it will last a lifetime. Life expectancy notwithstanding, the best rolling pins wear out and fall apart. You want one with encased bearings so that, if the chase wears out, those hard little steel bearings don't wind up

Quality products for the food industry

This is a fairly basic bake sheet with space on the left to write in the names and par amounts of items to bake each day, and space to show on-hand to to-bake for each day. It also provides a good record.

in the dough and cost you your bakery in a lawsuit. Soft doughs like pastries take a softer touch, so you want to use a smaller rolling pin, about 12 or 14 inches, some of which are just round pieces of wood.

Pizza cutters are very handy for cutting croissant dough and, of course, slicing pizza fresh out of the oven. When you roll up cinnamon-roll dough, you get a nice long log with cinnamon and raisins rolled in it. Nothing slices it better than a big chopping knife. Smaller knives are useful to score and shape items, and you always keep rectangular dough cutters at hand.

There is also a tool called a bun divider, a grid of metal blades a few inches apart inside a metal frame. The most popular divider is made by a company named Dutchess. Ours is round and looks like a stack of circular, heavy steel egg crates. A handle swings the top up. When you slide in a four- or eight-pound pan of rolled and floured bread, bagel, or cookie dough and pull down on the handle, the top part first flattens the dough, then the blades cut it into 36 equal pieces. It's a real time saver and we wouldn't be without it.

PROCESS

Most bakery production cycles are consistent every day, based usually on a master bake sheet and the previous day's bake. You know when you come in each day what you will bake. The procedure is to go through the master bake sheet at the end of the day before. It's a simple list that among other things shows what is on hand by a "yes" and "no" after each item. Chris goes down our list and marks each item "yes" or "no," depending on what has and hasn't sold. By reading the list the next morning and counting up the "noes," you are sure to bake everything needed. This permits baking just a day ahead of time. Some ingredients, like almond paste for the bear claws, will last a week or two. It would be pointless and time-consuming to make those items every day. So every two weeks you grind 30 pounds or so of almonds in the mixer's grinder attachment and extrude the paste into the bowl to mix with almost as much sugar by weight.

Even running a daily schedule, it's more efficient, as noted, to make some breads by mixing a large dough, freezing most of it, and baking off portions over the next few days. Most of our breads. sell out every day, but it's better to mix specialty bread doughs in advance. Danish dough, also as noted, should be made the day before. We divide the dough into seven pieces and roll butter and shortening into four or five of them. The term "rolling in the dough" means folding in butter or shortening or both. The dough gets four three-folds by laying the raw piece of dough on the bench, rolling it out to about two by three feet, smearing the butter or shortening on it, folding one flap over and the other on top, then rolling again. You roll it in three times. The two or three other pieces that don't get shortening or butter rolled into them, are for cinnamon roll danish. They have a different texture. Folding the dough, and rolling in butter or shortening again and again creates layers and gives the dough a flaky character, which you don't want in a cinnamon roll. After rolling in, we put the doughs in the freezer where they harden but don't freeze solid. In the evening you take them out and refrigerate them.

Danish dough has butter and other milk products, eggs, flour, water, yeast, and salt in it. You can be creative here. Danish dough is a little like soup—a great product to use up leftovers like whipped cream that is no longer fresh enough for icing cakes. If you add whipped cream; you pull out some of the butter or milk. Once you get the touch you can adjust it and throw in almost anything

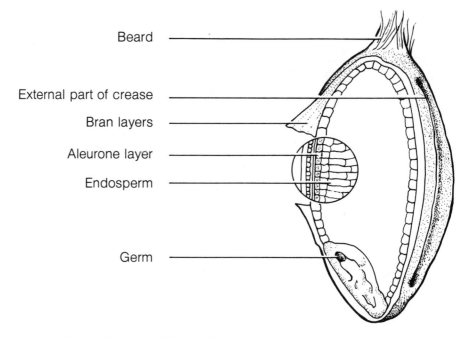

Beard

External part of crease

Bran layers

Aleurone layer

Endosperm

Germ

CROSS-SECTION: MAJOR ELEMENTS OF THE WHEAT KERNEL

within reason. You may have a scrawny leftover piece of danish dough to add to the next day's dough, so you just mix it back in and re-use it. There's no waste, it's still fresh, and it tastes good.

When the dough comes out of the refrigerator in the morning, the cinnamon-roll portion goes on the bench first. Then you roll it out flat, egg wash it, throw cinnamon and raisins on it, and roll it up. You then chop it up in big pieces with that big knife and throw them on the pan for the proof box and oven. If you're fast, there's enough flour on the dough and the board so the knife doesn't stick. It's more involved than that, but not much. If you've done it two or three times, you can make cinnamon rolls. You have to get the touch, of course. They can look a little clumsy the first few times, but they improve with practice. It goes very fast once you've done it a few times, and that's where a baker can move and make money.

With an approximately 18-pound piece of danish dough, half will be for bear claws and cheese pockets, and the other half will be equal portions of butterhorns, cinnamon twists, and pecan rolls or fruit danish. You cut the first piece in half and the other into thirds, and throw them up onto the shelf over the bench. Then, as you bring each piece down and work it, you know exactly what that piece will be. You roll it out to specific dimensions for butterhorns, or the like, pan them, then put them into the proof box. The next pieces are for cinnamon twists and so on. Although each piece is

WHEAT, RYE & BARLEY

There are about 30,000 known varieties of wheat and wheat-like grasses all over the world. The commonly cultivated wheats fall roughly into bread wheats and durum wheats. They split further into winter and spring varieties. In warmer climates, winter wheat is planted in fall to harvest early the next summer. Spring wheat is planted in the spring in colder climates to harvest at the end of summer. Seventy percent of wheat grown in the United States is winter wheat, and about 95 percent of the crop is bread wheat.

The wheat berry is creased along one side, with a beard of tiny hairs at one end. The bran consists of six layers of coating, including a nutrient-rich aleurone layer. Within the bran are the germ and the starchy endosperm. The endosperm comprises big granules of starch and gluten; how tightly it packs them in controls whether it is "hard" or "soft" wheat.

Rye's qualities approach wheat's more closely than any other grain, and it is the only one of them that used alone will make successful yeast bread. While its proteins resemble wheat's, and the two are nutritionally similar, rye flour makes a stickier, less elastic dough and a heavier loaf.

Rye flour generally comes in dark, light, medium, and straight grades. The dark flour includes some of the grain's outer husk, the light flour contains the starchy endosperm, and the medium grade is usually a blend of light and dark. Straight rye is the whole milled grain—about 30 percent dark and 70 percent light. Ordinarily, medium and straight grades are interchangeable.

Barley is one of the oldest cultivated cereal grasses. Deposits of it have turned up in the Stone Age lake dwellings of Switzerland. The Roman goddess Ceres wore barley ears plaited in the her hair. One of China's sacred books notes its cultivation there as early as 2000 B.C., and it grows wild in western Asia—probably its original home. Adapted to both warm and cold climates, barley covers more of the globe, including all its temperate zones, than any other cereal. Nutritionally it ranks very close to wheat. Little used as a cereal in North America, it is chiefly malted for brewing and distilling.

---

pretty shapeless when you look at it, you soon get a feel for exactly what the end result will be.

The croissant dough, which has been in the freezer and refrigerator with the danish dough, gets three three-folds and a four-fold at the end. Apart from puff pastry, croissant dough is the toughest to handle. It goes in the freezer like danish dough, and the next day you take it out, roll it thin and cut it into triangles with a pizza cutter. They're extra work and some bakeries have chosen to buy a frozen croissant dough pre-cut into triangles. It's a very efficient approach and not a bad product. Once your customers are accustomed to in-house croissants, however, you'll never switch because the packaged variety is noticeably inferior.

HAPPY HOLIDAYS

To approach production as you get busier for the holidays, you do the same advance preparation but think a little further ahead. By refrigerating or freezing the product you can prepare for the big jobs and maintain quality. Freezing is essential. We were unprepared for holiday production the first couple of times, and we found that if you don't freeze product in advance, you end up doing four days' work in one—for several days running. For example, we will make 300 to 500 pies for Thanksgiving, all by hand. This is a high-stress time. It's especially frenetic when you want to keep up the quality.

Most scratch bakeries use the same methods we do. We make the crusts ourselves, rolling them out, putting them in the pans, then freezing them. Beginning about the first of November, Chris will roll out ten pie shells a day. By the 20th we've got 200. Towards the last week I'll help him and we may roll out 50 a day; so by the time it's production day, those two or three days before Thanksgiving, we'll have all our pie shells done.

We'll have ordered all our pie fruit ahead of time. All of our fruit—boysenberries, blueberries, cherries—comes instantly frozen but not made up. We defrost the fruit, make up the fillings, and fill five or six pails with each variety, which we'll take to the local dairy. The dairy will refrigerate them for us, because we don't have enough refrigeration. The day before we bake, all the pie shells are in the freezer. The milkman brings in all our fruit fillings. All we have to do is fill them and roll out the tops, which are too fragile to do ahead.

Between Thanksgiving and Christmas there are office parties with orders for more pie shells again, large coffee cakes and the like, things that are fancier than day-to-day items. It's a bakery's busy time of year. Many retail businesses make or break during those months. That probably isn't as true for bakeries. It is a time when a baker can make money; but a bakery—at least a small one—will not see enough extra volume in the holidays to pull it out of a bad year.

It's always a good idea to decorate the bakery for holiday sales. For most holidays you need to display your specialties only a few weeks in advance to let the market know what's coming. You can sell hot cross buns from Ash Wednesday all the way through Easter. While most people want traditional chocolates and flowers for Valentine's Day, bakeries are handy for people who forgot. We make chocolate cakes, big and small ones, that say "Happy Valentine's Day," "I Love You," and so on—like the little candies. Everything with chocolate goes over very well then. You have to know your market. Soda bread is good for St. Patrick's Day, and we get very busy with parties around June graduation days.

All of the holidays—Halloween, St. Patrick's Day, Christmas—are good for cookies. There's a cookie for every event. The problem is you can't cut and decorate every shape of every holiday cookie, like those little leprechauns for St. Patrick's Day. They're too expensive to bother with while you're making all of your breads, pies, and everything else unless you or an employee can do them efficiently.

At that time we were working at the food store and baking in the kitchen back there, but Burt got busy. We had to wait till four o'clock in the evening to use the kitchen. So we'd bake bread till about two o'clock. I'd go home and catch a few hours sleep then I'd run it over to the coast and to Ukiah. I was working some terrific hours.
—BRUCE HERING
BRUCE BREAD

Some suppliers have contacts with large holiday cookie manufacturers. They're one thing you can justifiably buy from outside, as long as you're sure of the quality. And it gives you something to offer kids who want a special treat for the holiday. We let people know the cookies are from an outside bakery and we can sell them at a decent profit.

CHARITABLE DONATIONS

When your product has to be fresh daily, you bake most items for a single day's needs. If it's a day old you mark it day-old and put it on the day-old rack for sale at a reduced price, usually half. We wrap breads in plastic at the end of the day and put them in the day-old racks. Even items with a longer shelf life, like iced cakes require a rapid turnover. If you have extra danish left over after two days, you can crumb it up to use in different items like apple-pan dowdy and apple-nut bars.

Two-day old product is still good, but to ensure that your customers buy fresh you won't sell it. Instead, most bakeries donate unsold product to charitable causes that rely on bakeries to supply food for needy people in the community. There is probably not a bakery in the country if not the world whose product doesn't help sustain good causes on a regular and substantial basis. Donations are also a part of making contacts within the community. When you're in the community you have to give back to it. Much as you want to give to all the good causes, however, you have limit your generosity. Sometimes you'll be asked three or four times in a day. It's hard to say you can't spare three dozen cookies, because the organizations don't always understand that you've donated 20 dozen, about $75 worth, for the week. We touch on our donations policy briefly in Chapter 15, but you'll have to see what works best based on your own experience.

DISPLAY

Some bakers will tell you that if you have too much on display, people can't make up their minds and it slows down sales. There is also a trend in some shops to display one perfect this and one perfect that. There are two schools of thought on the subject. My brother Brian is fond of saying, "Stack 'em high and watch 'em buy." And it's great when people come in and say, Oh, just a second, I can't decide. It means they're scanning the cases and interested in buying something. When you load your danish cases in the morning, you can display 10 or 12 different varieties of danish. You wouldn't stack a bear claw pan next to another one. You'd put butterhorns next to the bear claws and so on. When you mix them up people look at the cases and may see only be those 10 or 12 different types of danish, but they'll look like a hundred.

There's an aesthetic side to baking that also comes with experience. People buy with their eyes. Anybody can make the same items, but you'll try to make your product look better by taking time on it and perhaps by offering a more generous portion. Instead of a well-bred little scone for 95¢, you might offer a big one for $1.00. Bear claws and other danish with the sliced almonds on them have an aesthetic appeal; so cover the danish with big slivered almonds and chocolate-chip muffins with extra chocolate chips.

You can do little things to make a product look better or more exciting. Take a full sheet of apple-nut bars, for example. It's like a two-inch thick cake that will be cut into squares. If you sprinkle a little powdered sugar on top, it will look much better because of the white powdered sugar against the brown apple nut bar. Bakers slash bread on top before baking so it will rise against the crust in a predictable and attractive way. Different slash marks also identify a bread and give it a special character. With some breads you can wash the cut with a little salad oil to give it stringy look in the cuts that you often see in a French or artisan bread.

Magazines are a great source of new ideas about how to make items look good. But baked items in magazines are always picture-perfect. The typical bakery's don't always come out looking quite that flawless. That's an aspect of the fresh-baked appeal. It didn't come out of a box or get pressed out of a machine. When you walk into a bakery where every item is a little different, quality can be consistently high while very item is handmade and unique.

TRENDS AND MARKETS

We've added bagels to our menu. People want something other than just sugar items when they go into a bakery. They want something that's a little healthier (so they can spread cream cheese on it). Trends are important for deciding on appearance and product mix, but customers get tired of trends and you have to be ready to change. People are getting away from mass-produced, and a neighborhood bakery will be flexible enough to shift and stay in tune with community tastes. Staying in tune is the key. A highly successful bakery in San Francisco called "Victoria Pastries" makes very high-end, luxury pastries. A bakery like that is a geyser of good ideas for the rest of us. Not all of them will fly everywhere, however, because, while there will be people in most markets who will pay for $35 for a champagne cake, there may not be enough in your area to keep you in business. You have to know the demographics and your market's buying habits. If you're in Hillsborough down near San Francisco, you want an elegant bakery selling the best in petits fours and champagne cakes—because you will get the money for them. If you're in South San Francisco, an industrial area, you would probably make more money selling donuts and muffins and bagels than trying to sell expensive pastries.

The old family bakery in Utrecht, Holland, in the 1930s. The building is still there, but the business has outgrown it and moved to larger quarters.

Any bakery worth the name sells quality. That's what its customers expect and, if they don't get it, they don't come back. There's no difference in time or effort if you use butter instead of shortening, and it's just as easy to bake high quality items as to make them second-rate. But the issue, if you want to stay in business, is whether your market will support a high-end *pâtisserie* or you need to scale your product to local pocketbooks. A working, successful bakery has to produce the best quality its customers can buy. That calls for a cost-benefit evaluation of whether you afford to be a purist about using butter only and still stay in business at your location. In the real world everyone's conclusion will be different. It's a conclusion that may change over time, so you need to stay aware of your market and change if it does.

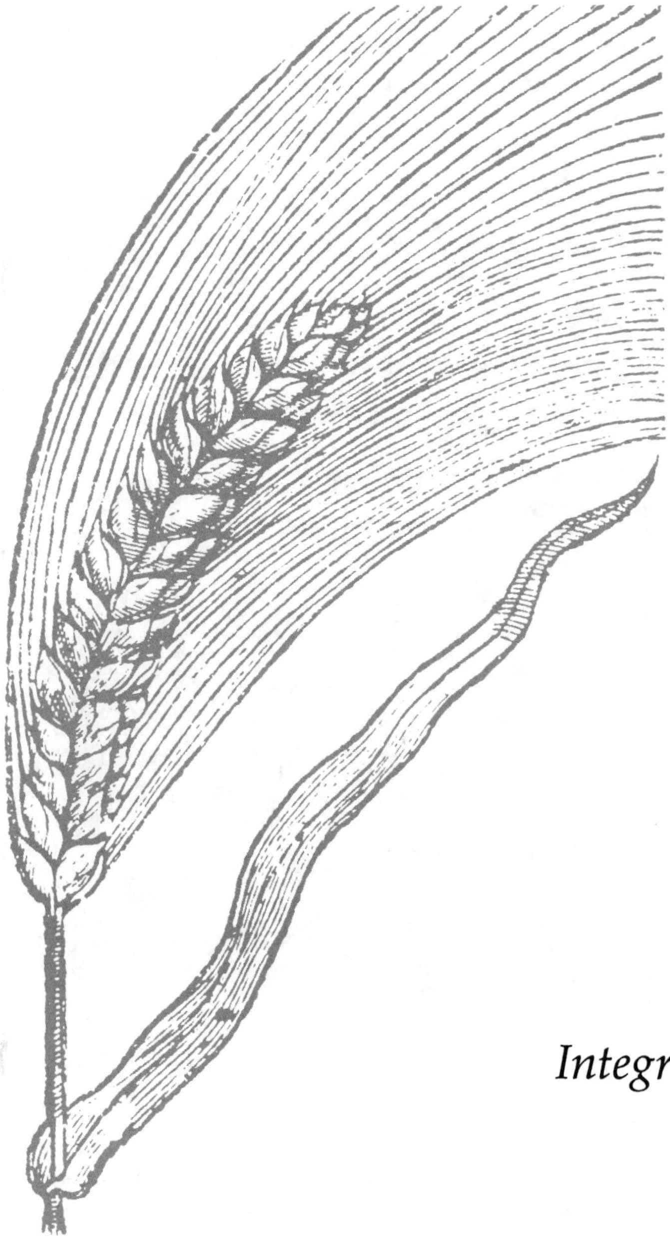

3

RETAIL SALES: THE PUBLIC AREA

YOU REALLY CAN'T SELL BREAD from the back of the bakery. You need a retail area, and it has to sell your product for you. That means designing a public space where your customers and product come together, and it's love at first sight. This chapter covers that with a bonus, a two-for-one: bakery retail space with a café attached. Readers who don't care about running cafés can skip all those parts and stick to showcases, lighting, floors, and so on. For the others this is where we introduce you to all the joys and grief of being a baker-restaurateur.

If the building in which you plan to set up your bakery is an empty shell, you have to decide first how much space to devote to merchandising—that is, your display, counter service, and customer space—and how much to set aside for production. The smaller the production space you can manage, while still able to produce in greater volume when necessary, the better—because you want plenty of room in which to merchandise and sell. If your plan includes seating, you need even more retail space. At the same time, however, you should leave room for production to grow.

Let's say that you have a 1,000-square-foot building and you divide it down the middle: 500 square feet for production and 500 for merchandising. If you plan to have seating, you would probably be cheating yourself of merchandising space. Or you might decide you could get away with 300 square feet for production, leaving 300 for counter and display space and 400 for seating. If you start to get busy down the road and acquire a few wholesale accounts, things will begin to get hectic in production and you'll find you don't have room for new equipment. So you have to plan for a reasonably sized production area. It's a balancing act and a judgment call.

We will discuss planning and design in more detail later. Meanwhile, it's enough to know that the best way to begin to plan how you will set up your shop is to learn from other people. Look at different bakeries to get a feel for layout. First decide on the product line you want to carry. Visit as many bakeries as you can to see how established businesses do it. Introduce yourself and just ask if you can look at and, perhaps, talk about their shop. Think about what makes a bakery work and ask questions, such as whether the owner would like more seating or production space.

I've been around family bakeries all my life, which has limited the variety of bakeries I have seen. When we decided to set up in the home-improvement center, I got more interested when leafing through *Bakery Production and Marketing* magazine in how people have arranged their retail spaces. When you decide to set up you'll be keyed in to viewing bakeries with a more critical eye. You'll want to know what works and what doesn't. You may feel a little uncomfortable about taking pictures on your visits, but it's a good idea. You need a record, because you can't remember everything. You might be on vacation, or out actually looking, and spot a great idea—something you definitely want to remember—but once you leave it's just gone. The least you should do when you go outside after talking to someone and checking out a bakery is to take notes right away, or tape record them, and draw a diagram. Whether you take pictures, and how you make notes, depends on you and the circumstances. Some owners may not appreciate your curiosity and taking pictures, or they may be flattered and let you go right ahead.

Let's take the Courthouse Bakery's retail layout as an example. We have an L-shaped display. The refrigerator case forms the leg of the L, and unless people want something out of it, they'll walk right to the other two cases without even a glance at it. What you want in a bakery's retail area is a better "flow." A good production area has a flow. The mixers are usually left of the benches, so that mixing bowls go from there to the benches where the product is taken out, divided, and rounded. Then it's put in a rack to go to a proof box just short of the oven. There it's proofed and goes into the oven. Finally it comes full circle from the oven into a rack, then to a packing area.

A good flow in front would have showcases running from the window back to the kitchen in one long line. A long line of cases gives you a chance to mix things up and put them all on display. People have to walk past them and look at the baked goods to get to the cash register. They would see nothing but showcases—refrigerator cases, two or three dry cases—with all the product in them. Getting people to look at your product is the first step in selling it. Or, instead of creating one long line of customers from the register all the way out to the front, you might try to have a register at every second showcase or on each side of one showcase so that you could spread them out. However you do it, the idea is to lead the customer past all the merchandise or as much of it as possible and get them to look at it.

The single line of display cases can also provide window access in which to stack bread. A stack of bread in the window looks great. We can't do that now because that's where our seating is. Taking away tables would take money out of the business, but one long line of cases would let you put tables where the cases might be. Everything could be behind the cases, an espresso machine, a coffee machine, soups, all serviceable from that one long flow. That lets you get the most out of your cases and retail space.

You want an impulse area near the cash register. Ours sits right above the cinnamon rolls and next to the cookies. (The perfect spot.) This works especially well for things like biscotti and chocolate-dipped shortbread, which sell well around the register as "easy grab" items.

You can also use the cash register—which is where all your paying customers have to go—as a place to do sampling. You should have a sample running almost all day long, especially in the beginning when you're trying to get things going. You will make more money by sampling than it will cost you to give a few things away. For example, say you put out a new type of bread. It could be a honey-wheat bread: 100-percent whole wheat flour, honey, water, yeast, and salt. You would point out that it has no white flour, milk, or egg products. People taste it, and it's heavy and good, and they buy a loaf. You want your fresh-baked samples out where the customer can't miss them.

Fresh bread is the best way to decorate a bakery wall. Currently it's also popular to pile things up in woven baskets. The effect is pleasing and gives a homey feeling. Put a big basket of fresh-baked bread out where people are standing in line, with one of each kind of loaf in it. The loaves are like a bouquet of flowers but it's a bouquet of bread, and you can smell it. We have all our bread on shelves behind the counter, which is a perfect place to display it. The shelves are slanted down to a guard rail so that you stack several rows of each kind of bread up each shelf. People will look at the basket and ask what kind of bread it is. You'll have labeled the shelves to identify the bread, so that the help can turn to the shelved bread, if necessary, and read the label to them. Then the help can grab a loaf, slice it up, and—boom!—it's sold.

You also have to make room up front on the counter for a packaging area. And you need a space for a bread slicer out in front unless you choose to slice your bread in advance or not to slice it at all. We always send all the bread out unsliced and without any sort of wrapping. It's fresh-baked that day, and we slice it on the spot if the customer wants.

Up on the wall behind the cash register we have a blackboard listing most of the items we sell, with each item's name and price. It also lets your staff turn around and see the price conveniently. The items on that board make a fairly permanent list. You can alter the prices or erase a discontinued item, but even if you don't bake the product every day it should stay listed if eventually it will make an appearance again.

The cashier's station raises its own set of questions. You can have an order counter that is strictly counter space to write out orders, to make change, and to let people write checks. We do all of that at our register, which occupies a flat space on top of a showcase, and it works well enough. It might be easier to have a little more room, but you have to be careful about tying up space in a small bakery for things that won't make you money. You don't want the customer to feel cramped and uncomfortable, but there are certain limitations people will live with. If it's a little tight around the cash register, they'll make do.

The biggest problem with our cash register system, and it may be one you'll encounter, is that no one person rings in everything. Our staff is trained to do everything so that everyone can cover anyone else. It's a policy that works best for this kind of shop. There is a problem in accountability, however, when the register tape and cash don't balance. Businesses that can afford to have one person at a cash register all day don't have that problem. Some cash registers give each employee a number, so that cash register employee No. 2 can show how many sales and over-rings the employee has had that day. It still doesn't limit the number of hands in the till. The only way around it is to have more than one cash drawer. If know you want only two people in the till, have two cash drawers. When person No. 1 is ringing a sale in, that person gets the top drawer, and person No. 2 gets the bottom drawer. Then when shifts change you put in a new bank and go right back and count the money.

SHOWCASING THE PRODUCT

The two most important sales tools in the front of the bakery are the people who are selling for you and the what's in the display cases. First you want people who are knowledgeable about what they're selling and who make offers to people by saying, "have you ever tried this?" or "do you know that this is not only a loaf of apple-cinnamon bread but is also great for French toast?" You as the baker will probably be the best salesperson in the store because you know exactly what's in every product. You'll be unable to spend as much time up front much as you may like to, however, and you'll be hard pressed to train your staff to know everything about every single item. What you aim for is to tell a customer what's in a product, what it's good for, and exactly how it tastes. Making sure your staff knows the product that well can be a big job. The help will

never be as closely involved with the product as the baker is, but you should teach good customer skills with that aim in mind.

Your showcases are your second most important sales tool. Unless they're full of appetizing items, and present an attractive display, you won't sell very much out of them. Used properly, they can be your best "salespeople" by the way they display the product. Guessing whether each day will be busy or slow, however, does make filling them a gamble. On some days you'll fill them in the morning and gradually sell out by day's end. Other days will find you left with sparse, unattractive displays by early afternoon. I hate half-empty cases, because they really slow down sales. But there's just no way to predict sales from one day to the next.

It doesn't matter much how old the display case is. The latest trend in new cases is a sleek, curved-glass style, which unfortunately is very expensive. Many of them are made in Europe. They aren't for anyone who is just starting out, unless he or she has plenty of capital. We have old cases, none of which match. They're completely different and just slapped together, but they work fine because what people are looking at is the product inside. Cases that might look funky and slapdash when they're empty don't necessarily look bad when they're full of good-looking baked goods. Naturally, you'd prefer your display cases to match but it's really not that important. My dad has had many a bakery with funky equipment in it and it just didn't matter. As long as the product's good, your customers will buy it; they'll never see the display cases as long as they are spotlessly clean and the product looks and smells appetizing.

Basically, there are two kinds of cases available. There are high-volume cases that allow you to load full bun pans or racks of cookies in them. There are also low-volume cases with single or double shelves that will take only a basket of cookies or an individual cake or pie. You also need refrigerated cases if you are baking products like éclairs, cream puffs, or cream pies that have to be stored cold. Again the best way to decide what kind of cases you want is to identify your product line. When you inspect a place that has the kind of products you plan to make, check out their display cases. Two high-volume cases and a refrigerator case work very well in our bakery.

The health code requires all the product on top of your counters to be protected by sneeze guards. Product that's up on the wall behind the service counter where the help can grab it can be left safely out in the open, but on top of the counter the only thing between it and the customers is a (we hope) not unattractive sneeze guard.

You want the bakery to be clean and free of dust or grime. Show me a bakery that doesn't get flour and dust all over everything, and I'll sign up to take a class where they teach the course. In any bakery there will be flour in the air; there will be dough spilled; there will be a constant mess. Anybody who has baked at home knows it's just a messy process. You always keep your hands clean, naturally, and wash them between jobs. You sweep and wipe up constantly in back where you're baking. But the process always wants to get away from you.

Keeping the retail area clean can be a nightmare, because every little kid leaves fingerprints on the cookie case. You have to wipe down the cases as often as often as needed, because it detracts absolutely from your product if people can't see through the hand smudges and whatever else is on the glass. If you have a café, coffee gets spilled, napkins float off the tables, and the crumbs fly while your customers enjoy themselves. It's pretty amazing what happens. You have to clean the dining area continually, because after awhile nobody will be able to sit and enjoy coffee and a roll amidst all that can pile up during the day.

Just as you need to keep the display cases spotless, you definitely also want to date your product, especially in a refrigerator case. Cookies have a shelf life of two or three days; but you can't serve pastries as fresh if they're a day old. We don't date the cookies because we go through them so fast. We do rotate them. When a new pan of cookies comes out it goes on the far left and we slide the earlier ones over. As they empty out, always check the product. If there are cookies left over from the day before, it's a good practice when you come in the morning to crack one open and eat it to make sure it's fresh. If it isn't, throw the batch out or put them in a bag labeled, "Two dozen for $1.00: Not-so-fresh cookies." The important items to date are the products in the refrigerator cases—cream pies, cream puffs, and so on. You don't want to neglect custard if you make your own fresh, because it can become poisonous, and you can't delay with whipped cream, because when it goes stale it's very nasty. You won't get any good customer responses to stale whipped cream.

The date goes on the back of the label that identifies the product. The customer sees the name of the cake. The back will have the item description and price for the employee: "Double layer white cake, chocolate frosting, custard filling, $15.95," and underneath it will say "4/23/97." Then we know its shelf life. The customer doesn't see that the cake was made on 4/23/97, and if it is 4/25/97, the cake, with its longer shelf life, is still salable at full price. If it hasn't sold in three days, we'll sell slices discounted. Otherwise we'll have it at lunch or throw it out.

THE TAKE-OUT BAKERY

A take-out bakery is practically all production and merchandising area without much need for customer space. It's my view that a bakery in a small-town commercial district would certainly benefit from café service even if it only wanted a take-out trade. A small bakery in a busy big-city downtown, however, may prefer customers to walk in and walk out, sometimes because of frantic urban activity but usually because of higher real estate costs. That is, a bakery-café combination might work there only when a high-quality, higher-cost product brought in enough money. Otherwise, it may not pay to have people sitting around in the bakery's valuable floor space. If you paid, say, 50¢ a square foot and could rent a 4,000-square-foot building at $2,000 a month, seating is worth investigating. If you had to pay $2.00 a square foot for a 1,000-square-foot building with a good walk-in trade, seating may just be out of the question.

Good use of limited retail space for a take-out bakery means making as effective a display of the products as possible. At a minimum, a take-out bakery would probably work in 1,000 to 1,500 square feet for both the baking and retail—that is, the merchandising and customer—area. Space for a few customers to stand and view the product without feeling crowded would be adequate. You could keep the pans looking full and appetizing with extra product from the back by continually turning it over. You could also show just one of each cake, pie or similar item; when you sold one you would pull another out of the refrigerator in back to keep the showroom stocked.

How much display area you need depends also on how much variety you want to carry. A full neighborhood bakery starts to need bread racks, refrigerator display shelves, floor racks, and so on. Still, you can do it in a relatively small space, with perhaps a three- or four-foot-wide refrigerator display case for cream puffs, éclairs, and a few cakes. One or two six- to eight-foot display cases for other products—including breads, pastries, muffins, cookies, and the like—would give a total of 12 to 20 feet of display. You could run it in a straight line or any shape that worked. A counter area to serve the customers is useful, but sometimes the top of the display cases will do.

Your day will be less complicated, too, if you forgo the café. Without it you would get by with less help, less space, and certainly fewer headaches.

AMBIENCE AND ESSENTIALS

Bakery smells — Any bakery should smell good, and there you'll have no problem. Bakery smells are chocolate chip cookies, fresh breads as they come out of the oven, cinnamon rolls, and the like. Everyone likes them. They're a bonus for you while you're baking; let the public enjoy them too. Many bakeries have a ventilation duct that runs from the production area where things are baked and siphons those fresh aromas right out onto the street or into the retail space. It's a great idea. All bakeries have that wonderful aroma; use it.

Ceiling fans are great in bakeries' retail areas. They help push the smells around and they're stylish. Those with lights look even better and they work for you. Lights directly over the baked goods—track lighting or hanging drop cord lights—highlight the product. Lighting inside the bakery cases is also very effective, as is lighting inside the bread cases on the wall. We don't have lights on the wall, but at other bakeries I've seen how it sheds a golden light on the bread and enhances the way the crust looks.

Floor Coverings — You should choose your floor surface according to the motif for the entire bakery. If you plan to have a country-style or home-style bakery you couldn't do better than a hardwood floor. At our new place in the home-improvement center the main activity is home-improvement retailing. The center has a beautiful, smooth concrete floor throughout with a gloss finish on it. For a bakery the health department requires seals on a concrete bakery or restaurant floor to make it *food safe*. To meet the health department's requirement, the center owners put a food-safe sealed gloss finish on the bakery floor and pigmented the seal to give the bakery floor a different color from the rest of the store and set it off. If you choose to work from a modern theme, a floor like this could serve you very well. It also substitutes for expensive ceramic-tile floors in the production area.

Interestingly enough, we tried a low-fat cheesecake about three and a half years ago. It was a lemon and white-chocolate cheesecake with 51 percent less fat and 65 percent fewer calories. It was pretty good for a low-fat cheesecake. We marketed the heck out of it. Usually, if a cake's not selling after two months we'll drop it, but we left this one out there for four or five months. It was the worst selling cheesecake we've ever had. We learned our lesson: That's not our market. We deal in a lot of sugar, a lot of butter-fat. If there's no fat in cheesecake, there's nothing in it. It isn't cheesecake. I talked to another cheesecake company in Chicago and one in Virginia. They all introduced low-fat lines with the same result. If you want half the fat in cheesecake, take half a slice. Or walk an extra mile the next day.

—PAUL LEVITAN
THE CHEESECAKE LADY

Vinyl flooring for the retail area is fine. Our Courthouse location has an old vinyl tile floor that came with the shop. As with all smooth surfaces, it is slippery at times, especially on rainy days, so we use a non-slip runner when necessary. While some bakers claim a carpet puts customers on their good behavior and helps maintain a cleaner shop, my experience is that it catches too many crumbs and ends up looking messy. And, if you have to roll supplies and equipment in and out the front as we do, it will tear up a carpet.

Restrooms — If you serve food on the premises, the health department will require public restrooms. Regulations require may new shops to set aside a certain number of square feet, say 50, for men's and women's bathrooms. The health department may grandfather in the restroom in your building if it predates current regulations. Even so, if you let the customers use your one and only restroom when they ask, you should warn them if the floor is slippery or there are other hazards. We've been lucky, so far. When you open your production areas to customers you assume a risk of liability. The last thing we want, with many of our customers being lawyers, is to have somebody slip and fall back there. They could be smothered under business cards.

You'll also have to keep after your staff to keep the restroom clean for your customers and make sure there are soap and papers in it. Bakers usually have flour all over them, and may track in something that was spilled on the floor. It's invariably some baking ingredient, not dirt, but it will look messy.

Central Air — Bakeries need central heating and cooling. We need the air conditioner, for example, when it's 108° in the shade outside. You'll need a heater all day in most places from late fall to early spring, but usually your oven will keep the morning chill off for the rest of the year. It's very important to have a constant temperature for the bakery, because doughs react differently when it's cold or hot. You also need it for your customers' comfort in the retail area.

Fire Codes — Finally, you have to comply with fire laws. There are guidelines that every fire department in the land will issue to control maximum seating. You must have fire extinguishers available and exposed. Your electrical panel must be free of any obstruction or debris. The building code and fire and health requirements that you need to comply with are necessary and beneficial. They also mean there is more than design and personal choice to take into account when you plan your bakery.

THE CAFÉ

The main advantage of combining a café with the bakery is the opportunity it provides to increase your gross revenue. Let's say you want to gross $1,000 a day, which is pretty good for most small bakeries. That's $315,000 to $350,000 a year. It's much tougher to do that on baked goods alone in a small town like ours than in a well-to-do suburban area. Since you have to price to the market, adding a café is a great way to increase your gross without raising prices. If you can generate $500 or $600 lunch business in a three-hour period, you can get a whole lot closer to that $1,000 mark.

As long as you control costs as you develop it, a café helps in two ways. First it adds directly to the gross by increasing the number of people who come into your shop. Not everybody will come into a bakery for a cookie every day. It's just not in their dietary plan. But people who otherwise wouldn't be your customers will come in for lunch. Or let's say you decide also to offer breakfast by serving pancakes, biscuits, muffins, or even hot cereals and fresh fruit. You will get more customers because everybody eats breakfast and lunch, and many people eat out. If they come in because you have the best lunch in town you may get 200 extra people a day to come in the door just for that sit-down meal.

Second, if you get 50 or 60 of those people to pick up a loaf of bread while they're in the shop, you're moving baked goods that otherwise you might not sell for lack of the necessary traffic. That's the true advantage, selling both lunch and over-the-counter baked goods to the same customer. And it's a natural combination as well, because if you have the fresh breads and can get fresh produce, meats, and deli, why not combine them all and sell them? It's the best sampler you can have. Your customers eat their sandwich on fresh sourdough, and it happens to be great bread. They look up and see it on the shelves and buy a loaf for $2.25. It works very well, and it's a clear trend for bakeries to follow.

It is true, you will find well-established bakeries that aren't combined with a café or a simple soup-and-sandwich place. They are often older shops that used to survive, and still get by, on cake and fine pastry sales. But it's not always the best choice. For example recently, while looking at other shops to plan for our new branch, I went to Gayle's Bakery & Rosticceria in Capitola, California. Gayle and her husband Joe Ortiz had just won *Bakery Production and Marketing* magazine's Retail Bakery of the Year award for the entire United States. And it was well deserved. They have one of the most imaginative, well-run, and successful retail bakeries I've seen in my entire life, and by now I've seen quite a few, both overseas and here. Our managers came along with me. We talked to the owners and got the grand tour.

Gayle's Bakery has been in business for 18 years. It has outdoor seating, indoor seating, and a great kitchen. It is three separate businesses in itself, a deli, a beautiful coffee area, with espresso and *lattes*, and it has a fine bakery display area. It occupies 5,500 square feet of space and employs 95 people. Ninety-five people! It's a great example of what a baker can aspire to. No one could open that on the first day, but it's a great motivator when you start out small and want something to aim for. It is a bakery that I highly recommend anyone in the business to see. It also somewhat illustrates a market shift to low-fat bakery products.

Joe Ortiz has traveled all around Europe and visited local bakeries there. He wrote a book called *The Village Baker,** which describes some of the wonderful breads that are native to certain areas of Europe. He and Gayle are reproducing many of them in their bakery. They also built their reputation on fine European pastries, and they had an upper-income market that could support it. They sell a key-lime pie, for example, a gorgeous nine-inch creation that goes for $22.50. If we tried to sell that key-lime pie in our town, even cutting the price a little for our lower overhead, it would sit there and sit there until it turned really green—with age. Gayle's had such a growing demand from their market for low-fat items, however, that even they finally had to cut back on rich pastries and build up their other lines, like the deli, and lower-fat products. So, if your talents lie in rich desserts and take-out pastries, watch out and research your market very carefully before committing all your capital to the idea.

INTEGRATING THE BAKERY AND CAFÉ

The Courthouse Bakery's Experience—When we first started at the Courthouse Bakery, business was slow enough to have one baker, one cook, a couple of counter people. But as activity picked up we had to define and work out how the café and bakery functioned together. They are essentially separate entities. In fact, we operate them as two separate businesses. From the beginning we have had people whose job description has been cook or prep cook and who work for the café, while the bakers' job has always been just to bake the items on our bakery list. It means two crews doing separate jobs, but the jobs complement each other. Each day the cooks place an order with the bakers for whatever rolls or breads they want for the lunch menu. Usually it's a standing order based on our regular bill of fare.

We work together. With just the one big oven we have to. The cooks have to bake off their pizzas and turkeys and roasts in the oven that the bakers use for bread, cookies, danish, and so forth. The cooks prepare everything. They give it to the us, the bakers. Then we put it in the oven when the temperature is right and we pull it out when it's done. That's about our only involvement with the cooks. We bake items, such as pizza or focaccia with fresh-

* Cited in the Appendix, and very highly recommended. Although we include a few favorite recipes, you can't find a better collection of commercial formulas than in Ortiz's book. It is a great resource on the practice of good baking, too.

chopped vegetables that the cooks prep for us. We don't have a written list of steps for getting out each product but we work from a close understanding of what each side of the business will do to get it out on time.

We keep the café and bakery separate right up to the point of sale and work out what percentage of the gross is generated by café sales and what percentage comes from bakery sales. It helps to have a register that lets you ring things up from different departments as a way to see which part of your business is growing and which needs attention. The two entities are complementary. If the baked items were not good, we wouldn't have as good a café business, and without high café sales we wouldn't move as many baked goods.

Deli Supplies—As with bakery supplies, the purchase of deli supplies must emphasize rotation, rotation, rotation, in order never to have too much on hand. You'll have to turn over the inventory of meats and cheeses and other perishables weekly. Always keep an eye on rotation—and food costs. Ideally you can have two suppliers for the deli for two deliveries a week. Inventory items like dry goods, canned tomatoes, and canned pizza sauce can be bulked up, letting you take advantage of sale prices. But you should still try to turn that inventory over every two weeks.

We use a set of inventory sheets—a page of which we show here —for every item we order from our suppliers for produce, meats, and dry goods. One of our cooks fills out inventory sheets every Tuesday. The sheets list each item, followed by three columns, and include, for example, "roasted turkey breast," which we order by the case when we buy it. The first column is for "par," or the amount we normally use per week. It may show we need three cases. The next column will have a space for "on hand," and the cook will mark how many are on hand. We may have two. Next there is a space to enter the amount ordered. It's simple math. You order one more case. There are times when you'll need halves and portions, and then you can only guess what you think business will be for the week—but the system itself is very simple.

Base your choice for deli meats on getting the highest available quality for a sandwich you can serve at a competitive price. Mainly, we prefer to roast our own meats, but there are times when we have to order top-grade pre-cooked turkey or ham. If you can't keep up, then substitute the highest grade of pre-cooked meats. It's a good back-up for very busy periods—because you can't always arrange to whip out another roasted turkey breast whenever you run short, especially in those seasons when the bakery is operating at capacity. Even if you can't justify the cost of pre-cooked deli items, you may be so busy with everything else that, in order to meet demand, you have to swallow some of the cost for the convenience of quality pre-cooked ingredients. This is also a matter of weighing the options.

		UNIT SZ	RZ=RITZ	H=HUDSON		A=RITCHIES		PS=PORT STOCKTON
			PAR	OH/O	OH/O	OH/O	OH/O	
				WK1	WK2	WK3	WK4	
DATE								
FETA CHEESE			1/2 EA	/	/	/	/	
BLUE CHEESE CRMB.			1/2 EA	/	/	/	/	
BLUE CHEESE CONC.			1	/	/	/	/	
PESTO			1/2 EA	/	/	/	/	
SHREDDED PARMESAN			1 1/2	/	/	/	/	
DRY GOODS								
LIGHT RED BEANS			1/2 BOX	/	/	/	/	
BLACK BEANS			1 BOX	/	/	/	/	
LENTILS			1/2 BOX	/	/	/	/	
SPLIT PEAS			1/2 BOX	/	/	/	/	
NAVY BEANS			1/2 BOX	/	/	/	/	
WHITE BEANS			1/2 BOX	/	/	/	/	
BARLEY			1/2 BOX	/	/	/	/	
LIMA BEANS			1/2 BOX	/	/	/	/	
SMALL RED BEANS			1/2 BOX	/	/	/	/	
PASTA			1/2 CS	/	/	/	/	
LINGUINI			1/2 CS	/	/	/	/	
SHELL MACARONI			1/2 CS	/	/	/	/	
FETTUCINI			1/2 CS	/	/	/	/	
GARDEN SPIRALS			1 CS	/	/	/	/	
FROZEN LASAGNA NOODLES			2 CS	/	/	/	/	
SPINACH FETT.			1/2 CS	/	/	/	/	
RADIATORE			1/2 CS	/	/	/	/	
LASAGNA			1/2 CS	/	/	/	/	
VINEGARS &OIL								
APPLE CIDER VIN.			1/2 GAL	/	/	/	/	
RED WINE VIN.			1/2 GAL	/	/	/	/	
SESAME OIL			1/2 GAL	/	/	/	/	
RICE VIN.			1/2 GAL	/	/	/	/	

This deli order sheet is typical of the forms suppliers provide. Eventually computers may simplify the work of ordering, but the forms will remain unless the industry adopts a standard print-out.

The Menu — The deli menu can double as a customer order sheet. Ours is a two-sided 7x8½-inch list with all our special and make-your-own sandwiches on one side, and all our salads, baked potatoes, and so forth on the other. There should also be a space to write in the special of the day. The customer comes in and takes a menu, circles a choice or writes one in from the specials board, then signs and hands it to the cashier. The cashier rings it in and gives it to the cook. When the cook prepares the order our counter help calls the customer's name and takes it to the table. The menu also goes out the door as advertising.

For our bakery menu, we're still working on a three-leaf flyer printed on good-quality colored stock with our logo on the front leaf, along with our name, address, and location—the immediate neighborhood. With any printed material you want to convey all the information you can. You wouldn't just say Schat's Bakery, but Schat's Bakery, address, Ukiah, California, and telephone number. Ours says "Courthouse Bakery," so it lets people know our immedi-

Courthouse
Bakery and Cafe

Schat's ™

113 West Perkins St.
Ukiah, CA 95482
(707) 462-1670

Lunch order for:_____

No. of Items ordered: _____

☐ **For Here**   ☐ **To Go**

Pick-up time: _____

Visit Us At Our Friedman Bros. Location!!!

See Reverse Side for Many Other House Specialties

Special Sandwiches

☐ **Legal Eagle** $4.25
  turkey, ham, jack, cheddar, lettuce and tomato

☐ **Melvin Belli** $4.25
  roast beef, cream cheese, pepperoncini, tomato, special red sauce on dark rye

☐ **Expert Witness** $4.00
  avocado, sprouts, onion, cucumber, tomato, spinach, carrots and jack cheese with special dijonaise sauce

☐ **Della's Delight** $4.00
  fresh croissant with tuna, tomato and sprouts

☐ **Perry Mason** $4.00
  Louisiana hot sausage served on a French roll with mustard, pepperoncinis and jack cheese

☐ **The Appeal** $4.25
  Italian dry salami, ham, turkey, provolone cheese, onions, olives, tomatoes, lettuce & Italian pesto sauce on a french roll

☐ **1/2 Sandwich** $2.50

☐ **1/2 Sandwich** *with a bowl of soup or side salad* $4.75
  ☐ *with side caesar add .25'*

Specials

☐ **Special of the day** *(check the chalk board)*

_____

☐ **Homemade Quiche** $4.95
  with dinner roll and green salad
  ☐ *with side caesar add .25'*

Large quiches made to order!

Or...Build Your Own Sandwich

☐ **Full Sandwiches** $4.25
☐ **1/2 Sandwich** $2.50

Breads:
☐ *Multi-Grain*
☐ *Sliced Sourdough*
☐ *French Roll*
☐ *Croissant (50')*
☐ *Sour Rye*
☐ *Sheepherders*
☐ *Skquaw Bread*

Meats:
☐ *Turkey*
☐ *Ham*
☐ *Pastrami*
☐ *Roast Beef*
☐ *Tuna*
☐ *Salami*

Cheeses:
☐ *Cheddar*
☐ *Swiss*
☐ *Jalapeno Jack*
☐ *Smoky Cheddar*
☐ *Jack*
☐ *Provolone*
☐ *Mozzarella*

Condiments:
☐ *Lettuce*
☐ *Tomato*
☐ *Mayonnaise*
☐ *Mustard*
☐ *Dijon*
☐ *Onion*
☐ *Sprouts*
☐ *Pickle*

Extras:
☐ *Avocado (50')*
☐ *Pepperoncini (50')*
☐ *Sliced Jalapenos (50')*
☐ *Potato Salad ($1.25)*

☐ **Pizza by The Slice** $1.75
  ☐ *with green salad* $3.25
  ☐ *with caesar salad* $3.75

_____

_____

_____

We Do Box Lunches For Large Get Togethers-Ask Us!

The deli menu for our courthouse location serves as an order sheet and provides information about the shop

ate whereabouts. You should print all of that on everything: on your menu, your business cards, your stationery, and anything else that takes ink or paint.

When you open up the menu there would be a list of all your baked goods, starting with breads and followed by other categories of baked goods. It needn't list prices because, no matter how often you reprint, prices always change when you still have plenty of old menus on hand. As a flyer it can also be advertising. People can take it with them. And you can drop it off places. Motels and tourist bureaus are great drop-off points if tourism is strong in your area.

A menu's form depends on how you handle your sales. Whether you have sit-down service with a printed and laminated menu, or have point-of-sale lunches with descriptive flyers as we do, will depend on the kind of place you have in mind.

Menu design calls for good layout, common sense, legibility, and simple arithmetic if it lists prices. Our bakery menu board is set up to list the price of each item individually and by the dozen, especially for the smaller products like cookies and danish. We cut the price per dozen by giving people one or two items free and calling it the "dozen" price. The price for one cookie is not necessarily the price for a dozen. For example, if we charge 45¢ each for a cookie, we don't charge $5.40 for a dozen. We charge $3.50 for a dozen. We always make deals on the dozen. That's how it's always been with bakeries.

The menu's size should be the minimum that allows for good legibility. Once you decide on size, you have to come up with the best way to get the most menus per sheet of paper. Paper is expensive and can be a make-or-break part of the printing bill. If a slightly smaller menu lets you get two to a sheet, where a larger one would take a whole sheet with an inch or so of waste, use the smaller menu. The printer will help you plan this. The printer can also help with graphic design if, like me, you are not strong in that department. You can hire a graphic designer. You can also brainstorm it with your staff. That works pretty well and is cheaper, too—something to keep in mind.

You should supplement menus and the blackboards with identification tags for each product. A pan of bear claws would have an identification tag in a plastic holder that said, for example, "Bear Claws, $1.20." In front of the cakes it would say, "Black Forest Cake," and might list the ingredients with the price. You want to have all those identification labels wherever you can, especially if you don't have a menu or menu board.

Dining Room Design —One reason we want visibility throughout the dining room is to keep the self-service area in view of the register and insure efficient service. A counter person 20 or 30 feet away from the self-service station can then see if coffee or sugar is out or make eye contact with a customer who may look around for someone to restock it. You also want to know if people are just walking in the front door to help themselves and walk right out again without making a trip to the register. I like our bakery wide open, anyway, without any cubby holes or corners. It has an airy atmosphere that fits the place. If you're trying to create a dimmer, trendy place, then you might want to create little nooks where everyone can sit down and enjoy a cup of coffee in semi-seclusion. A baker's personality is reflected in the bakery. Your bakery should reflect your personality, too, because you will spend most of your waking (and sleeping) moments there. People will get a good idea of who you are by the message you send with your bakery.

All this means planning for the feeling you want your customers to have. For people who want to kick back and relax, a place like ours might be too busy. Other people work, read, and respond well when it's busy. You can't please everybody. You have to get a collection of ideas, including your own, and just go with the best one. Remember it's your money and your deal, so don't be entirely swayed by what everyone thinks.

Furnishing a Dining Room — We like people to sit and enjoy themselves in our bakery but not to stay forever; so we make them comfortable enough to enjoy the meal then go. We offer nice places to sit and read a book if you want, but not the cushy booths where you can put up your legs and kick back for a long time. Our combination of rectangular, square, and round tables seems to work well for the purpose. Rectangular tables fit four to six people. The square tables suit four, and our smaller round tables, about 30 inches in diameter, take two to three. Sometimes people push tables together to seat more. Since we don't reserve tables, they have to come in early enough to ask if they can we put two tables together; then we'll pitch in and help them move furniture. Sometimes I've seen square tables next to round tables. It looks pretty funny, but people do whatever it takes to make themselves at home. It depends also on the mood you're striving for in your café. You incorporate whatever fits. If you are informal like us, you can accommodate a range of choices.

How long people will sit also determines how much seating you need. For example, we do as much business in the new store in the home-improvement center as in the downtown location. We know that the downtown location is where people want to hang out, however, so it has seating for 45. At the home-improvement center location people will grab and go; so we have seating for 25. More seating makes sense, too, if you serve meals, even simple ones. People sit down longer to eat breakfast or lunch than just to have a roll and coffee. So, with more leisurely dining and lower turnover, you also need more seating.

Our seating is comfortable—for the duration of the meal. That's the standard restaurant and café rule. You want to give people a strong chair that they sit in without feeling like they're going to fall through, but not so comfortable that they want to linger all day. A sturdy table is essential, too, so that, when people touch it, their espresso doesn't fly out of the cup. Basic considerations like that are all you need. If your food is good, people will settle in and be happy.

You also want your display cases to be relatively close to the seating so that the product can appeal to customers' visual and olfactory senses. While the customer shouldn't sit in a vast area out

Talking to other entrepreneurs I see that once you start a business you no longer get to do what you like to do. You have to do business instead of creating. I'm lucky because I'm here in the bakery. Even so, as small as it is, it gets to be a little factory after awhile; we're just cranking it out. In some ways I can be more creative because I can make different kinds of breads. But it's really hard, especially for a wholesale business, to say I want to make this today and put it out—because all the stores want a label, bags, and stuff like that.

—ELLEN HERING
BRUCE BREAD

in the open with no other customers around, you want to give them a little elbow room. This gets down to how much personal space people want. Some are happy packed in a crowd. It can add to the experience of coming in to get something to eat, although that's truer for a brief snack or coffee break than when someone wants a meal, or to sit and read awhile.

Merchandising racks are a good idea within the bakery seating area. Tiered display racks work well for that space, those with a small shelf on top and wider shelves toward the bottom. They're great for impulse items like bags of cookies, boxes of rolls, and packaged bread. If you have too much seating area, you crowd out display cases. On the other hand, you don't want to reduce or crowd the seating area. You have to balance display space and seating area. It's one more judgment call.

Mood — A bakery can be old fashioned, shiny and modern, 1920s sleek like See's Candies, or almost anything your imagination suggests. Ours is an old brick building and feels about as old-fashioned as they come. One of our brick interior walls is painted white, which helps to open up the small space. If you stay with dark colors you might give people a sense of claustrophobia. They also make it a little darker and can affect your lighting bill, which is something to consider. If your customers want a quiet cup of coffee with a bagel and a place to sit and read for a long time, you might expose the brick, and have it dark red. That gives a nice warm feeling, despite any other drawbacks it may have. Our place is small and usually crowded, so we want to make it seem a little bigger than it is. If you get the balance right, it will be very comfortable.

Table cloths are the easiest way to change the mood of your bakery if it has seating. Pick out a colorful print from the fabric store and cover it with either glass or plastic. Also, table cloths let you change the mood for the seasons. You can use a holiday design for Christmas, and a brighter color when winter turns to spring, and you want to get people in a spring mood.

Don't forget, however, that you are providing an atmosphere, so you want to make it pleasant. It's part of why you charge $4.00 to $5.00 for a sandwich. If everything walked out the door, and all you had to do was wrap it, you could sell the sandwich for $3.50 to $4.00 and not have to charge for table service, atmosphere, and the cost of your added square footage.

Music — Mainly we use a CD changer for background music and load two dozen disks to play randomly all day. You can put in six classical, six soft rock, six jazz, six blues, or whatever, push "random," and get a nice blend of music all day long. When we use the radio we tune to a soft-rock, blues or jazz station. You want to keep close control of music. The kids who worked for us would occasionally tune to their favorite station, and I've walked in when somebody was playing Metallica. You want pleasing music for the people you work with, but it's really for the customers' benefit. Also you don't want the sound to drown out the talk.

Outdoor Service — An outdoor seating area is a great idea. The Courthouse Bakery has only a garden bench and a table with two chairs out in front. The home-improvement center shop will have a 200-square-foot patio. Outdoor seating not only provides an attraction for your customers from spring to fall, but increases your seating. The baker around the corner from the Courthouse location converted a backyard trash area to a nice garden. Gayle's Bakery has terrific outdoor seating; they built a small patio and furnished it with furniture that can handle the elements. Heavy duty plastic tables and plastic chairs with umbrellas work fine and meet all the health codes. The new plastic furniture is designed so well now that you just wipe it down, and it should last as long as your indoor furniture. If you sell beer or wine, your liquor purveyors will sometimes give you free beer or wine umbrellas. Gayle's also has a heating element in the patio. They are not cheap, but Capitola is on the northern California coast where it's usually chilly year around. Elsewhere it would extend the outdoor dining season.

Disadvantages of a Café — A café is labor intensive. That in turn increases your payroll. There is a higher risk factor in a café because the cost of goods is higher, the margin is lower, and you have to meet your café payroll out of that margin. A café is more subject to

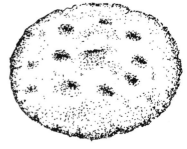
Barley bread, ancient Egypt

Egyptian raised wheat bread, 1200 B.C.

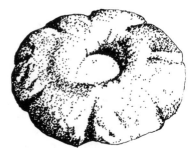
Ring bread, Greece, 580 B.C.

Roman bread, 200 B.C.

BREAD AND CIRCUSES

The Romans got leavened bread in about 300 B.C. from the Greeks, who got it from the Phoenicians three centuries earlier. By the Second Punic War (218-201 B.C.) the Romans were importing wheat and by 170 B.C. commercial bakeries began to appear. By 25 B.C. Rome had 329 bakeries.

Fear of hungry, restive city dwellers led the Romans to create bread doles and to invent large-scale milling. A Greek slave, Arcus Virgules Euryasaces, invented the first large mechanical dough mixer, one powered by a donkey or horse walking in circles to turn paddles and knead the dough in

a large stone bowl. The bread-dole roster grew from some 40,000 recipients in 72 B.C. to about 300,000 in A.D. 275. Eligible citizens carried bronze or lead ration tickets.

Roman miller-bakers had formed a corporation or guild in 168 B.C., and in the Second Century A.D. the government organized them into a "college" subject to official rules and regulations. It made the trade hereditary and obligatory, and drafted bakers as civil servants in thrall to the bread dole.

---

health codes and requires more staff training. You need more paper supplies, such as napkins and wrappers for sandwiches to go. All of a sudden you need ceramics—to serve lunch on ceramic plates and soup in bowls—and where you were once washed pots and pans in a big sink, you now need that dishwasher which, at $3,000 or $4,000, is not cheap.

The café puts extra pressure on the bakery to supply everything it needs, and getting the bakery to supply the café in a timely manner involves careful coördination. The cooks need their food prepared well in advance of serving it; but they need to get their orders and ingredients ready on time. The bakers can't wait for the cooks.

Finally, any time you go into the restaurant or café business you face more competition. If you open a bakery in a likely neighborhood or small town, and there's no other bakery there, you've got a corner on the market. If you go into the breakfast and lunch business in the same place, there will be plenty of competition and nobody will have a corner on it. You also enter restaurants' higher failure-rate bracket when you open a café. So, if you're making money and doing well without a café, you may not want the headaches that go with it. But, if you think you can do a little better with a café and it will make you more money, then go ahead. You can do it gradually by introducing soup and salads, work up to a full menu and follow it up with specialties like baked potatoes, pastas, pizzas, or whatever strikes your market's fancy. However you do it, it will be uniquely yours.

In a wholesale bakery business you don't have to worry about stimulating sales with your merchandise display area. In fact, if you bake only for wholesale distribution, you can and should set up in a low-rent industrial area, with only production space and perhaps an office or somewhere to meet business customers. If you bake only wholesale, your profit margins will be lower and you need to keep your costs low, too. Even if you don't plan on any wholesale business, restaurants and possibly small groceries may ask if you want to sell to them. That's flattering in its way, but presents a whole new set of problems, one of which, as mentioned, is how the retailer presents your product. Finally, as a small bakery owner out to develop a wholesale business, you have to get the product to your customers. Wholesaling also means deliveries. Somebody has to bake the product while somebody else delivers it. You can't do it all unless, perhaps, you sell to restaurants that are open only evenings. Then you can bake all day, fill up your van, and deliver the product on your way home. It means being very resourceful and meeting the demand in any way possible.

It's a good idea to find out beforehand what product the potential customer is already using. Taste it and make sure that yours is better. Most of them will want to offer the best product possible. Some accounts seem to be concerned only with price, which is why some restaurants serve fairly good food but nondescript bread. It happens more often than you'd expect. You wonder how a restaurant can serve a nice piece of salmon and vegetables, and then give you such a bland piece of bread. It's either because they're cheap, or because nobody has gone to the owner and said, Your bread is really awful.

That might be a direct way of opening a sales pitch: Your bread is awful, try mine. It gets the idea across, but we don't recommend it. A better approach is to pick a target area, research what bread your potential customers use, and know your own product thoroughly. If you are small, you have to go out and sell personally. It means either cold calling or just walking in, introducing yourself, and offering a sample of your product. Buyers want to meet the owner, anyway. You have to prove to them that you're a reliable person and that you have a superior product at a good price. If you can show all that, then getting wholesale customers will not be difficult.

If you want to get into supermarkets, you need more sales skills and much greater production. Even if you identify your product as a superior item that should command a high price, however, the store probably will not make much money on it. Most of them work on a very low margin and require producers to share a little of the operating costs by paying for shelf space. Chain supermarket managers exercise very little control of their own. Usually you must deal with the head office wherever it may be. Profitable wholesale distribution to markets means high-volume baking, with low costs and a low profit margin. Starting out, at least, you would ordinarily restrict wholesale accounts to low-volume, higher-profit production for specialty stores.

The hardest part of wholesaling is taking orders and filling them without making mistakes. It's very easy to discover that you are a great salesperson but have more orders than you can handle. You should either delegate the paper work to an assistant or focus on trying to avoid mistakes. Mistakes will happen in a bakery at every turn. It's in the nature of the business, as with any other, but customers are not very tolerant of bakeries' mistakes. Usually they have just purchased an item they hoped to consume right away or very soon after, and their disappointment is fairly immediate if not instantaneous.

As long as you're small and working on low-volume production you can do almost anything. The trap is that you will think you can keep on doing it. When you increase your volume you have to adjust your methods or you will get over-extended and come to grief. Wholesale business is a sure way to get over-extended fast. If you pursue a potentially large wholesale market, be prepared to hire new people and reorganize the way you handle the bakery's products. Keep monitoring staff, equipment, and procedures.

Or plan to get up earlier.

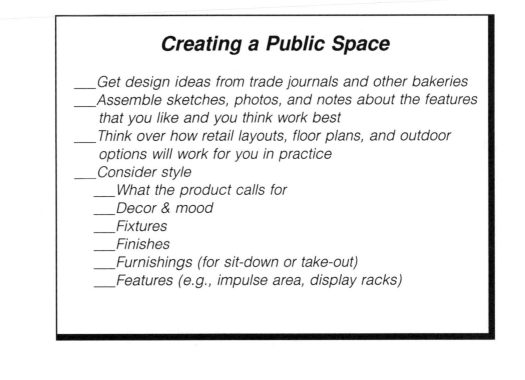

Creating a Public Space

___Get design ideas from trade journals and other bakeries
___Assemble sketches, photos, and notes about the features
    that you like and you think work best
___Think over how retail layouts, floor plans, and outdoor
    options will work for you in practice
___Consider style
    ___What the product calls for
    ___Decor & mood
    ___Fixtures
    ___Finishes
    ___Furnishings (for sit-down or take-out)
    ___Features (e.g., impulse area, display racks)

4

PREP WORK: SETTING GOALS

L ET'S SAY you've now decided either that you want to change your career path and become a baker or that you've been involved in so many bakeries it's time to go out on your own. That's where you need to stop, take a personal inventory, weigh your choices, and determine what kind of bakery you will have. To make your business a success from the outset you'll need a number of personal skills but, above all, you'll need to be organized. You need to approach your idealized bakery in an organized way and build sound business organization into it even before you start.

If you're like most of us, you probably haven't organized your life much beyond getting up at about the same time every morning. While spontaneity is an appealing and probably healthful personal trait, it has no place in your business. You will need to develop a system for every part of the business, regardless of how creative and untrammeled your personal life has been or remains.

GETTING ORGANIZED

You can't expect to get those organizational skills all of a sudden, just because you're in business. If you're lucky, you'll have learned from somebody in a good bakery or acquired organizational skills in another profession. If you are *not* totally organized, your work will be chaos and your working life will go crazy. Laying the groundwork for organization while the business is still small and going slowly is a last chance, because when you get busy and start suffering those growing pains you may not have time to set up the systems you need.

For many of us beginners there will be times when our whole business life feels like it is going out of control and will fall apart.

It can be overwhelming, and, like many people starting businesses, you'll want to cut and run. That's when you have to remind yourself that you're making progress every day and you're still finding ways to improve. If you have a good product and you face the task, you'll make it. You'll begin to acquire filing cabinets and to take care of your paperwork. And that will be because, at some point, you'll lock the office door, shut the windows, and actually do the paperwork. If you ignore it—this is a guarantee—it will only get worse.

There's a strong temptation when you open to just move. But then, as you need more equipment, get more charge accounts, and branch out into more activities, you'll learn that the lack of systems wrecks efficiency and eats up income. You need to establish your systems early. That means, for example, establishing a system for charge accounts as soon as you have one charge account. Then, when you have fifty accounts there is a system in place. That goes for everything. Before you get rolling, preferably before you open your doors, you should have set up your accounting system, your ordering system, your production schedule, inventory systems, and everything else necessary to keep track of the dozens of things that go on all at once during business hours.

You may ask, why be so organized to order 100 pounds of flour and a few hundred dollars of bakery supplies? The reason is that when you start ordering $2,000 a week or $3,000 a week, you'll need a way to compare supplier A's costs to supplier B's. With a system in place, no matter how enormous or complicated your orders get, you can always make the best deal. On everything.

BUSINESS SKILLS

You need to be as good in accounting as you are in baking before you go into the business, unless you have a great relationship with someone skilled at it who is going into business with you. It could be your spouse or a partner, and you may decide that one will be the bookkeeper and the other will do the baking. But even then, know your numbers, know percentages, know operating ratios. Partners and spouses often die or part company. Enroll in business accounting courses so that you know accounts payable from accounts receivable. Many of those courses, especially in community colleges, are taught by professionals who are in business themselves. You may be able to get good practical advice from them. Have them explain whether something works in the real world or is just a theory. Everything should be as simple as possible, because you need to know it will work on a daily basis when you've got 20 minutes to post daily sales and make deposits.

Don't take just accounting courses, take business management courses, marketing courses, personnel management courses, take basic economics and personal finance. Read all the self-help books you

*We called it Mendocino Sourdough from day one. We've always done some sort of baguette or white sourdough, but I wanted our version of a **pain au levain**. I wanted to put our signature on it. I like the flavor of barley in different contexts, so I thought it would be interesting to add a little barley flour. The actual [sourdough] feeding schedule and the proportions of barley and whole-wheat flour all have changed over the years, as we've learned more and reacted to how it's come out, but it's probably our oldest surviving product.*
—CHRISTOPHER KUMP
CAFE BEAUJOLAIS, THE BRICKERY

can find. You need all these skills, as well as an organized way to do things, and you need them preferably before you open your doors. When you go into business for yourself, there is no big company to look out for your interests. You are the company; but *your* company can look out for your interests better than any other if you organize it right.

Trade journals, trade shows, and consulting firms are good sources for acquiring skills related specifically to bakeries. There are numerous trade shows—big ones—for bakeries and restaurants. The Retailers Bakery Association (RBA) is a major trade association. It offers several days of valuable seminars at its annual convention, and attending the convention is definitely worth the expense. The RBA and the American Institute of Baking (AIB) are on the Internet now. There are also a handful of first-rate trade journals, among them *Bakery Production and Marketing*. We have listed it and a few other sources in the Appendix. Between RBA and a regular look at the trade journals you can get all the specific trade information you need.

BAKERY SKILLS

If you want to get bakery experience by starting as a baker's assistant, and are lucky enough to land a job at it, you won't make big money. If you have an expensive lifestyle—with a growing family and a mortgage—you'll have to cut back on your expenses unless you have unlimited capital or investors to see you through. Consider the low pay your tuition. Expect it to continue when you open the bakery, too. Some businesses seem to take off, and make money from the very beginning; but don't *you* count on it. You'll hear story after story from business people who made no money until about their second or third year. What you must do is conserve capital. You'll need money to pay your bills and put food on the table until you reach break-even two or three years down the line. At break-even there's no profit, but at least the business will stop draining your capital.

If you're employed at a successful bakery, pay attention while you're on the job and try to do everything. Learn what works for the bakery. That's what you want to duplicate, but you also want to look at its weaknesses. Maybe it lacks good flow in the bakery line, but resistance to change keeps it from doing better. When you set up your place you would duplicate the best part the procedure but switch things around to relieve the problems you see every day. Every place will have a few problems. Try to get rid of all you've seen before you set up.

Stay after hours to put in extra time and learn all you can. Tell the boss you know he can't afford to pay you overtime, but ask if he or she will let you stay on a couple hours. If you like the work, that will be a joy. It's like going to a baking class. If all you do is roll the dough and make breads, you could stick around after work and hang out with the cake decorator just to decorate cakes. Say you just make roses for half an hour; that's how you learn things.

FIND A NICHE

To start building that profitable business a few years down the line, you need to begin thinking right away about your market, your product, your equipment, and your shop. They are all interdependent and inseparable. Research what market you want to reach and how best to reach it. Your market determines what product will move well enough to support your business, and your product determines what equipment and kitchen layout you need.

Think about your chief product. Every bakery should be identified with something special. Even bakeries that make everything superbly produce something by which the market knows them. It helps even before you start to know how you will highlight your best skills. For example, our bakery makes what's known as a sheepherder's bread. It's not fancy but it's our signature bread. People come in to buy Schat's Sheepherder Bread. We've made it for generations from a formula my grandfather acquired, and it's been a huge favorite with people who know the bread. It's superior to other bakeries' sheepherder breads, it's what identifies us, and it's how many people hear about us. You want to try to attract customers with one unique item and then let them explore everything else you make.

EXPERIMENT

When you experiment to develop your product-line, find people for a test market. Just because you like an item doesn't mean it will taste good to everybody. Your test market can be family or friends, but don't hand over a sample and say, "Here is the best scone you've ever had, give it a try." You need honest criticism. Plant a little doubt. Tell people, "I'm trying this out for a new product but I'm not that sure about it." Reassure them that they won't hurt your feelings, because you don't want to serve a bad scone. They will tell you "Well it's a little dry" or "It's just not sweet enough." Get as many people to taste it as you can. It will be the best information you can possibly get. Because if you sample widely enough that test market will be a representation of all your potential customers.

You can't rely on trade journals alone, but they are surprisingly good guides to a profitable product mix. Every other issue of *Bakery Production and Marketing* magazine, which is free monthly to people in the industry, will tell what's on the rise, what's on the skids: "Danish and muffins are taking a dive, bagels and scones are going through the roof." It's a hot tip that tells you why and lays out a whole market analysis. You may decide not to go into the danish,

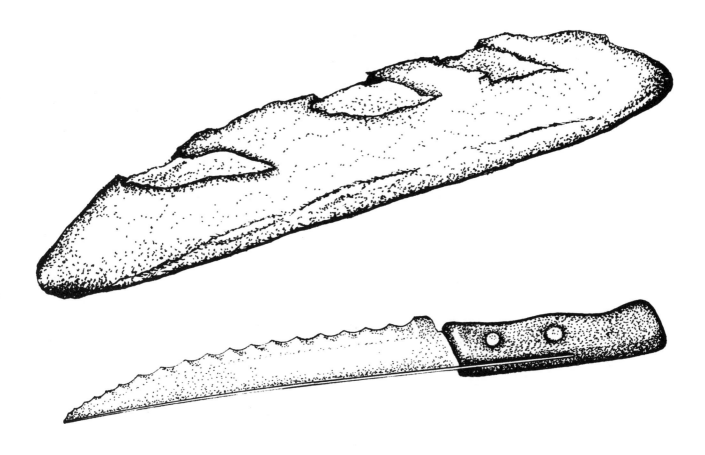

muffin, and croissant business but to set up in the scone and bagel trade. That depends also on your market. We'll discuss that below.

There are bakers who started out selling products from their kitchens. We mentioned Mrs. Fields Cookies. There's also a company called Cinnabon World Famous Cinnamon Rolls, which sets up in malls. It does strictly cinnamon rolls. Its founder apparently had a great recipe for home-style cinnamon rolls. She was able to duplicate them in quantity and get them into one store. It was one of those rare items that took off immediately. She recently sold the company for $400- or $500-million: On cinnamon rolls! Still, being a baker at home doesn't prepare you for being a commercial baker. You can develop good quality items at home, but you have to be able to transfer those items to large-scale production. First, you must be prepared to bake for 400 instead of four people a day. Second, as a corollary of that, you won't be able to be involved in everything you make when you move up to large-scale production. The work is very different in many ways.

If you're moving up from a teaspoonful of this and a capful of that to pounds of this and quarts of that, you need to learn your conversions. With some ingredients the proportions change as you scale up. The amount of vanilla you may need for a small-batch recipe increased ten times will not be a tenfold increase of vanilla, because a little bit of it will permeate the whole product. If you increase vanilla proportionally it's like adding tankards of it, and that's all you taste. You have to watch out for the little items: spices, salt, yeast. Sometimes the more you scale up the product, the less of certain ingredients you use.

There is no problem increasing flour and water ten times in weight; but, while you will usually get the same texture, the equipment you need for large batches makes a difference. What you whip up with a mixer or hand whisk at home will have a different texture from what you combine in a large commercial mixer. If you pay $10,000 or $12,000 for a machine specifically to incorporate ingredients into a dough, it will make a whale of a difference in the result. That's also where experimenting comes in. There are as many different pieces of equipment as there are bakery products. You need a heavy-duty mixer for bagels but not for pastries and danish dough. There are different ovens for different products. First you decide what you plan to bake, then select the equipment you need, not the other way around. Otherwise you may spend too much money and not get what you need for your products.

PRICE FOR A LIVING WAGE

Finally, an acceptable recipe must command a price high enough to cover the labor, materials, and overhead necessary to prepare it. That's the point of being in business. You have to come up with a price per item that will cover all its costs with a little over for profit. Don't count your own labor as free. Cost out everything as though somebody else were doing it. Your own wage is a cost, not profit. Profit is to compensate for the risks of being in business. You have to decide what profit you want to see from each item.

You also have to base expected profits on what the market is willing to pay. The market will pay $2.50 for a loaf of bread even though it costs you 50¢ or 60¢ to produce. That is what the market sets as the price of a loaf of bread. If you have an item that costs you $1.80 to make and you wanted to see the same margin as on a loaf of bread, you would have to price that high-cost item at $7.00 or $8.00. The market probably won't pay it, so you might have to sell it for $3.50 by cutting your profit margin to half what you make on bread. If you sell a high volume of low-mark-up items, however, they could bring in sufficient money despite the lower margin. Those are calculations you always have to make. We will get into a little of that in Chapter 14.

Once you work out product mix and profit margins, a simple way to project income is to guesstimate how many people a day you expect to walk through the bakery door. If you can sell each person $3.00 worth of goods and you expect on average 300 people a day, that's $900 every business day. The industry estimates maybe 35 to

40 percent food costs, 25 percent in labor, 15 percent overhead on the average item; so say it costs $700 a day to make $900. That's a profit of $200 a day. This is a very simple projection but it may be enough to tell you roughly whether you want to get into the business at the location you pick out. You have to know how much you can charge for the products you plan to make. That depends on who's buying.

YOUR MARKET

The first consideration in a projected market is average household income, but you also want to learn about people's eating habits. Go around town. Is every lunch place busy? We operate in a town where every shop is busy at lunchtime. People here decided—fairly recently as I understand—that there is not enough time to go home and eat. So everyone goes out at noon and spends $5 for lunch. There is not much of a dinner crowd here; the number of lunches served daily is hugely overwhelming compared to dinners served. Other places might still be good lunch towns, but everybody also goes out for happy hour and a salad or something, or the practice is to eat dinner in restaurants and tell friends whether the food there is still good. It's a peer-group sort of thing.

There are different food-service environments. In a college town, for example, you can do great volume on small-ticket items but you won't sell high-end party desserts. A well-off suburb may buy all the party desserts you can make. Today, however, you can't go wrong with fat-free, low-cal items in the bakery case. Most people these days are careful about sweet or fatty things. If you plan to open a donut shop, your prospects may not be very rosy, because donuts are fried in one or another kind of fat. You can't get away from their effect on the waistline and arteries. But if you're a full-scale baker you can play off all the variables. You can substitute fruit purees for shortening, and honey, or raisin or fruit juices for sugar. You can flavor items while you're experimenting and have a whole line of low-fat, non-fat, non-dairy, diabetic, or low-sodium food. There is a growing demand for that cuisine, and it's worth testing for in your market.

What your potential customers will buy depends somewhat on income level and food preferences. Look at the neighborhood closely. Walk into the shops and surrounding businesses where you plan to set up. Take a look at the clientele. Are they blue-collar workers who may spend $5 or $6 tops? Are they white-collar middle-management people. Or do the ladies and gentlemen of the community park their Infinitis or BMWs downtown to spend $15 or $20 on baked goods without a blink of the eye? Perhaps the neighborhood has unemployed people or public-assistance recipients who can only afford items for between 75¢ and $1.50. While you probably shouldn't bother with a donut shop in a classy downtown, its prices may help satisfy people's wants in a low-income area.

A mix of wholesale and retail sales can be part of setting your goals. What percentage of your business, if any, do you want to be wholesale? You can predetermine wholesale business by getting the accounts before you open. Say you want 50 percent of the business to be wholesale. If you anticipate doing $200,000 a year, you have to put on your selling shoes and go out and sell $100,000 worth of wholesale goods. It's easy to calculate. The customer tries the product and says, "I go through 200 loaves of bread a week, and I'm going to need them every week." You simply work it out and calculate how much you'll do a year on those accounts.

YOUR PRODUCTS

Your market will determine what products you can sell, but be sure also to consider whether your shop will complement or compete with other bakeries in the market. Healdsburg, for example, is a small community in Sonoma County just to the south of us. While Healdsburgers may not like to think of the town as a suburb of Santa Rosa, a city of about 130,000 a few miles further south, many including myself would consider it that. Healdsburg is also a favorite tourist spot with antique stores, art galleries, boutiques, and bed-and-breakfasts set around a leafy town square. It had three bakeries.

Cousteau's Bakery, an old-fashioned crusty-bread, artisan-style place a block or so from the square, has been there for years. It makes croissants, French bread and rolls, and does a sandwich trade. It recently remodeled its premises and now sells wholesale, as well. "The Upscale Downtown Bakery and Creamery"—the actual name, it's in the Yellow Pages—was set up by a baker from Chez Panisse in Berkeley, so it's mainstream nouvelle and gourmet. Downtown produces frankly decadent deserts, pastries, and ice cream for when people choose to indulge themselves to the max. The third shop called the "Home Bakery" just went out of business. It was a small place, which is all right, but what killed it was its lack of character and variety.

To stay competitive, a successful bakery has to both specialize and offer variety. Home apparently didn't do either and failed to distinguish itself for any particular market, or at least for one broad enough to support it. If you're in a small demographic area, even with a tourist trade, you can't copy the shop right down the road. You need to do something completely different so that you share customers. A new baker has to think, what kind of baked goods can't you find here? There's no other way. Unless each of, say, three bakeries concentrates on different specialties, the best will drive the other two out of business.

TWENTY-FOUR PIECES OF SEASONED OAK

When the Cafe Beaujolais Brickery's baker—who was also a stand-up comic—got a theater engagement in Germany, he left. Tim Bottom, his assistant of two weeks, offered to fill in and has been the Brickery's baker for the past seven years. Every weekday he stokes up the brick oven for which the bakery is named with 24 pieces of oak firewood. It will then produce about 35 loaves of bread at a time for as many as seven bakes a day. Bread from wood-fired brick ovens is a crusty, chewy loaf that other ovens cannot duplicate. The Brickery's latest product—enthusiastically received by its growing retail and wholesale market—is a sourdough bagel. The bakers first boil the bagels in the restaurant kitchen, which is housed next door.

Cafe Beaujolais is a highly acclaimed restaurant in the town of Mendocino on California's north coast and a favored destination of tourists from around the world. In 1983, Margaret Fox, its owner since 1977, established the "Cafe Beaujolais Bakery" in Fort Bragg just up the coast to produce panforte, fruitcake, and other specialties for wholesale and mail-order sales. In 1988, as the restaurant's dinner trade grew, husband and co-owner/chef Christopher Kump suggested offering good quality bread from a traditional brick oven to complement the meals. He contacted Alan Scott, a designer, builder, and authority on brick ovens, to design and help build one. It was named the Brickery so people would not confuse it with the "Bakery."

Cafe Beaujolais, The Brickery
961 Ukiah Street
Mendocino, California

"I wanted to bake good crusty bread for use in-house," Kump said. "I've eaten a lot of great bread and I had done research in books on baking and breads. But the books are all for home ovens or are textbooks for huge-scale commercial operations. A brick oven falls betwixt and between, and does not react like either. So, once I'd built the oven, the baker and I spent the better part of the first year getting to know it—figuring out its temperature curves, how it responds, and when to start baking after raking out the ashes. We learned a lot the hard way. Simultaneously, I started working on bread recipes, garnering what I could from books, extrapolating, and playing around.

"These ovens are idiosyncratic. It takes finesse to get your product to come out consistently well. Tim's definitely got it down. But we've had, six or seven bakers come through. None could bake like Tim. Our weekend bakers, Zac and Tomás, have been with us just over a year, and I'd say that in the last three or four months they're getting close to Tim's consistency. My own bread came out pretty well early on, but that's just because I have a longstanding background in working with food. I knew how it should come out, and I'm used to experimenting."

"Tim once said that the thing that's kept him interested here is the nature of the work. It's never exactly the same from one day to the next. You build a fire, and one day it's going to be a little cooler, one day a little hotter. And your doughs, because they're living things, are always going to react slightly differently. I think he really enjoys having that challenge of getting people to come to the window and say, this is absolutely the best bread I've ever had in my life."

Any time you put together a business plan, you need to know what you will bake—what products will sustain your income. You don't *really* know your market until you start baking things and getting responses. You will plan to bake the most profitable and competitive product you can, but once you open your doors you'll have to just try things. When they sell you stay with them, and when they don't you move on. Your marketing strategy gets very pragmatic: Put it out under the collective public nose. If people like it, keep it on your daily bake sheet. If you make 30 of something and 25 are left—and after two more days they still don't sell—take them off the bake sheet.

Once established, you might find you're selling only a few of a once popular item but think you have to keep making it because you always made it. It's an easy trap to fall into. You should drop unprofitable products. If it irritates a few customers, try to introduce them to something else. If you lose them, remember that you're changing to attract different, more numerous customers. This is something you might never say publicly, but among bakers it may not be a bad attitude to have. Getting rid of unprofitable items for those that make money makes sense. You're in the business to make a living.

Many people who think "bakery" visualize wedding cakes, party cakes, and items for special events. There are birthdays every day, after all, and it seems like a good trade on which to base a bakery. I personally would not focus our business on those items but might add them later if the market seemed to want them. If a bakery is successful with one line of products, the shop's market will grow. Then, if it decides to add a line of cakes, people will come to it for weddings, birthdays, and special events. You want to be sure, however, that anything you add does not hurt your everyday traffic. Develop and cater to your regular customers first, and then add the frills. For another baker—and depending on the market, of course—cakes could be the leading product and bread might follow.

Here's another approach. You can do specialty breads for expensive restaurants, or you can do breads for cheap restaurants. Most people may think about getting their name and bread out in some of the fancier, upscale places to identify it as an upscale item. But we also sell buns to a little hot dog stand that was around the corner but has moved to a new location. It has the best hot dogs in town, partly because they're made with our fresh product. The stand is not expensive but it makes a better hot dog. The buns and the hot dogs support each other and produce a little synergy for both places. Marketing like that works.

It's a great idea to get your bread on the health-food rack of a good grocery store where you can promote it as made fresh daily with no preservatives, and run it there every day. Don't bother initially, however, trying to sell to the average supermarket until

When I decided to go into a bakery I realized I had just been in the kitchen doing it myself. So I contacted the people in the Arcata Co-op. I told them what I was doing and that I was thinking about starting a bakery and didn't have any idea what I was doing. They said, well, if you want to come up and spend the day here, you can work with us in the bakery and you'll learn a lot. So I went up there and they put me up, and I started at 5:00 a.m. I learned more in that space of time from 5:00 a.m. to midnight than I could ever learn on my own about the reality of how you do this on a bigger scale.
—BRUCE HERING
BRUCE BREAD

you can make money on their low prices, pay for the shelf space, deliver four or five times a week, and swallow the cost of stales.

Ethnic specialties are fun, but neighborhood dictates that as much as anything. In North Beach in San Francisco you would without doubt sell a lot of Italian bread. Here we advertise as a Dutch bakery with an American flair, but you wouldn't consider it an ethnic bakery. Baking strictly in an old-country style works better when the ethnic market exists or enough of a general market wants to experiment. A large, very ethnically diverse market might let you specialize like that. A small, homogeneous community like ours won't.

YOUR SHOP

That promising neighborhood is a good place to set up, however, only if you can find space there to rent or buy. We'll discuss acquiring space in considerable detail, but remember above all to keep your options open and be on the lookout for unexpected opportunities. If the building you rent or buy has extra space, consider a sublease. It may not bring in much extra money directly but could have other advantages like increasing traffic. Along that line, I know of some very good bread and pastry bakers who did not want to do cakes. They had an opportunity to rent out their baking area to a wedding-cake caterer. She explained that she had done only wedding cakes out of her home. All of her cakes were special orders and she was expanding into cheesecakes and pies as wholesale accounts. They rented her their production space, but only for the hours after they had finished their own baking. She would come in during the off-production hours and do her special-order work. Her product didn't interfere with theirs or vice versa. If they ever decided to expand their line to cakes, they could purchase them from their tenant to sell in their cases at a mark-up.

This kind of opportunity lets your otherwise idle facilities make money. You may not see a great deal of money from it, but it can provide a way to expand your product-line and attract more customers without taking on extra tasks. This works best, however, only if the tenant is in a related business that uses your space and equipment but does not compete with your products. For example, if you have a breakfast and lunch trade, a small restaurant may be a compatible evening tenant. It's a good idea to be sure that your evening tenant's plans mesh with yours if you decide to do this. The only restaurant I ever heard of that rented space from a bakery eventually left because it needed to expand. You must also make sure that the quality of a tenant's product reflects favorably on your own business. You could call this renting time like space. But you shouldn't overlook renting extra space, either.

YOUR COMPUTER

I use a computer regularly and think it belongs in any business today. All of our payroll goes on it, and we are now experimenting with a bakery program that does everything from inventory control and costing to formula keeping. All of our formulas are loaded into memory. With ingredient price changes, the program will adjust the cost of the formula and suggest what to charge for the product. Setting up the program at the outset is expensive, but it looks like it will save enough money over time to pay for itself. We discuss computers and these specialized bakery programs in Chapter 14.

Our cash register is not tied into the computer but that's a very good idea, especially if you're an absentee owner. I know an owner of several franchise pizza parlors who can access each of his computerized cash registers from a laptop and see exactly how much each has sold for the day—broken down into kinds of products: pizzas, soft drinks, soups. Believe me, it's a comfort to know what's going on.

YOUR PLAN FOR SUCCESS

This transitional chapter only hints at the tasks a beginning baker faces. It raises important questions. For usable answers you'll need a written business plan. The plan is not only to set you on the right path and let you step back to see how you are doing, but to help you get the financing you will no doubt need. You'll base the plan on many of the things this book says you need to know and on all the research you'll do to find them out. The plan doesn't have to be fancy. There are even a few sources and aids to help you draft it. We'll go over them at the end of the book when you're ready to put the plan on paper. But you do need the plan.

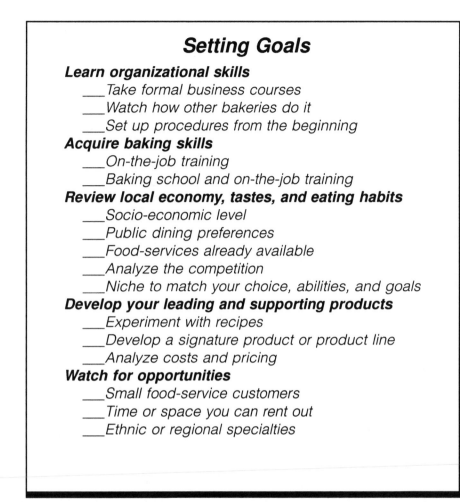

Setting Goals

Learn organizational skills
___Take formal business courses
___Watch how other bakeries do it
___Set up procedures from the beginning

Acquire baking skills
___On-the-job training
___Baking school and on-the-job training

Review local economy, tastes, and eating habits
___Socio-economic level
___Public dining preferences
___Food-services already available
___Analyze the competition
___Niche to match your choice, abilities, and goals

Develop your leading and supporting products
___Experiment with recipes
___Develop a signature product or product line
___Analyze costs and pricing

Watch for opportunities
___Small food-service customers
___Time or space you can rent out
___Ethnic or regional specialties

CONVERSION TABLES AND RECIPES:

No book on baking would be complete without a few recipes. So we've included a few along with some volumetric and weight equivalents. No list of weights and equivalents has everything. This list is no exception. You will have to start your own list and add to it as you go. The recipes represent a handful of favorites (although not the family secrets) and a little promotion for pears, one of our area's leading products. We offer these, like the rest of these pages, as a beginning, something to build on.

The bread recipes are based on the quantity of liquid. Flour measurements are approximate and will vary. Add flour until you get the right consistency.

CONVERSION TABLES

MEASURES:

60 liquid drops	= 1 teaspoon (tsp)	
3 tsp	= 1 tablespoon (tbs)	
2 tbs	= 1 fluid ounce	
16 tbs	= 1 cup	
2 cups	= 1 pint	
2 cups (liquid)	= 1 pound	

EQUIVALENTS:

1 tsp	= 1/6 oz
1 tbs	= ½ oz
1 oz	= 2 tbs
2 oz	= ¼ cup
4 oz	= ½ cup
6 oz	= ¾ cup
8 oz	= 1 cup

INGREDIENT EQUIVALENTS:

	TSP	TBS	¼ CUP	½ CUP	¾ CUP	1 CUP	1 POUND
Shortenings:	1/6 oz	½ oz	2 oz	4 oz	6 oz	8 oz	2 cups
Wheat flour:							
Bread	1/12 oz	¼ oz	1 oz	2⅛ oz	3¼ oz	4¼ oz	3¾ cups
Cake/Pastry	1/12 oz	¼ oz	1 oz	2 oz	3 oz	4 oz	4 cups
Graham	1/10 oz	⅓ oz	1-1/6 oz	2⅓ oz	3½ oz	4½ oz	3½ cups
Milk:							
Fresh whole	1/6 oz	½ oz	2 oz	4 oz	6 oz	8 oz	2 cups
Pwdrd whole	1/5 oz	½ oz	1⅛ oz	2⅜ oz	3½ oz	4¾ oz	3⅓ cups
Pwdrd nonfat	1/12 oz	¼ oz	1 oz	2 oz	3 oz	4 oz	4 cups
Sugar:							
Granulated	1/6 oz	½ oz	2 oz	4 oz	6 oz	8 oz	2 cups
Brown	1/9 oz	⅓ oz	1⅓ oz	2⅔ oz	4 oz	5⅓ oz	3 cups
Powdered	1/10 oz	⅓ oz	1-1/6 oz	2⅓ oz	3½ oz	4½ oz	3½ cups

INGREDIENT WEIGHTS:

Cocoa	1 lb = 4 cups		Almonds	1 lb = 4 cups
Chocolate	1 lb = 16 1-oz squares		Almonds, ground	1 lb = 2⅔ cups
Walnut halves	1 lb = 4½ cups		Almonds, slivered	1 lb = 3½ cups
Rolled Oats	1 lb = 3½ cups		1 lemon	= 2-3 tsp juice
Cornmeal (& farinas)	1 lb = 3 cups			= 2 tsp zest
Raisins	1 lb = 3 cups		1 orange	= 6-8 tsp juice
Prunes	1 lb = 2½ cups			= 2-3 tsp zest
Dates	1 lb = 2½ cups (60)			
Figs (dried)	1 lb = 3 cups (44)		Eggs/lb	
Bananas	1 lb = 3 (approx.)		8 lg in shell	= 1 lb
Cream cheese	1 lb = 2 cups		Eggs/cup	
Cottage cheese	1 lb = 2 cups		Whole: 6 large, 8 med., 10-11 sm.	
Mashed potatoes	1 lb = 1¾ cups		Whites: 8 large, 10-11 med., 11-12 sm.	
Molasses (& syrups)	1 lb = 1⅓ cups		Yolks: 12 large, 13-14 med., 15-16 sm.	

Milk Dough

YIELD	25 1½-lb loaves
PREPARATION TIME	25 minutes
SOURCE	Schat's Courthouse Bakery
COMMENTS	Milk dough is a sandwich loaf base, softened with shortening and enriched with milk, eggs, and sugar. It's good for dinner rolls, calzone, hot dog and hamburger buns, raisin bread, cinnamon-nut bread. You can add parmesan cheese, and minced garlic, onions, and herbs to it, then divide and put it in muffin tins for good bread-like muffins. Or you can add sugar or other sweeteners to use it for sweet muffins.

INGREDIENTS

	Whole		*Scaled*
Water	16 lb		2⅔ c.
Eggs	4 lb		2-3 lg
Bread Flour	30 lb		9 c.
Sugar	3 lb		½ c.
Shortening	3 lb		½ c.
Milk Powder	2 lb		½ c.
Dry yeast		14 oz	1 pkg
Salt		11 oz	1¼ tsp
Egg shade	Dash		Optional

METHOD

Pour water and eggs in the mixing bowl. Add flour, sugar, shortening, yeast, flour and salt. Add milk powder late or it will lump up in liquid. If you use fresh milk, reduce the water by that amount. Don't mix the yeast and salt together or the yeast will burn out.

Incorporate the ingredients in a 15-minute mix, 10 minutes in first gear with five minutes in second to finish.

We use fresh yeast for a better result, although this recipe is based on active dry yeast. To convert to fresh yeast substitute one pound for every 7 ounces of dry yeast. The recipe also calls for a shot of egg shade—a food color—which you can dispense with if you can use farm-fresh eggs with a dark yolk.

Scale into 1-lb 12-oz loaves and bake in a pre-heated oven for 40 to 50 minutes at 375°.

For the scaled recipe (two loaves) combine with a whisk then a wood spatula until stiff enough to work by hand. Let rise in the mixing bowl, punch down twice. Remove knead, shape, and let double in size before baking. These loaves are slightly larger. Bake a very little longer, until thumping the loaves produces a hollow sound.

Molasses Multi-Grain Bread

YIELD   25 1½-lb loaves

PREPARATION TIME 25 minutes

SOURCE   Schat's Courthouse Bakery

COMMENTS   This is a rich, flavorful, full-grain bread that's very easy to prepare. We've sold it for a few generations, and it's a hit with our customers.

INGREDIENTS

	Whole	Scaled
Water	16 lb	2⅔ c.
Bread flour	10 lb	2¼ c.
High gluten flour	11 lb	2½ c.
Bran	3 lb	1½ c.
Whole wheat flour	5 lb	1½ c.
Rye flour	2 lb	½ c.
Brown sugar	2 lb 8 oz	½ c.
Honey	⅔ qt	¼ c.
Oil	⅔ qt	¼ c.
Molasses	½ qt+	3 tbs
Dry yeast	7 oz	1 pkg
Salt	9 oz	1¾ tsp

METHOD   Add all the ingredients with the mixer in first gear using the dough hook for seven to eight minutes. When everything is combined and the dough is the right consistency, finish by mixing in second gear for about seven minutes.

Divide into 25 loaves about 1¾ lb each. Round and let rise. Bake at 350° for about 50 minutes.

For the scaled recipe (two slightly larger loaves) combine flours, salt, and bran with a whisk in a separate bowl. Mix them into the liquid gradually and add yeast while the dough is still thin. Mix with spatula until stiff enough to work by hand. Finish by adding bread flour if necessary. Let rise in the mixing bowl, punch down twice, then remove knead, shape, and let double in size before baking in a preheated oven as above.

Eight-Grain Bread

YIELD

12 1½-lb loaves

PREPARATION TIME

25 minutes

SOURCE

Schat's Courthouse Bakery

COMMENTS

This is the richest, grainiest bread we sell. It's less sweet than the Molasses Multi-Grain and takes a little advance preparation, but it helps us provide a wide range of choice for our customers.

INGREDIENTS

	Whole		Scaled
Water	8 lb		2⅔ c.
Bread flour	8 lb		2½ c.
Rye flour	1 lb		½ c.
Eight-grain flour mix	5 lb		1 c.
Flax seeds	2 lb		5 tsp
Bread shortening		4 oz	2 tsp
Brown sugar	2 lb	8 oz	⅔ c.
Dry yeast		5¼ oz	1 pkg
Salt		6 oz	½ tsp

METHOD

Soak eight-grain mix and flax seed for 15 to 20 minutes in the water. Add all the other ingredients, beginning with the liquids, in a 60-quart bowl with the mixer in first gear for 10 minutes using the dough hook. Don't add the milk powder until the dough is thickened, otherwise it will lump up. When all the ingredients are combined and the dough is the right consistency, finish by mixing in second gear for three to four minutes. Divide into 12 loaves about 1¾ lb each. Bake at 350° for about 35-40 minutes.

For the scaled recipe (two loaves) combine with a whisk at first then a spatula until it is stiff enough to work by hand. Let rise in the mixing bowl, punch down twice, then remove knead, shape, and let double in size before baking in a 350° preheated oven as above. It is done when thumping it gives a hollow sound.

Chocolate Macaroons

YIELD	12 dozen 2½" cookies	
PREPARATION TIME	25 minutes	
SOURCE	Schat's Courthouse Bakery	
COMMENTS	This formula is done in two stages but is not complicated, and the cookie has gotten raves from confirmed chocoholics.	

INGREDIENTS	*Whole*		*Scaled*
First Stage:			
Powdered sugar	12 lb		7½ c.
A good Dutch cocoa	1 lb	4 oz	¾ c.
Egg whites	4 lb	8 oz	12 lg
Cream of tartar		1½ oz	1 tsp
Numoline		3 oz	½ tsp
Second Stage:			
Shredded coconut*	6 lb		1 lb (7 c.)
Salt		2 oz	½ tsp
Vanilla	Dash		½ tsp

METHOD

Combine the first-stage ingredients—powdered sugar, cocoa, egg whites, cream of tartar and Numoline (an invert sugar that keeps everything moist)—in a mixing bowl using first gear. Once combined, put the bowl on the stove and double boil, hand stirring with a spatula or the mixer paddle, until the ingredients reach about 125° or "very hot to the touch." When the ingredients reach the desired temperature, put the bowl back on the mixer and add second-stage ingredients in second gear. Mix for approximately 3 minutes in second gear. Finish in third if you wish.

Bag with star-tip or without and drop on greased cookie sheet in chocolate mounds. They look like big Hershey's kisses. Bake at 325° for about 20-25 minutes.

The scaled version for about two dozen cookies is made in exactly the same way. The Numoline is an option that won't affect the cookies' flavor if omitted.

* This recipe calls for dessicated, unsweetened coconut shreds, which soak up some of the moisture.

Macaroons

YIELD	8 dozen 2½" cookies	
PREPARATION TIME	25 minutes	
SOURCE	Schat's Courthouse Bakery	
COMMENTS	These macaroons can be served plain or dipped half or fully in chocolate. The formula varies slightly from the chocolate macaroon but uses the same two-stage method.	

INGREDIENTS

	Whole	Scaled
First Stage:		
Powdered sugar	3 lb	3¾ c. (1 lb)
Granulated sugar	3 lb	2 c.
Egg whites	3 lb 12 oz	10 lg
Cream of tartar	1 oz	1 tsp
Second Stage:		
Shredded coconut*	5 lb	5 c.
Salt	½ oz	½ tsp
Vanilla	Dash	½ tsp
Butter flavor	Dash	Dash
Rum flavor	Very little	¼ tsp

METHOD

Combine the first-stage ingredients—powdered sugar, egg whites, and cream of tartar—in a mixing bowl in first gear. Once combined, put the bowl on the stove and double boil, hand stirring with a spatula or the mixer paddle, until the ingredients reach about 125° or "very hot to the touch." When the ingredients reach the desired temperature, put the bowl back on the mixer and add second-stage ingredients in second gear. Mix for approximately 3 minutes in second gear. Finish in third if you wish.

Bag with star-tip or without and drop on greased cookie sheet in mounds that don't look like Hershey's kisses. Bake at 325° for about 20-25 minutes.

The scaled version will also make about two dozen 2½" cookies. Baking plain macaroons along with the chocolate variety makes it easier to judge doneness by eye.

---

*   This recipe also calls for dessicated coconut shreds.

Butter Spritz Cookies

YIELD	20 dozen 2-2½" cookies		
PREPARATION TIME	20-25 minutes		
SOURCE	Schat's Courthouse Bakery		
COMMENTS	If your market dictates, you can cut the butter up to one half with a high quality shortening, the change will be undiscernible.		

INGREDIENTS

	Whole		**Scaled**
First Stage:			
Granulated sugar	6 lb		2⅔ c.
Butter (room temp.)	9 lb		3 c.
Salt		2 oz	1 tsp
Vanilla		2 oz	1 tsp
Egg whites	1-2		As needed
Lemon flavor	Dash		6 drops
Yellow color	Optional		
Second Stage:			
Bread flour	6 lb		3½ c.
Cake flour	6 lb		4 c.

METHOD

Combine all but the flour in the mixing bowl with a paddle for 5 to 7 minutes in first gear. Scrape down sides of bowl often to combine ingredients thoroughly. They will get a smooth, almost glossy, spreadable texture.

With the first-stage ingredients still in first gear, add equal parts of the flours (scaled: all-purpose flour) in three separate stages, combining the first third for 10 minutes and later thirds for 2 or 3 minutes each until you get a fluffy, light dough you can extrude from a pastry bag. Total mix time: about 14-16 minutes. Egg whites will loosen the dough and make it more workable. If it is stiff, you made a mistake. *E.g.*, ingredient proportions could be right, but cold butter has stiffened the dough.

Extrude the cookies with a star tube on a baking sheet with a circular motion bringing the last bit into a tip. Top with nonpareils, chocolate, or nuts. Or press the cookie to spread it out, then poke the bag down to make a depression for raspberry, lemon or other flavors. The the scaled version for about two dozen cookies calls for the same techniques using a hand mixer at low speed. Bake for 18 to 20 minutes at 325°.

Blueberry or Chocolate Chip Scones

YIELD	3-4 dozen 5-oz. scones
PREPARATION TIME	8-10 minutes
SOURCE	Schat's Courthouse Bakery
COMMENTS	We use two scone recipes for variety. This is the denser but easier one. It's the basic mix for our chocolate-chip and blueberry scones, and will work for any sweet scone mix. When you mix the dough, and pull half of it out and leave half in the bowl. You can add any kind of frozen berries in the first half, and chocolate chips and walnuts in the remainder.

INGREDIENTS

	Whole		*Scaled*
Bread flour	2 lb		1 c.
Cake flour	2 lb		1 c.
Brown sugar		13 oz	⅔ c.
Baking powder		3 oz	1½ tsp
Baking soda		1 oz	½ tsp
Butter	1 lb		¼ c.
Buttermilk	1 lb	8 oz	½ c.
Eggs	6 lg		1
Vanilla	Dash		¼ tsp
Frozen (blue)berries	2 lb	8 oz	¾ c.
OR Chocolate chips	2 lb	8 oz	¾ c.
Walnuts (chopped)	2 lb		¾ c.

METHOD

Combine sugar, butter, flour, and baking powder & soda in second gear for two minutes to blend loosely. Next, mixer off, add buttermilk, eggs and vanilla to make the dough. Mix liquid in for about one minute to make a dough. Mix for another minute in second gear; dough will start to come away from sides of bowl. Add berries frozen hard so that they won't crush and color the dough. Blend frozen berries or the chocolate chips and walnuts briefly—just enough to blend evenly throughout the dough without smashing them.

Put the dough on the bench and for round scones roll it into a 2½"-thick log and chop it into about ½" thick patties. For traditional pie-wedge scones flatten a 5-lb piece of the dough into about a 1½"-thick round and cut it into eighths. Bake for 15 minutes at 350°.

In the scaled version combine dry ingredients in all-purpose flour. Cut in butter with fork, knives, or (very quickly) food processor. Add liquid ingredients then berries or chips and nuts with a few strokes. It's a wet dough. Shape on a floured board. Bake 25 minutes.

Fruit and Cream Scones

YIELD	32 scones
PREPARATION TIME	20 minutes
SOURCE	Donald Pittman
COMMENTS	This is the richer scone recipe, compliments of our pastry chef. You won't make this one on the mixer, and the quantities are smaller. Compare the recipes and see which you prefer.

INGREDIENTS

	Whole	*Scaled*
Bread flour	3 lb 12 oz	7 c.
Baking power	6 tbs	3 tbs
Salt	1 tbs	½ tbs
Sugar	11 oz	¾ c.
Heavy cream	3 lb 12 oz	3¾ c.
Dried Fruits	1 lb 12 oz	2½ c.

METHOD

Mix the fruit (apricots, raisins, cherries, candied orange peel, or the like) with the heavy cream to separate the fruit. Use just shy of ¾ cup of sugar. Make a well in the combined dry ingredients and add the cream and fruit mixture. Stir lightly, just enough to combine everything. Divide the dough in half. Pat one part of the dough into a round, about ¾" thick, and cut the round into eighths. Do the same for the second half of the dough.

Brush each scone with cream and sprinkle with coarse sugar (AA sugar). Arrange on a sheet pan and bake at 400-425° for 15 minutes.

The scaled version is half the full recipe. You'll want just slightly over ¾ cup of the heavy cream, otherwise the method is exactly the same.

Danish Dough

YIELD	6 dozen danish		
PREPARATION TIME	20 minutes		
SOURCE	Schat's Courthouse Bakery		
COMMENTS	This is a straight cinnamon-roll recipe, before rolling in shortening or butter. It's another two-stage recipe.		

INGREDIENTS

	Whole		*Scaled*
First Stage:			
Water	4 lb		2 c.
Eggs	1½ quarts		9 lg
Dry yeast		8 oz	2 pkg
Nutmeg		2 oz	1 tsp
Cake flour	4 lb		4 c.
Granulated sugar	1 lb	8 oz	¾ c.
Butter (softened)*	1 lb	8 oz	¾ c.
Second Stage:			
Bread flour	7 lb ±		6-7 c.
Salt**		3½ oz	1 tsp

METHOD

Mix all but salt and bread flour with paddle 8 to 10 minutes in first gear. The ingredients will look almost soupy. Slowly add bread flour in two stages in first gear. Then mix in second or third gear for one minute. It is now cinnamon roll dough. To make danish, divide it into 5½-pound pieces, refrigerate for a few hours, roll out to about ½" and spread a *thin* layer of butter, shortening, or both on it, then roll it in. Roll it in once with a three-fold and roll it out to the original thickness. Repeat twice. It gets four roll-ins—the first roll-out and the three-folds.

Shape, add fillings (nuts, etc.) egg wash, then proof at 110° for 10 to 15 minutes. Use all-purpose flour for the scaled recipe of about a dozen and a half danish. Bake 375° until golden brown. Ice while hot.

Recipes for icing and cheese filling follow.

* Again, your market will determine whether to use pure butter or a combination of butter and shortening. You'll have to cost out your formulas.

** Don't add salt in first stage because, when mixed that long with yeast, it can severely inhibit the yeast's action.

Danish Icing

YIELD	Enough for 12-14 dozen danish	
PREPARATION TIME	10 minutes	
SOURCE	Schat's Courthouse Bakery	
COMMENTS	This is the basic recipe. It's quick, easy, and very satisfactory.	

INGREDIENTS		*Whole*	*Scaled*
	Water	4 lb	1 c.
	Powdered sugar	22 lb	9½ c.
	Honey	½ cup	1 tbs
	Vanilla	1 oz	¼ tsp
	Salt	Pinch	Pinch

METHOD — Combine everything but powdered sugar with wire whip in a 20-quart mixing bowl. Start mix in first gear. *Slowly* add the 22 lbs of sugar. Mix in first gear for 4 minutes, then mix in highest gear for 15 minutes. Apply thinly with spatula on danish as soon as out of oven.

Cream Cheese Filling

YIELD	Enough for 12-14 dozen danish	
PREPARATION TIME	10 minutes	
SOURCE	Schat's Courthouse Bakery	
COMMENTS	Cream cheese filling for cheese pockets is not just cream cheese.	

INGREDIENTS		*Whole*	*Scaled*
	Cottage cheese	5 lb	2 c.
	Sour cream	5 lb	2 c.
	Cream cheese	9 lb	2 c.
	Powdered sugar	7 lb	3 c.
	Granulated sugar	4 lb	2 c.
	Instant starch	1 lb	2 tbs
	Crushed pineapple	#10 can (drained)	1½ c.

METHOD — Mix together for 3 or 4 minutes and that's it. There is just enough pineapple to give an elusive little tang.

Banana Nut Bread

YIELD   14 1-lb loaves

PREPARATION TIME   About 20 minutes

SOURCE   Schat's Courthouse Bakery

COMMENTS   Mix, scale, pour, and bake. What could be easier? The key is to use extremely ripe bananas, fruit almost too soft to handle but not yet brown and liquefying.

INGREDIENTS

	Whole		*Scaled*
Bread flour	4 lb		2¼ c.
Granulated sugar	2 lb		⅔ c.
Baking powder		1 oz	½ tsp
Baking soda		1 oz	½ tsp
Salt		1 oz	½ tsp
Cake shortening	1 lb	12 oz	½ c.
Super ripe bananas	4 lb		1 c.
Eggs	1 lb	12 oz	1 lg
Buttermilk	1 lb		⅔ c.
Nuts	1 lb		⅔ c.
Vanilla		1 oz	1 tsp
Banana flavor		1 oz	Optional

METHOD

Mix everything together in third gear for 3-4 minutes. Divide into 1-lb 2-oz. portions, and bake for 30 minutes at 350°.

The scaled version for two loaves works best by combining the dry ingredients in roughly the order of appearance, then creaming in the shortening. Mash the bananas and add them with the eggs, buttermilk, and flavorings. Omit the banana flavor if the bananas are very, very ripe. Yoghurt will work for buttermilk in a pinch. Mix with a hand mixer at low speed for 2 to three minutes, adding the nuts at the end. This is a fairly stiff batter and may tend to climb up the beaters, but a little less so at low speed.

Pour into greased pans and bake in a 350° preheated oven for about 30 to 40 minutes. Remove from pans and cool on a rack.

Bran Muffins

YIELD	4½-5 dozen 5 oz. muffins
PREPARATION TIME	About 20 minutes
SOURCE	Schat's Courthouse Bakery
COMMENTS	This is another straightforward matter of mix, scale, pour, and bake. Buttermilk and pineapple provide an intriguing piquancy.

INGREDIENTS

	Whole		*Scaled*
Bran	1 lb	8 oz	1¼ c.
Bread flour	2 lb	8 oz	3⅓ c.
Granulated sugar	1 lb		¾ c.
Brown sugar	1 lb		¾ c.
Raisins (pre-soaked)	1 lb		¾ c.
Salt		1¼ oz	½ tsp
Baking powder		1 oz	1½ tsp
Baking soda		1 oz	1½ tsp
Buttermilk	4 lb		2 c.
Eggs	1 lb	6 oz	2 lg
Salad oil	1 lb		⅓ c.
Honey	1 lb		½ c.
Crushed pineapple	⅓ - #10 can (drained)		1 c.

METHOD

Mix with paddle in second gear for 8-10 minutes. Pour into muffin tins. Bake in an 375° oven for about 30 minutes.

For the scaled version of about 3 to 3½ dozen cupcake-sized muffins, combine dry ingredients in a large mixing bowl. Soak the raisins for an hour before using, then drain. Add liquid ingredients, including beaten eggs, using a hand mixer or whisk until batter is smooth. Yoghurt will work in place of buttermilk. Pour into greased or paper-lined muffin tins and bake 25 to 30 minutes.

Editor's note on the following pages: Pears were the fruit of the aristocracy; the rest of us had to eat apples. But while apples burgeoned into an abundance of flavors and culinary roles, pears seem to have slipped into a backwater along with the nobility. Because we're in a center of pear production, we've included a few recipes on the following pages from a recent pear bake-off to give our local wares a little boost. We think you'll be pleasantly surprised.

Simple Pear Pie

SOURCE   Geri West

INGREDIENTS:

> 3 to 4 pears
> 1 cup sugar
> ¼ cup melted butter
> ¼ cup flour
> 1 tsp vanilla

Peel, core, and halve pears, lay in crust. Mix filling, pour over pears. Bake at 350° one hour.

Pear & Polenta Tart

SOURCE   Sarah Kennedy Owen
COMMENTS   This entry will give an idea of how keen the competiton was in the bake-off.

INGREDIENTS   *Crust:*

> 2¼ cup all-purpose flour
> ¾ cup good quality polenta (or cornmeal)
> ¼ tsp salt
> ⅔ cup sugar
> 1 cup margarine or butter
> 3 egg yolks
> 2 to 3 tbs water

Filling:

> 5 to 6 pears
> ¾ cup sugar
> 2 cup red or white wine
> 1 stick cinnamon

METHOD   Peel, core and halve pears. Simmer with clove, cinnamon and sugar in wine partially covered for 5 minutes. Add pear halves and water to cover pears completely, then heat just below simmer for 10 to 20 minutes or until tender. Let cool for at least one hour or up to several days refrigerated.

With a fork or wire whisk combine flour, polenta, salt, and sugar in a large mixing bowl. Drop the butter in small pieces into the mixture and cut until it resembles grated parmesan cheese. Stir egg yolks and 2 tbs of water into dough. Add water until dough coheres. If using a food processor, don't run it longer than 30 seconds. Halve and roll out halves between two pieces of floured waxed paper for top and bottom crust. Line pie pan with crust, add pears and top crust, seal, and bake in preheated oven at 375° for 35 minutes.

Lucie P's Pear Cheesecake

SOURCE
COMMENTS

Nancy Stamback Prescott
This recipe won first prize in the pear bake-off.

INGREDIENTS

Crust:

> 1¼ cups all purpose flour
> 7 tsp butter
> 3 tbs sugar
> 3 drops vanilla
> ½ beaten egg

Filling:

> 1 lb can pear halves, undrained
> ¼ cup kirsch
> 9 oz cream cheese
> ½ cup plus 2 tbs sugar
> Juice of one lemon
> 1 envelope unflavored gelatin
> 1 cup whipping cream
> 4 tbs crushed praline (see below)
> ⅓ cup currant jelly

METHOD

Crust: sift flour and salt into bowl. Cut in butter. Add sugar, vanilla, then egg to make a dough. Refrigerate in foil or plastic wrap two hours. Preheat oven to 400°. Roll out dough for 8" pan with removable bottom. Prick with fork, cover with pie weights, and bake for 10-15 minutes. Remove weights and bake about 30 minutes more until golden brown. Cool on rack.

Filling/topping: Drain pears, reserving 3 tbs of juice, and moisten with kirsch. Beat cream cheese, ½ cup sugar, lemon juice and remaining kirsch in bowl. Dissolve gelatin in reserved pear juice over low heat. Cool slightly. Stir into cheese mixture. Drain, slice, and fan pears over pastry shell. Cover with filling. Refrigerate.

Whip cream with 2 tbs sugar. Combine ⅔ cup cream, 3 tbs praline and half the jelly, and spread the mix over the cheesecake, using the remainder to decorate with piped rosettes, then garnish rosettes with the remaining jelly and praline.

Crushed praline: ¾ cup sugar and ¾ cup coarsely chopped almonds. Heat the sugar and almonds in medium saucepan over low heat until the sugar melts. Boil slowly until the mixture turns golden. Pour onto an oiled baking sheet. When cold, crush the hardened mix with a rolling pin.

Pear Tart

SOURCE Mary Rhodes and Heidi Hildebrand
COMMENTS This ran a very close second in the bake-off.

INGREDIENTS

Crust:
>   *1¾ cup all-purpose flour*
>   *10 tbs unsalted butter*
>   *¼ cup sugar*
>   *2 egg yolks*
>   *¼ tsp water*
>   *4 drops vanilla*

Filling:
>   *2 pears*
>   *1 cup plus 3 tbs sugar*
>   *6 tbs flour*
>   *3 eggs*
>   *¾ cup melted butter*

METHOD

Blend crust ingredients with a fork, knives or briefly with a blender until they form a ball. Refrigerate for at least one hour. Roll out and place in 8" tart pan. Peel, core, and slice pears, then fan out on the pie crust. Combine other filling incredients and pour over the pears, bake at 375°for one hour. Dust with powdered sugar before serving.

Thomas French Pear Pie

SOURCE Alex R. Thomas family
COMMENTS This is from one of the oldest pear farming and packing families in the region.

INGREDIENTS

>   *⅓ cup sugar*
>   *1 egg*
>   *¼ tsp salt*
>   *⅛ tsp nutmeg*
>   *1 cup sour cream*
>   *½ tsp grated lemon peel*
>   *2 lb peeled, cored and sliced Bartlet pears*
>   *8" pie shell*
>   *Streusel topping*

METHOD

Beat egg until foamy, add all ingredients but sour cream. Pour into unbaked pie shell, top with sour cream, bake 25 minutes at 400°, add topping of streusel and sour cream.

GETTING STARTED

5

START-UP FINANCES

QUESTION NUMBER ONE for starting a bakery or any business is whether you have enough money in the bank and elsewhere to cover not only start-up costs, but to carry the business to break even. Most of us have to start on our own and borrowed funds. A friend of mine, for example, is very able and experienced in the restaurant business and wants his own café. He had done the preparatory work we recommend in the next chapter, and he drafted a business plan; but, since he didn't adequately evaluate the cash reserves needed to open up, the bank turned him down for a loan. That's how it is. No matter how good you are and how sound your plan is, no bank will go out on a limb if you can't afford to invest substantially in the business. The bank wants *you* to take the risk. It's there to pick up the pieces and recover its money if you can't make it. Banks cover themselves pretty well where money is concerned; that's the business they're in. They'll make sure that you spend enough so that, if you bail out, the bank doesn't lose.

WHERE THE MONEY IS

Institutional Lenders — Even if you don't need a loan right away, get involved with a banker early. You may need one later to expand if things break out better than you anticipated. Talk to the banker to find out what the chances are of getting a loan based on your idea. Banks want numbers, so you need projections. You say, "I will see $250,000 in sales this year. This is how I will do it. I will sell this much this month, this much more the following month," and so on. Each month you show how much your developing business increases your bottom line so you can repay the loan.

You have to establish the cost of the project and get an idea of how much of it your own resources must carry. That means, first *over-estimating* most costs as you evaluate the plan, then looking at how much money you have. Say you have 30 or 40 percent of the cash your business plan requires. Is it enough? To find that out you have to meet with your banker and ask how much you must come up with for the bank to lend you the balance.

Paying back a loan is an added burden and risk that becomes part of your overhead. If you plan to pay the loan back in five or 10 years, you have to amortize out what you plan to borrow and enter the monthly debt service in your plan as a fixed cost for every month. And you won't see any income for the month until the bank does.

We've been very lucky in dealing with a small bank and making friends with people in the loan department through the bakery; so we haven't had to go out loan hunting. Not many people have that advantage. My understanding, talking to other small-business people, however, is that most small banks or small-town banks are aggressively trying to make loans. If you don't get money at the first bank, definitely do not give up. Most people will tell you that a small bank is readier to loan money than a large one. This view holds that all banks have to get their money working, that the big, well-established, high-profile banks grab the prime deals, and that the little ones have to take what's left. That's an over-simplification. You won't be dealing with Bank of America or the Hometown Savings Bank. You'll get your own loan officer no matter what the bank is, and the loan officer's job will be to find a good place to put the bank's money. You have to convince your loan officer that you're a good risk with a good idea and capital of your own, and that you'll make money for the bank.

The bank, essentially becomes your partner. As partners go, a bank is the least intrusive of them. It will want you to provide it with acceptable balance sheets and financial statements, of course. It may even help you set them up. Some banks will even suggest ways to make your business more profitable. But a bank won't stick its nose in the door and suggest that you move the potted palm to the other side of the retail area. You can't say that for every "silent" partner.

Contact commercial lenders and work through their loan applications. These in themselves are an education, if only to focus your ideas and sharpen your knowledge about start-up financing. In drafting a business plan you should have set up a start-up costs worksheet, and your estimate of needed working capital will determine the size loan required. The bank will want to know certain asset and liability ratios, as well as what you'll take in and what you'll owe. It wants to have a good idea whether your net worth will be adequate, based on your outgo and income. Before you go

I would suggest that anybody who was starting from the ground up have a very happy backer—or a lot of money—because bakery equipment is not cheap. If you find some cheap, you'd better figure out what's wrong with it.
—MURIEL GLAVE
THE LANDMARK BAKERY

to the bank you should prepare your own personal financial statement, get your income tax returns for the past few years, provide an indication of your financial net worth, show any other sources of income, and offer all information about you and your experience. You should also review your credit report, which you can order from TRW or the other major credit reporting bureaus. That will let you anticipate and resolve any problems before you see a lender. A credit history that shows you're accustomed to borrowing money and paying it back counts here. If you can't get a credit card, you probably won't get a bank loan.

Here's how to look like a pro when you borrow money: Put all the above data into an information package. Essentially, you will extrapolate a loan application from your business plan. The bank will know that you're shopping around and that it will have to compete for your business!

Try not to take the loan as a lump-sum amount. For our home-improvement center branch we got a line of credit. I went to the bank with our proposal showing how much it would cost to put the project together, the cash flow to carry the loan, and our need for as much as $40,000. We weren't sure we would need the whole $40,000, and we didn't want to start paying interest on all of it the minute the bank approved the application. I asked for a line of credit up to $40,000, so that we could borrow the money as needed, while the bank charged interest only on each new amount borrowed. A *revolving* credit line lets you keep borrowing on the same money if you meet certain requirements, such as owing nothing for a 30-day period.

While a commercial loan is safely impersonal, a bank or commercial lending institution may want the loan secured with additional resources. If you don't object to encumbering an asset, consider a loan against your life insurance policy or a home equity loan or second mortgage. At least the interest rate on a secured loan like this should be lower than on a personal loan.

"Silent" Partners — If you find that you're $10,000 or $20,000 short of qualifying for a loan, you may consider either taking on a silent partner or asking family to kick in. As noted above, silent partners are not entirely silent. And, based on my own experience and all I have heard, asking family for money is the worst way to go. Money problems have probably broken up more families and friendships than anything else. You do *not* want to involve family in a business project. If you do borrow from friends or relatives despite my warnings, draft a formal loan agreement and *follow it exactly*. That's the only way it will possibly work.

There may be no such thing as a silent partner. Anybody with money invested in your venture will be inclined to meddle. They will either question you or will just walk in and look around. They'll scrutinize you much more than you want, especially in the beginning when you are nervous enough without a 30-percent silent partner showing up. If you choose to pursue silent partners as a source of funds, you'll have to pick and choose very carefully. It all depends on your circumstances and whether you want the bakery so badly that you're willing to go out and get 10 partners at 5% each. Some people do and it works for them; it won't for everybody.

If you need a cosigner on a loan, be careful. The cosigner's potential liability is greater than yours in case you default. Even if you had to discharge your debt through a Chapter 7 bankruptcy, the cosigner would still be liable. A cosigner can be protected through a Chapter 13 or 11 bankruptcy, in which debts are paid off from future income—provided there is any income at that point. This may never happen, but it's something to keep in mind when you invite friends and relatives to share in your new venture.

Government Programs—It may be worth your contacting the Small Business Administration (SBA). One curious role the SBA has recently stepped into, according to the *Wall Street Journal*, is to underwrite "town cafés." In small rural communities, people from the countryside rely on exchanging information at the one café in town. If it goes out of business, an important feature of civic life goes with it; so the SBA has undertaken to finance new "town cafés" where they have disappeared. It's something for a baker to inquire after. Even if the SBA drops the program, it could be a good argument for getting a loan in the right small town.

The SBA has a number of programs available, but its funds are often hard to tap. At this moment the SBA's primary loan program is its 7(a) Loan Guaranty Program, by which it will guarantee as much as 80 percent on loans up to $100,000 and 75 percent on loans up to $1 million. It is up to lenders to ask for SBA backing on a loan if the borrower appears to qualify. The SBA's guarantee assures the lender that the government will reimburse it if the borrower can't repay the loan. To qualify, the small business must meet 7(a) criteria and the lender must certify that it could not fund the loan without the SBA guaranty. CAPLines is a specialized program under 7(a) for meeting short-term and cyclical working-capital needs. Under it the SBA will guarantee 80 percent of loans of $100,000 or less and 75 percent of a loan up to $750,000. There are other programs for fast turnaround loans (FA$TRAK) up to $100,000 guaranteed to 50 percent, low-documentation loans up to $100,000, loans for small firms adversely affected by defense cuts, and loans for export firms. Its 7(m) microloan program makes money available in amounts from $100 to $25,000 through intermediaries which process the loans in less than one week.

An SBA pilot program for minorities and women lets intermediaries, who may charge a fee, write a loan application, which if approved by the SBA gives the borrower a pre-qualification letter to show a lender. The SBA guarantees 75 percent on such loans up to

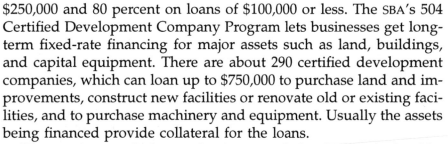

$250,000 and 80 percent on loans of $100,000 or less. The SBA's 504 Certified Development Company Program lets businesses get long-term fixed-rate financing for major assets such as land, buildings, and capital equipment. There are about 290 certified development companies, which can loan up to $750,000 to purchase land and improvements, construct new facilities or renovate old or existing facilities, and to purchase machinery and equipment. Usually the assets being financed provide collateral for the loans.

The SBA is a good place to begin a search for that kind of public funding. It also licenses independent small-business investment companies (SBICs) to lend to small-business people. The local SBA can provide a list of them in your area. If nothing else, the SBA is a good source of information on starting and managing a small business.

Other sources to investigate are grant and loan programs from such government agencies as the Farmers Home Administration, the Economic Development Administration, the Department of Housing and Urban Development, and even the Department of the Interior, which makes grants to restore historic buildings.

Equity Financing — If you need extra capital but can't or won't borrow the money, you might investigate equity rather than debt financing, that is, find that silent partner or a limited partner to be paid off from the business's proceeds, or consider a corporation and sell shares. Even a small S corporation is complicated and expensive, however, and needs professional assistance to set up and run. Limited partnerships are less complicated than corporations but still more complex than a sole proprietorship or general partnership.

Kamikaze Financing — Some people have put small businesses together using credit cards that offer $10,000 at 5.9%. It's an introductory no-fee offer good for a year and apparently an easy 5.9% on borrowed money. That 5.9 percent jumps up to "normal" credit card rates of between 12 and 18 or even 21 percent after the first year. If you haven't paid it off before the year is up, the interest will devour you and your bakery. It's a scary way to do business.

Second Incomes — A final source of added financing would be a second income, like your spouse's or "significant other's." It will be absolutely impossible for you to work another job while operating a bakery.

BEFORE AND AFTER START-UP

There are actually three phases of financing you will need to consider. So far we have discussed only start-up capital. Before that you need "seed money." That refers to the money you spend to travel to potential markets, to acquire data, to take people to lunch in order to learn from them, to shop for space, supplies and equipment—everything necessary to sound out the market, estimate start-up costs, and determine where to set up.

After the business gets going you may need "growth capital" to expand it with a new branch or product line. Growth capital may be available from yet another source. I've never dealt with "venture capitalists" but have met people who come up, after seeing that the shop does well, to express an interest in being a partner in future development. There are people who want to get their money working for them. Either they feel that bank interest does not make them enough money, they may not trust the securities markets, or they may just want to diversify their investments. Some investors have done very well that way and they may offer a better deal than the bank. You won't meet them, however, until you have started the business and it proves to be successful. They can be an excellent source of funding for expanding the business, but keep in mind the problems of dealing with any silent or limited partner.

INITIAL CASH RESERVES

Initial cash reserves must include: set-up expenses (fixed capital); operating expenses to break-even (working capital); and a contingency reserve. Be sure you have enough to cover all of those items. Starting out will be a fairly stressful time even at best, so don't make it worse with empty pockets.

Fixed Capital for Set-up Expenses — Costs for setting up a food service business are so much higher than for others that once a space is converted it will command a premium sale or rental price. If you buy an existing bakery, your entry cost—whether a lease or purchase—will be higher than for the same size shoe store, for example, but it will still vary with how much of the existing equipment you need to replace or refurbish and other planned or required physical changes. Most of the expenses apply even with an existing bakery, because you will probably change at least the sign and façade. Setting up your first bakery may look daunting but it's like moving into a house. If you haven't done it enough before to feel comfortable about it, read all you can about the process, use all the professional help you can rent or borrow, and give it serious thought.

If you plan to set up even an average bakery, you will need in the neighborhood of $150,000 to $200,000, possibly more. Equipment alone can cost $50,000 unless you take time to shop carefully for good used items. We'll go into greater detail about acquiring equipment later, but remember that you may not be ready to buy when the best deal arises, so keep your options open and your cost allocations loose, in case you have to spend more than rock-bottom for your oven, mixer, display cases, and major fixtures.

It's still possible to pinch pennies and set up for under $50,000, the very low-end range for start-up. My dad's done it plenty of times. The upper range can go as high as you let it. My brother Brian recently opened a bakery 25 miles north of us for $30,000 by buying used equipment and doing much of the work himself (and getting some of Dad's hand-me-downs). You probably won't be as lucky, but you can still be a thrifty shopper who is ready to work and do things you would usually hire people for. It also helps to know the business and sources of supply.

Costs in addition to equipment, fixtures, and furniture can include rental advances and security deposits; demolition and space renovation; locks and security systems; signage and façade; packing materials, other paper supplies, menus, and register tapes; telephone and utilities deposits; insurance; legal and accounting fees; publicity and advertising costs; a myriad of permits and licenses, pre-opening sanitation and trash pick-up. As you go through the steps of actual set up, make a note of every new cost you encounter—fees, licenses, needed purchases—and add it to the projected start-up amount. Then increase everything *conservatively* by 25 percent.*

Working Capital to Make Ends Meet — Working capital is what you need to cover short-term operating expenses to break-even and later to even out cash flow. Accountants define working capital as current assets minus current liabilities. You will always need working capital because of the irregular flow of cash into and out of the business. You will probably have an outflow until break-even, but even after that you'll experience cash shortages from seasonal sales patterns and shifts in consumer demand, and you'll have to

---

*   There is a list of start-up costs in the Appendix. Think of the costs listed mainly as suggestions. You will probably have to add to them as you draft your business plan and run up against actual costs.

buy inventory, pay wages and salaries, carry credit sales, and often cover unexpected emergencies.

Remember that "capital" is any kind of wealth used to produce more wealth. Working capital is only one of four kinds. "Fixed capital" is to buy permanent assets that are not for sale but to generate goods and services. "Growth capital," is a separate fund, as mentioned above, to pay for expanding or diversifying the business. The lender, incidentally, wants to see that any growth capital it lends will increase the business's earnings at least enough to pay off the loan. Finally, I like to set aside "reserve capital" for emergencies and opportunities. You can include it in working capital.

Working capital can keep you current if you find yourself over-extended, a common problem starting out. We bought many of our supplies on credit when we were putting the place together. It costs plenty to fill your refrigerators and storage areas with raw materials. And if you can get those products on credit, it saves having to borrow the money. To do this, you have to sell yourself to your suppliers. You get a good list of suppliers and tell them, "I'm starting a new business and I'll be one of your best customers but you need to give me a line of credit for 60 days, so I can get on my feet and start generating income to pay you." You can fill up your store that way, but all of a sudden you're 60 days into the project and you start getting the bills. That's when it is comforting to have working capital to help start paying off those bills in case your income hasn't taken off fast enough.

You should base the working capital you need at start-up on revenue and expense forecasts. Ideally, they'll be part of your business plan. To calculate needed working capital you have to project your income, then subtract fixed and variable expenses from it. The income and expenses are all admittedly guesses, but you should develop a set of figures that you can revise as you settle into the business. If the business grows as you project, the working capital you need to help cover operating expenses should reflect a declining monthly amount until you break even. Then you should maintain it at a minimum to cover the variations we noted above. This, incidentally, is the kind of projection you should try to learn about in business courses before you open up. If you're uncomfortable making that kind of projection, see a bookkeeper or accountant who can help you work it out. You may also be able to find a computer spreadsheet or dedicated program that will help. The time for reaching your break-even point is only a projection and may not come as early as you anticipate.

Fixed expenses are fairly easy to calculate. They include rent or mortgage payments, other loan repayments, utilities, telephone, fire and liability insurance, maintenance and cleaning, linen service, permits, licenses, and special taxes, trash and garbage removal, janitorial and cleaning services, advertising and promotion, professional

The bank wouldn't touch us because we didn't have any kind of documentation or a business plan or anything. So I just started moaning to my friends around here, and there are people here that are willing to finance a small business. Maybe not $100,000 worth, but I was looking for like $5,000 or $10,000. I don't want to overplay it, but there are people who, if you've got a reasonable business and you're part of the community, are willing to give you unsecured loans. We've always been able to make our loan payments, and it's 9 or 10 percent interest. For an unsecured loan that's great. . . . But even so, I can't over-emphasize how much our business has suffered, and still does, from the lack of initial capital.
—BRUCE HERING
BRUCE BREAD

services like accountants or bookkeepers and lawyers, and depreciation or cost recovery.

I include my own salary in the cost of wages. Some sole proprietorships don't include the proprietor's wage but consider it to be pretty much whatever "draw" the boss takes home every day after paying for everything else. Some partnerships operate that way, too. This can work for a simple operation, but remember that what you take home from the business as a draw is an expense to the business like any employee's salary, rather than profit over and above all expenses including your take-home. Profit, as compensation for the risk of enterprise, is income in excess of all expenses, including your wages. We operate as a corporation and include my wages as a salary expense. That's because (1) it reflects part of the fixed cost of our payroll and (2) it keeps up payments against quarterly estimated taxes during the year without the surprise of discovering at tax time that we neglected to put aside the money to pay those estimates.

As "variable expenses" suggest, they vary directly with income, because they represent the cost to make and market each unit of product. Variable expenses include things like salaries and employee costs, supplies, paper and packing materials, delivery costs, and everything else that changes with your output, including occasional expenses like equipment maintenance and repair. It means that each item produces a gross income. Gross income, after deduction of its share of production and sales costs, becomes your *net* operating income before taxes. And do not forget to factor in taxes once you compute your net.

When you've computed all your projected costs, you can calculate how much you must sell to cover them. To calculate that you have to know how many items you expect to sell, the cost per item, and what you can charge for each, wholesale and retail. That also means estimating what product mix—how many of which items— you will sell. This is pretty slippery ground and you'd better make a few alternative projections before selecting a likely product mix.

Reserve Capital: The Frosting — Reserve capital is what it sounds like. Among other things, it pays for mistakes during start-up and learning: Putting things in the wrong places, those 200-pound doughs you have to toss out, the Health Department saying it won't approve your refrigerator because it doesn't comply with the NSF (National Sanitation Foundation) standard,* unexpected new regulations, or a key piece of used equipment breaking down, which happens constantly. Reserve capital also lets you take advantage of opportunities such as someone's getting rid of used equipment you

---

* The "NSF" standard to which we refer throughout this book is shorthand for the standards of a number of testing organizations, including the NSF, which state laws consider qualified to evaluate equipment by those standards.

need. The nice thing about a line of credit at the bank is that it can also supplement your reserve for problems and opportunities like these. That's why I separate it from ordinary working capital. It's a matter of choice and of what works for you.

There is another very important advantage to working and reserve capital. It's convenient, even desirable, to establish credit with every company you work with, but once you get over the start-up hump it's better to stay caught up on your bills by paying cash. You sometimes get 1% or 2% discounts by paying cash for items when you get them. It also keeps everything current, almost like a daily balance sheet. Remember that it's just as important to keep track of your books as it is to be good baker, and, although it's a good idea to hire a bookkeeper when you start out, you may find it's an unaffordable luxury. Whether or not you have a bookkeeper—and I do recommend having one—you need to use all the shortcuts available to help you to spend less time keeping books. When you take in cash every day and pay all the bills as they come in, you know exactly where you stand. Most small businesses like ours can't pay much attention to their balance sheet all the time; we work from day to day. When the bills come in you just hope there's enough in the kitty to pay them. If there is and you can pay the bills, your books are much more manageable. If you can provide for adequate reserve capital, cash shortages should not be a major problem.

Finances

Get "seed money"
___Review how you will analyze potential markets
___Calculate how much that will cost
___Set aside the money to do it
___Keep cost records in the pre-opening year for tax purposes

Calculate need for start-up money
___Initial cash reserves: Fixed capital, Working capital, Reserve Capital
___Use a start-up cost spreadsheet for the business plan
___Estimate all costs and add at least 25%

Get a copy of your own credit report; look for problems

Investigate potential sources of capital:
___Institutional lenders
   ___Use business plan with estimated start-up costs
   ___Show how you will earn money for the lender
___SBA for assistance
   ___Loan programs
   ___SBICS
   ___Instructional aids (seminars, SCORE)
___Government programs
___Equity financing
   ___Incorporate
   ___Form a limited partnership
___A last resort, private money (family and friends)
   ___Draft formal loan agreement
   ___Follow it to the letter
   ___Be aware of loan co-signer's greater liability

Determine which source or sources of funds will be best
___Use a good small-business lawyer, if necessary, to advise and help draft loan terms

6

EXPERTS AND TECHNICALITIES

BEFORE you begin looking for start-up money you'll need to have dealt with a few legal and technical matters. Among them are the business's name and what form the business will take: that is, whether it will be a sole proprietorship, partnership, or corporation. You'll address these issues in your business plan and loan application. They tend to precede the search for financing, but we're taking them up in this chapter along with a few other technical items.

After you get a commitment for financial backing, you'll have to tackle a few more important details: You'll need to get all the necessary business licenses. You should have an accountant or bookkeeper, a good insurance broker, and possibly a lawyer. Look for them by referral. Whether or not you know anybody where you plan to set up, talk to a variety of business people. Tell them what kind of business you're starting and exactly what you want from your accountant, bookkeeper, lawyer, or other professional.

BOOKKEEPERS AND ACCOUNTANTS

Our accountant, whom we found through referrals, costs $210 a month, and it's a good deal. I handle the basic numbers by preparing completely tabulated daily reports of our sales, expenses, payroll less taxes, and so on. The computer is set up to the analyze payroll and the rest of our books. Then once a month we send the accountant all our daily reports. From those we get back a monthly general ledger and balance sheet with everything broken down into percentages. What this $210 buys us is peace of mind and time to run the bakery. We need to know the business's money performance on a monthly basis; but, even though we track all our income and expenses every day, we can't waste valuable time crunching them to see how much we pay the government, suppliers, or employees, or how close we are to industry averages and our goals for the business. That's what we hire the accountant to do.

Incidentally, in about 30 states, including California, there is a difference between who is a bookkeeper and who can call himself or herself an accountant. This majority of states limits the term "accountant" to public accountants and certified public accountants (CPAs). Public accountants and CPAs in these states can perform a number of functions that bookkeepers are legally barred from doing. Professional bookkeepers there can still do most things you would need from a CPA and they usually charge less. But don't base your search on cost or on titles. Figure out what you need your numbers person to do and find out who can do it best by talking to each one's clients. Then talk to the accountant or bookkeeper and get the one you like best, regardless of designations.

You don't want an accountant who does nothing but huge corporate jobs. Find an accountant or bookkeeper who at least specializes in small businesses like yours. At first we used a local practitioner who did a great job but eventually we saw the need for specialized services. Our current accountant is in Walnut Creek about 150 miles south of us. He is very familiar with grocery and food service businesses. He was involved with restaurants for a long time and does almost exclusively that kind of account. He can tell us, for example, what the average of payroll expense should be for a bakery like ours, and based on his experience he can lay out what payroll different size bakeries and restaurants usually run. Experience like that is invaluable not only because it tells you if you are on track financially, but because your accountant or bookkeeper will have ideas based on his other clients' experience and how they dealt with common problems.

Our accountant is also a Certified Financial Planner (CFP). This designation is available to anyone who passes a qualifying exam from the Institute of Certified Financial Planners. The advantage is that a CFP will keep track of your business and personal life, and tell you where you can make changes to plan for a better future.

Finally, the accountant does the bakery's yearly tax returns. While he gets our dailies once a month, he requires only one office call every five or six months for me to examine the books under his microscope. At the end of the year, he charges about $500 to do the corporate returns. Altogether, bookkeeping costs us about $3,000 annually and we get an expert who is up on what happens in the business throughout the year. It's money well spent.

LAWYERS

Unfortunately, as my dad likes to say, everybody has to have a lawyer sometime. When I needed one I used referrals again. Yellow Page advertisements are not much help, although they may be the only way to get a list of names to run by other people in business. If you still can't get people's opinions, ask the lawyers to give you clients' names as references. Be sure to check the references; word of mouth counts here. I was lucky enough to find a lawyer through someone whose judgment I trusted. The name he gave was of a smart and aggressive practitioner who handled the job quickly and economically. We've used his services only two or three times. You won't need a lawyer on a day-to-day basis, but it's nice to have that contact.

FICTITIOUS BUSINESS NAMES

If you use other than your own name for the bakery, the law will require you to file a fictitious or assumed business name—sometimes called a "dba," for "doing business as." Usually you file with the county but in some places with the state. If you used your own name or a variation of it—*e.g.*, Joe Smith, Baker—you might get by without filing a dba. But adding almost anything else to it would almost certainly require a filing. In California, for example, a fictitious name includes one that does not use your surname or suggests additional owners, as in "& Company," "& Son," or "& Daughter." You needn't do more than *select* a name until you get financing or open a bank account, but your bank will want you to file a statement. Some may not open an account for the business, even with your own name, unless you've filed a dba and can provide all the necessary licenses.

If you use a fictitious or assumed business name, you have to file it and comply with the other legal requirements. California requires filing a Fictitious Name Statement with the County Clerk, at $25.00 per named individual, and publishing the statement in a local newspaper of general circulation. If you use a fictitious business name in California but don't file it, you can't sue in its name. Recording the name also lets anyone else know that using it might infringe on an active trade name. It also lets the public know who owns the business in case someone decides to sue you and the business. Fictitious business names have to be renewed periodically. In California that's every five years. The laws in your state are undoubtedly different.

Be creative with the name. Pick one that no one else is using, of course, but that also describes the bakery, projects the image you want, and is easy to remember and say. Pick a name the business can grow into. If you sell the business, the buyer would be buying name recognition. What you are selling in addition to the value of your equipment is the business you've built with that name.

We've had an advantage in using the family name because my dad and uncles built their businesses and a good reputation for the name well before we set up in Ukiah. You can use your own name for the bakery, if you like. Then it just becomes a matter of establishing it over time. The business name doesn't matter greatly at the beginning, but it can help you out as you build on it. If you do use your own name, remember that you probably won't get as good a price for the business's goodwill if you sell the business without your well-established name.

BUSINESS LICENSES, LOCAL TAXES

You'll have to take out a local business license. These are regulatory and revenue generating devices; you needn't take an exam or qualify for one. A business license fee will be a certain percentage of gross projected income for the first year. For every year after that it will be based on gross sales for the previous year. The local government will want to be sure that you comply with all local ordinances, including building, zoning, and property tax laws. Proof of compliance with some of these may require a permit, variance, or waiver. Typically there will also be a tax on your business equipment if you don't own your own building, or a property tax on the building if you do.

Most states charge a sales tax and will require you as a retailer to get the equivalent of what the California Franchise Tax Board calls a resale tax number. That means that you won't pay a sales tax on taxable items that go into your product because you will pass the sales tax along to your customers. You may want to get a federal tax ID number. It's also called an employer identification number (EIN), and, while you don't really need one until you become an employer, it's free and you might as well get it when you're starting up. There are other things you have to check besides taxes and licenses before you can assume you can start ordering supplies and equipment. We will touch on them as we go through the start-up process.

FORMS OF BUSINESS

Choosing the form of your business is one of the first steps you will probably take. It will be right up front in your business plan, and you will approach your banker with your form of business already settled.

Sole proprietorship —A sole proprietorship is the easiest form of business to set up. If you just open your doors without anything more, you're a sole proprietor. This form also has the easiest paperwork because all the income the business makes is your personal income. You need only fill out a few extra tax forms. The big drawback is its unlimited personal liability. The business's losses are your losses up to and beyond the limits of all your personal assets. You also have to do everything yourself until you can hire out work like bookkeeping, tax preparation, promotion, publicity, marketing, ordering, personnel, clean-up, and the hundreds of

If you do decide to get a partner or do it in a partnership—Don't! I took accounting classes from Emmett Jones at the college and I remember him saying, whatever you don't go into a partnership. He came in one day, and I said to him, I should have listened to you! It was just a hard deal. My ex-partner and I are still friends. It just didn't work out business-wise. But it would be nice to have somebody, a partner, to do the business side.
—JACQUIE LEE
THE GARDEN BAKERY

other chores for running a business. Taking vacations is also a problem until you develop a skilled and reliable staff to run things in your absence.

General partnerships — Starting out you may be able to take on a great baker or someone who is good at the business end as a partner. The first time I ever needed a lawyer in my baking career, however, was to get out of the partnership with my brother. If you intend to develop a partnership or a corporation, then by all means do it through a lawyer who is familiar with that practice. You should have all your agreements put in writing by a lawyer, because anything you and your partner or partners cook up will probably collapse when push comes to legal shove.

A partnership's obvious advantage is that it lets you pool your resources and skills with at least one other person. Partnerships are deceptively easy to set up. You can do it on a handshake. All states have adopted the Uniform Partnership Act, which controls the relationship if you don't have a written agreement. Although there are a few tax and statutory formalities, you can change things informally as you go along. There is no need to register with the state, although you must protect some partnership assets by filing a recorded document. You can cover each other for time off, you often learn from each other, and earnings are divided and taxed like personal income.

Consider a partnership, however, only if you know that the other person's personality, skills, and goals complement and are compatible with your own. Agree in advance on who will do what. Put everything in a written agreement. Easy as that seems, however, have a good small-business lawyer prepare the agreement, or draft one yourselves from a partnership book and have that lawyer review it. A good introduction to partnership problems and agreements is *The Partnership Book*, by Denis Clifford and Ralph Warner, published by Nolo Press. You should also provide for the partnership's dissolution by death, disability, or incompatibility by executing a partnership buy-sell agreement. It should state how to appraise the partnership's value and how the remaining partner will pay for it. A buy-out usually provides for financing or carry-back financing.

Partnerships are like marriages. You can never foresee the problems no matter how well you think you know your partner. Going into partnership with my brother, we assured each other that we would never have a problem. We would work through it. He would learn what I knew; I would learn what he knew, and so on. But that's not what happened. As business picked up and demanded more of our involvement in it, we crossed paths more. Little problems grew large, and we began to toss blame and accusations back and forth. There are as many ways for a partnership to fall apart as there are potential partners. Partnerships can work

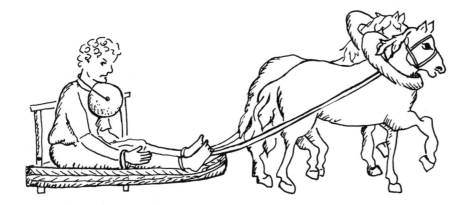

Mistaken scaling of the product could be a very vexing problem for medieval bakers.
(Illus. based on a manuscript of the period.)

and be hugely successful; so it's worth considering them, but keep the hazards in mind and make plenty of provision for them. My brother and I are still great friends, but we would never go into business with each other again.

One final and serious legal disadvantage of a partnership is that each partner is personally liable for all of the partnership's debts and liabilities, no matter whether the partnership or only one partner incurred them. It is the same complete liability as with a sole proprietorship—but you probably won't always know everything your partner is doing.

Limited partnership — A limited partnership is a good way to raise money. It's complex enough to require professional assistance to set up, but it's not as expensive to form and run as a corporation. A limited partnership comprises any number of general partners who run the business—as in a regular partnership—and no more than 35 limited partners. Limited partners must be real people, usually residents of your state. Although the general partner or partners will still have unlimited liability for the partnership's obligations, limited partners are liable only to the extent of their investment in the partnership. In order to retain their limited liability, they cannot participate in running the business. It's a good way to silence these silent partners.

There may come a time when a limited partner says, You know, I just don't like the way Zach's running the business. Fine. That partner can do the only thing he's allowed to do without becoming fully liable for the partnership's risks, which is to sell the partnership share to someone else the general partners approve of and get out. The general partners have complete control. The disadvantage as a practical matter is that usually the 35 people who invest are 35 people you know and who know each other. They may even be

THE BAKER'S DOZEN

In 1202, during the reign of King John and 13 years before Magna Carta, England enacted laws to regulate the weight of bread. In 1266 the laws became the Assize of Bread, which controlled the weights and prices of bread for almost the next 450 years.

Under the Assize, bakers had to base the weight of a penny loaf on the prevailing price of wheat and the grade of flour they used. So a penny loaf would have three different "weights" at any given instant. A baker convicted of breaking the Assize laws would be drawn on a "hurdle" (a sled for dragging the condemned to execution) from the Guildhall to his house, through the city's busiest and dirtiest streets with the evidence hanging from his neck.

Given flour's variable performance even today, bakers very reasonably considered the Assize rules cruel, capricious, unjust and oppressive. To avoid risking punishment they would add an extra loaf or bun to each dozen. This was the "baker's dozen," of which the 13th was the "vantage loaf."

The term acquired a slang meaning in "giving someone a baker's dozen," that is, a sound thrashing: all the person deserved, plus one more.

---

family, and while blood's thicker than water, money's thicker than blood. It has a way of ruining all sorts of relationships.

Corporation —Our bakery is incorporated. The corporation works well, because for one thing the boss is on salary and gets paid every two weeks like everybody else. He also gets his payroll taxes taken out every two weeks, too. The bakery has to match the payroll tax, based on how much money comes out of everybody's paycheck. On the other hand, the boss doesn't have to pay the 13-percent self-employment tax that would be required if he were self employed; so it's a wash.

You don't need a high income to justify a corporation. Many businesses incorporate for the so-called corporate veil that separates personal assets from those of the business. It's like an insurance policy. Other advantages of a corporation are that you can get workers' compensation as an officer of the corporation, you can give yourself better pension plans, and it is a good way to raise capital to expand the business. Say you have 100 shares, you take 55 shares and hold back 45 unissued shares. If you ever want to take somebody on, you issue shares. That's the part where you get professional advice.

Now for the disadvantages. Corporations can be expensive and complicated. You need a professional to set one up and to check on it from time to time to ensure that you are running it legally. Regular corporations, or what the tax laws call C corporations, are taxed twice—once on corporate income and again on shareholders' dividend income. One way to avoid double taxation is to set up an S corporation, which is what we have.

We didn't go through the California system but incorporated in the State of Delaware for reasons that aren't important here. A small business should seriously consider an S corporation. One person can be the entire corporation: the president, the secretary, the board of directors, the whole annual meeting. There is strong official encouragement for starting an S corporation whether you do it through Delaware or California or any other state. Government realizes that many S corporations are just sole proprietorships with a corporate veil. The so-called corporate veil, which is to protect you from personal liability for your corporation's acts, is very thin. In fact, it may be illusory. You will probably have to personally guarantee all your corporation's contracts. If you don't comply with the corporate formalities, you may lose the corporate status and revert to a sole proprietorship. If you permit a dangerous condition on corporate premises, an injured person may be allowed to pierce the corporate veil. Still, economic and tax advantages could justify converting your bakery to an S corporation at some future date.

INSURANCE

You will need to insure the bakery against risks of doing business, but you should also insure yourself as the sole source of your own and your family's income. Statistically you're seven times likelier to become incapacitated and unable to continue to work in almost any age group than you are likely to die. If you're accidentally disabled you'll be unable to make a living, and if the bakery is your only income and there is no one or nothing else to fall back on, you will need disability insurance. Even if you run a safe shop and there isn't much chance of an accident happening at work, the world is full of dangers, from driving to and from work every day to fixing things around the house.

You'll need standard business coverage, like premises loss and liability insurance. We have two separate policies. Since I own the building, I have a comprehensive insurance policy that covers it against fire and other losses. As a tenant, the corporation needs a policy that covers the landlord's building and its contents as well. If the corporation as tenant were to start a fire that burned down the building, it could be liable for the loss; so it needs a policy for that. It also needs liability insurance in case someone slips on butter and falls in the bakery. You might also want to look into business interruption insurance to guarantee an income if your building or equipment is damaged; overhead insurance to cover fixed expenses, including salaries, rent, and utilities should you be incapacitated for a long time.

One risk we have to live with is that working in an old, unreinforced masonry building in California we haven't a prayer of getting earthquake insurance. Any damage an earthquake causes will

This guy, the chef from the Hopland Brewery, came by after he had a hamburger on one of our buns over at the Anderson Valley Brewing Company here. He came over and said, I want to get some. I said, okay, maybe a couple dozen or something like that? And he says, no, I want three hundred or four hundred. And I thought, yeah, yeah, I've heard that before. But he wasn't kidding. It became a regular thing. That and the Harvest Market gave us a real basis for getting off the ground.
—BRUCE HERING
BRUCE BREAD

Ken Moore started his flour mill, bakery, and deli in 1983. But not all at once. First he acquired a shady lot on Ukiah's main business street by persuading the owner to borrow money so he could build the mill and to give him a two-year option to buy. The result is a striking wild-west style general store. A two-story water wheel on its north wall powers millstones that grind between 2,000 and 3,000 pounds of Montana wheat each week. The Flour Mill, Bakery & Deli is a remarkable asset in so small a community. It sells its own stone-ground flour, other flours, whole grains, spices, vitamin supplements, and sandwiches on its fresh-baked bread of fresh-ground wheat. The Moores live in a large house behind the store, a good way to economize. Moore's business is firmly rooted in economy, hard work—and risk. He races cars at Sears Point Raceway on weekends and trades in the commodities market.

"The mill idea," he said, "started in Redding in 1974. I was just out of the service and my dad had this great idea; so he roped my brother and me into it. We were all in it for about three years. I left to build houses. Then my dad went to Portland. My brother has the mill in Redding now. My dad's got one in Portland. When the housing market collapsed in the early 80s, I sold my house in Redding and got back into it over here. When I did I put everything on the line.

Moore's Flour Mill & Bakery
1550 South State Street
Ukiah, California

"We had three kids when we moved here. All we owned was our car and our clothes. But I had sold a house I hadn't borrowed a lot of money on. That put me ahead of the game, because selling the house provided money for the mill and bakery.

"The bakery wasn't in the original plan. I had planned to have a local bakery do the bread. There was none in Ukiah at the time, so I went to the Landmark Bakery in Willits. Landmark didn't want to do it, so I ended up baking bread here. I put the bakery together for a just few thousand dollars. It helps in this business to be mechanically inclined. I buy the cheapest stuff I can find and fix it to keep it going. Our first mixer cost $200. It didn't work but it only needed to have the clutch adjusted. I got the manual and adjusted the clutch, and it worked fine. Same with all of our equipment. . . . Then I had to learn to bake."

"Bakeries can be a lot of work, but I've kept ours pretty simple. We do cookies and about 200 to 250 loaves of bread a day. It isn't that difficult, but you're not going to learn until you do it. You can tell somebody what happens if you don't put the salt in or don't do this, but you're not going to learn all those things until you do them. And that's where it takes the time. . . . Take our new baker. He started by working three nights with the other baker. On the fourth night he could do it by himself. The bread came out fine. He may not understand a lot of things. If he had a problem he might not be able to figure out what he did wrong. But once he did figure it out, he'd know next time. After a couple of years he will probably have made all the mistakes, and then whatever happened he'd be able to handle it."

"We started the deli about five years ago. It was something I always thought about. It seems to go well with the bakery, and we do a lot of sandwiches. If you were going to open up a little bakery, a deli would be a good idea."

be entirely uncovered. It's goodbye building, contents, everything. We couldn't sustain a loss like that and would have to stand in line and hope for federal aid. But, as they say, what's enterprise if not risk?

Umbrella policies offer coverage in excess of other plans and can be acquired in increments of a million dollars for a very reasonable extra charge. As you get busier and your contacts spread, your risk of becoming the target of a lawsuit—justified or not—becomes much greater. So, the nominal sum necessary to carry an umbrella policy might be worth the money.

When you hire help you will have to carry workers' compensation. The law requires it, and it's a good idea but it can be expensive. Workers' compensation rates are based on how dangerous an employee's work is. When we first started business it cost $7.81 for every $100 of gross payroll expense. Since California deregulated workers' compensation it has become available on the open market, and buying it is like shopping for automobile insurance. We pay $3.56 per $100 for workers' compensation. If we went down the street to another insurance agent, his rate might be $5.25. You'll have to see if your state's program permits shopping. Also, you can sometimes qualify for industry rates by belonging to a group of bakeries. The group's rate might be eligible for a year's policy at reduced rates, subject to inspection and rate adjustment every three months. It's a way to get cheaper insurance.

An employee's employment and insurance rights are complicated and detailed. Chapter 11 considers hiring and using employees. Before you become an employer, you should consult someone, perhaps a good attorney, to help you understand what the employee's rights are. The time to start learning about employee rights and laws is before you are an employer and have a problem on your hands.

Before consulting a lawyer about employment problems, you might want to read Fred S. Steingold's *Legal Guide for Starting and Running a Small Business*, published by Nolo Press. We keep referring to this publisher's books. They are written in plain English by lawyers for non-lawyers and are very reliable. They will at least save you money by helping to organize your questions before getting legal help.

Your local Chamber of Commerce is another resource to investigate. California's has a good catalog of reasonably priced booklets and pamphlets that deal with employee matters. Those in other states may provide similar services. It's a good idea to join the local Chamber, anyway, as a way to get involved in the business community and become known locally. Your state's department of labor or labor commission is also an excellent source of material on your responsibilities as an employer, and often the materials are free for the asking.

Insurance is pretty arcane stuff for most of us. If you don't know much about it, you should get an expert's help; but watch out for the difference between an expert and a salesperson. Salespeople will offer you pre-packaged plans they guarantee will suit you perfectly. To avoid that, see a broker whose advice is fee-based instead of paid as a commission on sales. For example, there is a bookkeeper here who combines his financial planning services with stock and insurance brokerage. He earns his fees by setting up retirement and insurance plans that best suit his clients' needs. *Ask* if your insurance person gets a fee rather than a sales commission. Then at least you're likelier to get an unbiased analysis of your needs and not a sales pitch.

Technicalities - Lining Up the Experts

___Record fictitious/assumed business name
___Take out a business license
___Go to the health department
    ___Ask for all information and instruction sheets,
    ___Return with all forms filled out, and
    ___Provide menu, plans, and all other information the department requests
___Get a resale tax number, and possibly a federal tax ID number.
___Get a bookkeeper or accountant who knows about bakeries
___See an insurance broker for insurance
___Look for a lawyer, even if you don't need one now
___Select a form of business (Sole prop., partnership, corp.)

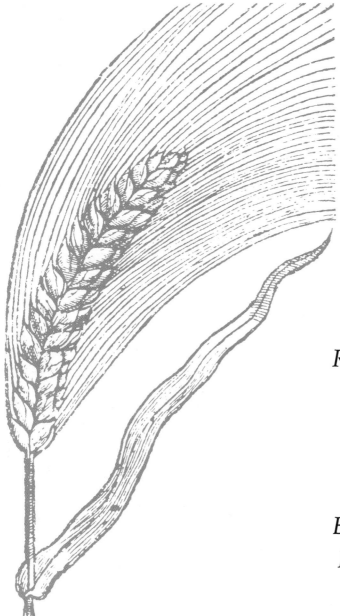

7

FIRST STEPS

WITH ALL THE PRELIMINARIES out of the way, you're ready to get your bakery off the ground. The first important step is choosing a good site. Typically, you settle on the region where you want to set up, then the city or neighborhood, then the street, and at last where to locate on the street. Setting up in a large shopping mall involves the same steps but there are extra wrinkles to consider.

Let's start with a look at street location because it's the easiest and most familiar. Bakeries and cafés depend on walk-by and drive-by traffic, plenty of it. That's the basis of the old real estate saw location, location, location, and it's a primary rule of retail business.... We should qualify that. If, say, you were opening your second bakery, location might not be as important as it was to begin with, because once you've established a name that's popular at its old stand it will probably do well in some less familiar place, too. It will attract people to the new site and do just fine as long as it's not too hard for people to find or get to. Your first business, however, will want the guaranteed walk-by traffic that other retail stores generate. Some of the people who walk by will walk in—partly because they are curious, but also because they're out shopping already and some will want bakery goods. That's how you build the business, by making regular customers of those passersby.

One-way streets are not the best on which to have a business because they get half the traffic. We happen to be on a one-way street, but our central location seems to make up for some of it. It's undesirable also to be on too busy a street. You want your customers to have parking, particularly when they're picking up $50 or $80 cakes. We're lucky enough to have a fair amount of diagonal parking right around the corner, but it can mean up to a one-block walk. In some places you can't help it. As you analyze and select your site, you have to make compromises every step of the way. Try to make sure things balance out as you go. If there are no parking spots, for example, you'll need more walk-by traffic.

Locating in a thriving retail center catches people while they're in a shopping frame of mind, which is why there are food places in malls now. Partly it's convenience. While people are already shopping for clothes and furnishings, they don't want to leave the mall and go somewhere else to eat. The malls don't want them to leave, either. People walking around and shopping are also building up an appetite. So those little food courts are extremely busy. That can be a guide for locating your bakery: Look for hungry shoppers in a buying mode.

If possible, downtown shops should adjoin major office buildings for morning coffee, lunch, and other breaks. We have a great coffee business early in the morning because we're right across from the courthouse. We're not far from the bank, either, so we get bank employees who also drop by on their 15- or 20-minute breaks. It's a real comfort, especially starting out, to know there will be a break at 10 o'clock, lunchtime, then 3 or 4 o'clock. It's like three guaranteed times when people will come into our place, get coffee and a roll, and perhaps take home a loaf of bread.

Some bakeries do well in neighborhood shopping centers, especially right next to good supermarkets—including those with in-store bakeries. People are already there to buy food, but, while it's convenient to have access to in-store bakeries, quality is not their long suit. You could probably do very well with good bakery right next to a supermarket, because it would attract people who are considering the purchase of a loaf of bread, cookies, or dinner rolls. It only takes them a few more steps to go in your door and buy better quality.

Corner markets and popular restaurants are worth seeking out, too, because their customers already have food in mind. The best place to set up a new food establishment is usually near the best restaurant in town or a high-quality grocery store. That way you become associated with the place where people go for something good to eat, and they may decide while they're there to get bread, dessert, or even their meal, at your place.

REGIONAL MARKET SURVEYS

Before picking the street location, of course, you have to decide on a regional or city location. As you plan to set up, you should do research on locations, population growth, and the economy before you commit any money or effort to your project, even if it's in your own town.

You can get the demographics for an area by going to the local library. The reference librarian can help you get started. You would look at the latest census to see if the area is growing. The standard indexes are *Cities of the United States* and the *Statistical Abstract of the United States*. They give population trends, average incomes, and major industries. If you're looking for a new place to live, check out *Forbes* magazine's annual ratings of cities and Savageau & Loftus's *Places Rated Almanac*. If you can't find these, check for similar guides in the catalog at the library under the subject heading "Cities and Towns—United States—Ratings." If you can get each potential location's telephone book, you can check the Yellow Pages for how many bakeries are already there.

Then go *look* at the places you research. You need to get the feel of a town. Does it welcome business? Most places do. Our town would love to get more big money makers and wage generators in those empty downtown buildings, which every city seems to have nowadays. It helps the whole area. If people come downtown and see prosperous businesses with people walking the streets, it gives them a good feeling for the town. It helps sell the town; it helps sell homes; it helps build businesses, including the one you plan. If you drive into the downtown and see that six of its 25 buildings are empty, it's not a promising sign. On the other hand, things could be turning around. There may have been eight empty buildings last year and two more may be ready to sell or lease out now. You have to talk to people and ask that kind of question.

You should also talk to people to find out if there are anti-growth sentiments in the community and which way people think the area is going. An anti-growth attitude may be all right if you know you can do well enough within the core of that community. Otherwise, the market you hope for may never develop.

Retail and wholesale business owners can tell you about the area's economic vitality. If you belong to a community service club like Rotary or Lions, or so on, attend the local chapter's meeting and ask the same questions. Radio and television station advertising salespeople can also tell you about business in the area. Credit bureaus probably have the clearest picture of the financial characteristics of the area and its residents. Go to chambers of commerce for a broad analysis of local consumers and types of businesses. A chamber is also a good way to connect with city officials, leaders, and programs.

Finally, confirm the status of planned growth with the companies that will do the growing. The big employers here are Masonite Corporation and Louisiana-Pacific Lumber Company. This is an old lumbering region. Most of the old-growth timber is gone, but the industries are logging managed forests. Anybody here knows that if Masonite or L-P closed down, however, it would affect many families directly and everybody indirectly. To compound the problem those two employers here are local branches of national corporations. Decisions about expansion and contraction won't be made locally. But there are other bright spots in the economy. There is a local high-tech metals processor, Retech, which was purchased recently by Lockheed. It does specialized metals fabrication for recycling hazardous wastes and has a promising future. The same is true of two high-tech employers in Willits, Advanced Manufacturing & Development and Microphor Corporation. Mendocino Brewing Company, a craft brewer 12 miles south of town recently expanded production and moved its plant to Ukiah. Finally, wine-grape growing and wine production are expanding and pumping money into the area. These are new industries that are springing up outside the old timber-based economy. That kind of new business activity, as well as stability or growth in old industry, is what you want to look for. You can't get a better feeling for growth in an area than by talking to the people who run those businesses.

Customer Dispersion — You want a local base of customers. If you're in a rural area you don't get the benefit of that foot traffic we talked about. In bad weather it would be worse. Here, although there are only 15,000 people within the city limits, the population jumps to 35,000 or 40,000 within a 10-mile radius. People in outlying areas will come to town for special birthday cakes and other specialty items. It helps to have both a local market and a surrounding rural customer base. Although the rare bakery can be a real magnet and attract buyers from miles around, it is not a good idea to set up in the middle of nowhere and expect that to happen.

The Labor Pool — For the bakery business, as with other food service concerns, the ideal employment pool includes a community college with plenty of bright, hardworking kids who are looking for part-time work. Part-time work is what you will offer and that's the kind of labor pool you want. Turnover is high in this business because there is a cap on how much you can pay. You'll find people who will be very happy to make $5 or $6 an hour—about all you can pay—but they'll be happy for only six months or a year, then they go. So it's nice to have a large employment pool to help you deal with that turnover.

Proximity to Suppliers — It helps to be close to your suppliers. If you locate too far out, you can get supplied but only at higher rates, and with the risk of missed deliveries from bad weather, failed connections, and other problems. Suppliers have a way of getting goods to you no matter where you are and most are very reliable, but sometimes a delivery can be a cliff-hanger. Also I know that we get better rates than a bakery in Gualala, which is a town in a remote spot on the coast. If you chose to live somewhere like Gualala for its beauty and isolation, you would have to pay more to make your product. In turn, however, you could charge more. People have to eat, and, if they choose to live in Gualala as you do, they will pay

The spice trade fueled expansion of the Roman Empire and opened the New World to Europe. Spices identify cuisines and define certain foods. What, after all, is gingerbread without the spices? Spices' fragile aromatic oils soon fade, but so little spice is needed, that you can and should buy the best and replace it often.

(Illus.: *Fanny Farmer Cookbook*, Little Brown, 1918)

higher prices just as you do. Just make sure they can do it on a regular basis.

All of the above information assumes a small-town business because it reflects our current situation and my perspective. But it applies to setting up in a city as well. Most cities in my experience are aggregations of neighborhoods and communities within a city. You have to isolate and define your community and market. Don't bother with political boundaries. Your market may jump city and county lines; it may be a social stratum or ethnic group within the entire city. It may be one middle-sized town and a handful of crossroads. If you ask the same questions of the people who operate within the market you are investigating, you'll get the same information as if you were to set up in a small town.

Municipal Services — You want to find out as much as you can about local regulations, especially if you're building or extensively remodelling. You'll probably be unprepared for the layer upon layer of official and unofficial standards you have to meet for various state and local agencies. Almost everywhere you have to deal with environmental concerns even in a bakery business. Local trash service, for example: How much will it cost you to bind all your cardboard, and separate all your cans and bottles? This is good for the environment, but some procedures can be more expensive and time consuming than others. You have to get a little hard-hearted and cost out all these good works as a part of doing business.

Look into fire and police protection, planning, and health regulations and inspection. Even if you don't plan to look at more than one locality, pick out another potential place, perhaps where you are now, and compare those municipal services. Better services by themselves may not cause you to choose one place over another, but you will have to live with them and they are one of the criteria that will help you select where you finally settle.

ZONING AND PLANNING

Go down to city hall and the county administration center. Talk to the planners. Talk to the development agency. Tell them your idea. They may tell you you're fine, that you picked the perfect spot for your bakery. In a small town it can be that easy, but it isn't always.

Get a feel for how much control the planners want to exert by laying out your plans verbally. Find out what the requirements are by stating exactly what you plan to install. Ask what you have to show up with in order to get approval. The planners will explain what kind of blueprints you'll need, what kind of health code requirements you'll have to meet, what kind of fire safety requirements will apply to the kitchen and public area. They'll probably load you up with documents and send you to two or three other departments for more. You had better take notes if you're comparing several localities.

You should get copies of zoning regulations and at least look at the planning document or master plan. If you can't get the answers you want at the planning department, the local public library ought to have a copy of the master plan and allied documents you can read. The more you know, the less you'll be surprised. This is where you find out how your potential site is zoned, and whether an existing bakery you're looking at is grandfathered in. Be careful, because in most localities, a grandfathered-in improvement that is destroyed or torn down can't be replicated but has to be rebuilt to code. See how the local authorities will treat a nonconforming site that you might seriously be considering.

If you're considering a site that's questionable or you need a variance or conditional use permit, you might also want the names of planning commissioners and the planning director. You may have to fight for your project all the way to the top. Your task is fairly easy if you're setting up downtown where the local authorities will welcome your business. If you're on wetlands or specially protected space where you have to deal with environmentalists, local supervisors, council members, citizens' groups, and the like, you'll have to consult experts, like lawyers or contractors or architects, who have actually dealt with these problems before. They can tip you off to what you're letting yourself in for. I've never had to deal with that kind of a situation but have heard hair-raising tales about them. It's a good idea to learn in advance what they can involve; so take your time and do it up front. All this looking, incidentally, is what you spend "seed money" on. You may need plenty of it.

Also inquire about any unofficial citizens' planning organization, a save-our-community group. Get its name and telephone number; talk to the members or the president. You don't have to worry about that in most communities, but in some expensive and popular scenic towns people can get very touchy. I've heard about a place that had five coffee houses on one street serving nothing but gourmet coffees. Another one wanted to set up, and the townspeople said, "No, we won't have another one. This town needs a bakery, restaurant, or ice-cream parlor, not another coffee house." You want to find out that kind of thing before you get too far along in your planning.

RED TAPE

Now that you've found the perfect place for your bakery, get ready to roll up your sleeves. The hard work begins here. Be prepared for long, daunting, and unfamiliar labor before you open your doors.

Buying or renting a building with a bakery already in it won't necessarily free you of red tape. Sometimes a change in ownership or tenancy is when the new regulations kick in. If we were to sell the bakery today or turn over operations to someone else, the new business would have to bring many things up to code. Health regulations are the toughest and will require the most changes. You may think that you're setting up a bakery. What you're doing is stepping into rat's nest. When you see a going concern you're interested in you can't imagine why it would have to be different when you take over, but it can and it's worth thinking about.

Because a grandfathered-in place will have to be rebuilt to current regulations if it's destroyed, you'd better see about insurance to cover new construction. Check out building and health codes very closely to determine what a new place will need. Our local health department uses a new-business plan-review checklist to approve everything. It's just a simple list the inspector uses to see that you have, for example, a suitable hood and ancillary system for making donuts. You can get a copy of the checklist in advance. I recommend it if your local department uses one. California has what it calls its Uniform Retail Food Facility Law (URFFL), to which the checklist refers. The health department will probably be happy to give you a copy of its checklist, but our department's only lists the code sections. You'd have to go read the appropriate codes to see if the shop measures up.

You want to know sign regulations. At the north end of town there is a sign 50 or 60 feet up in the air for "Fjord's Restaurant." It's visible from way off on the freeway. Fjord's has been out of business for at least 10 years, but the sign is still there because if the building's owners remove it they won't be able to put up another one. Whoever moves in gets to put a name on the existing sign. Once it's torn down, nobody can put up a new one.

This part of start-up will take all the patience and persistence you have. You won't get approval on a one-time visit. Get used to the idea. First you meet and find out who you have to meet next time. You may get no answers at all until you've seen everybody. There will be a swarm of little-known, almost secret rules to plague you. You hand over your plan and have one part of the bureau approve it just to have someone at another desk disapprove it.

You have to play by these rules, but sometimes being too agreeable is just opening the door for the government to help you make decisions for the rest of your business life. You'll have to walk a fine line between resistance and compliance. We're lucky enough to deal with very cooperative and helpful local officials, but in some places you'll have to stand up for your rights all the way. Be firm, of course, but if you have a short fuse burn it off somewhere else—not in a government department. You need to build a working relationship with the people you'll deal with. Get them on your side. Leave no doubt that you rely on, appreciate, and need them. You won't necessarily like all they ask you to do, but do it when you must. Just grin and bear it.

Towns like ours want business downtown for all the reasons we mentioned. Approach the city and ask how it can help you. It may have federal money or know of local funds, like our Main Street Program, to help finance you. It may also have enough leverage to get you through the regulations. You can also try to get waivers or see if the building falls under a historical district exemption.

Here in California, if we had to rebuild the bakery we would have to retrofit to seismic standards. One clause in the law says that if any single remodel constitutes 50 percent of the building's value, you must retrofit the entire building. The way around them is to bid out jobs in little chunks. Instead of one big $60,000 remodel on a $100,000 building, do it over time with four different contractors at $15,000 apiece.

LEASED SPACE

Most start-up businesses lease their buildings. Everything in a lease is negotiable. Sometimes the landlord has the bargaining edge, sometimes the renter does. It depends on the area. If it's a real hotspot, the landlord may be able to get the rent demanded. If you're downtown where there are eight empty buildings and the one you want is 50¢ or 75¢ a foot higher than one a couple of doors away, don't let on that it suits your needs better. Remember, your bakery can provide a place where people gather, sit, and relax. If the landlord's property—maybe it's a shopping center—doesn't already have such a place, you'll bring in traffic it might not otherwise get.

I paid extra to be on State Street but I realized that was important since I was giving up a central location. I made one sacrifice by being away from the middle of town but made up for it somewhat by being on the main street. If we were on a side street way south of town here, we'd have been dead. A location may be a $100 a month cheaper, but it may cost $1,000 a month more in advertising to let everyone to know where you are. If you're out there on the main street, they see you when they go by. That's why I tried to make our place more eye-catching with the water wheel and old-time design.
—KEN MOORE
MOORE'S FLOUR MILL, BAKERY & DELI

You're providing an asset. That's what you should base your bargain on to get the market rent.

Negotiate everything, the price per square foot, the term of the lease, and any options. An option to renew is one of the most important. Never get in a corner where at the end of the two years, after you've built a valuable site, the landlord can refuse to renew your lease or say, now it's $3.00 a square foot instead of $1.00. He or she becomes your partner. The harder you work, the more money the landlord makes.

If you lose the lease, it's goodbye to nearly all of your investment. You want a lease term that lets you recoup those costs. Also, if the building gets a higher tax assessment because of your improvements, the landlord might try to pass it on to you. Ask if the landlord will share some of the remodelling costs. Many will, because it's in their own interest. Some leases give rent allowances for tenant improvements (TI), often signaled by the term "divide to suit." Or perhaps the landlord will forgive a few months' rent if you put a few thousand dollars into the building. There are always trade-offs worth raising and exploring.

You also want to be able to back out of a lease. If you're committed to a five-year term and you see that you can't make it, you want a clause that lets you give the landlord two, three, or even six months notice to vacate without being responsible for paying rent for the rest of the five years. Try for the best of both worlds: the right to get out if things are bad but to renew on good terms if all goes well.

Many landlords will ask for a percentage increase each year, usually based on the Consumer Price Index (CPI). We're locked into that at the home-improvement center and our rent will hike up every few years. The owners felt that they gave us a pretty good starting rate, so that's how they plan to recoup. You can try to negotiate a little more slack in this by trying to get the first two months either free or get the first payment moved back a few months to help you get started.

Setting up in some commercial environments, particularly a mall or a shopping center, might require a triple-net lease and a percentage of your gross. By contrast, landlords in many downtowns are so pleased to get steady tenants they may offer much better terms, and you'll see those lease requirements less often there. Triple-net means that you pay all expenses, including maintenance, insurance, and property taxes. In a center or mall you might also have to pay "association fees" for "common area expenses"—parking lot clean-up, lighting, security, and other things. Triple-net leases and association fees are two-sided. If you're in a popular location with a good product and high profit margin, the foot traffic may justify the extra cost. But keep the costs in mind, and when you compare leases make certain what the rent does and does not cover. Then adjust them before you make comparisons. The fees that are common in malls are not a factor in a city commercial center, so those costs don't become part of your rent. That's what taxes are for.

Percentage leases can be another drain on your income, but they may help if you're uncertain about your start-up cash flow. They let you begin with a low fixed rent. The percentage payment doesn't kick in until you reach a certain level of sales. Later, however, when you're doing well, the percentage on sales could be substantial. Do a simple calculation. If the going rate is $2 per square foot, a 1,000-square-foot building would rent for $2,000 a month. If you can rent at $1,200 per month plus 6 percent of sales over $10,000, your rent at $20,000 of monthly sales is $1,200 plus $600, for a total of $1,800 a month. If you gross $25,000 a month, you pay $2,100 a month. It goes up from there, so you have to be willing to pay the premium for that low starting rent. Most percentage leases use declining rates as sales rise, but figure it out in advance. You could try to get out of a percentage lease when renewing, but usually you can't negotiate them away.

Also check on:

• What condition the building is in. If you're going into, say, a former clothing store, find out if the building can be brought up to code economically.

•What fire and safety regulations govern the permitted capacity for any seating.

• Whether you can get insurance on the building if you put a bakery in it.

• Whether you or the landlord will pay for improvements to bring the building up to code, or will share the expense. They will increase the building's value, after all.

• Who will maintain the building's outside, inside, mechanical and electrical equipment, plumbing, plate glass.

• Who will pay for garbage, trash and snow removal, and gardening.

• Who pays if the air conditioner goes out.

• Who pays to replace a broken hot water heater.

• Who pays if someone runs by and throws a brick through the window.

• Who takes care of off-street parking.

• Whether there is a delivery area with back-door access or a nearby loading zone that offers good front-door access.

• What kind of zoning and conditional use permits apply?

• What are chances for expansion? There's a building next to ours that would have been perfect to expand into but was one of three owned by the same landlord. He had a lease clause with a coffee-shop that forbade leasing to another coffee shop or the like in either of the other two buildings.

• What past restrictions are there on recent tenants' licenses? If you want to have live music at night and serve cappuccino and bagels, or even serve beer and wine with a café, find out if you are far enough away from any residential area.

Look for everything you would look for if you were leasing a house. Look for more.

BUYING PROPERTY

When I got the chance to acquire our building I did a rough buy/rent analysis, comparing the cost of rent against the costs of owning: mortgage, taxes, insurance, any expenses the landlord paid. Then I weighed the negative aspects of purchase against plans for the building and bakery. Essentially, the question was whether to rent and put $30,000 into improving a rented rather than an owned property. That made it an easy decision to buy for a little *more* than the equivalent of rent and spend to improve the bakery's value. The decision-making process should take into account the risk of a long-term financial commitment, the write-offs you get for owning property, the equity build-up you get, the effect of appreciation on an improved structure, and how long you plan to be at the location. Sometimes, the figures just can't support a buy decision, and at other times, there are personal or other non-economic reasons involved. Usually, if you can acquire your own building, you're money ahead. You build up equity, you have security for a loan if you need it, and you have stable payments if you can get a fixed-rate mortgage.

When you buy, check out all deed restrictions and conditional use permits that might expire on change of ownership. As mentioned, the authorities may throw a curve ball at you and say you are no longer zoned commercial or for your kind of business. There will have to be a structural pest inspection and report, flood plain reports, reports of assessed valuation and of taxes on the land and improvements. You want a complete list of all the equipment and fixtures, and you should double-check it before and just after you buy to make sure that you got all you paid for. For instance, are you getting the air-conditioner? Are you getting the stainless steel shelving that's attached? The oven and sink? Ordinarily, fixtures attached to the building are included in the sale. Most real estate sales are through agents who should check all these things. But whether or not a professional is involved do your own research and checking, because ultimately you will be responsible for confirming that you are getting everything in the contract.

Also, I bought the building as an individual. My corporation now rents it from me at a fair market rent, which is more than my mortgage payment. The rental income supplements my salary and is not subject to payroll tax, although it is subject to taxation in our quarterly estimated returns. It's good business and a perfectly legitimate way to supplement income. Also, you can give the business the option of not paying rent if it's hurting. Finally, you may have a chance to purchase more space than you need and lease out part of it as a way to cover mortgage payments.

Not many people starting their own bakeries have the money to buy, but the opportunity may turn up later on, as it did for us. Even if you're starting out and unsure whether the business will fly, you should try to get a lease with option to buy when you rent a good location. These should be drafted and executed by an experienced commercial real estate agent or a lawyer. If you can't get a written option to buy, at least let the landlord know that if the building ever comes up for sale you would like first crack at it.

Whether you buy later through a lease-option or otherwise, the seller sometimes will carry back a loan at a below-market interest rate. Then, try to get a right of first refusal to buy back your note if the seller decides to sell it later at a discount.

BUYING A GOING CONCERN

Buying an existing bakery can be less stressful because it offers immediate income. If it's doing very well, however, you won't get it for the price of the equipment alone. You'll have to pay for its business activity as goodwill. When the Courthouse Bakery was starting up, the present site with all of its out-of-date equipment had very little goodwill. That's why it sold for only $85,000. Also, in the rare case where a baker has taken care of his or her retirement and just wants to quit business, you may be able to buy for little more than the price of the equipment. Otherwise, count on paying for goodwill, and be sure you can run the business with a low enough overhead and sufficient potential for increased sales to cover the cost of the goodwill on top of the equipment price. You need at least to cover all the expenses, including your salary, and to pay off any business loan. Ideally, the business would do even better than before.

Reputation and recipes are part of goodwill along with business activity. The owner may not want to sell you all the recipes handed down through one or two generations. Many bakers won't give them up; so you'd be buying the bakery, all the equipment, and the customer walk-through trade—but not the recipes. Whenever you purchase a bakery or any business be sure to get a covenant not to compete. You don't want your seller to take the recipes two doors down and cash in on the sale with a new bakery. A non-competition covenant would prevent your seller from starting a new bakery within a few-mile radius of you for a certain number of years.

Any time you buy a business, look at its books for at least the last two years, but preferably more. You may find, for example that sales grew strongly in the first year, less strongly in the second year and even less in the third. See the accompanying table. The seller

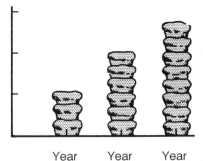

A "Declining Increase" in Sales

Year 1   Year 2   Year 3

will emphasize growing sales. You would counter with slowing growth. Partly it's striking a good bargain, but mostly it means figuring out *what kind of income stream* you're paying for. If you looked at two years, the business might appear to be growing but it could be on its way down. It could have made $750,000 for the two years you look at the books, but did $1,000,000 the year before. Try to see enough of its history to know where it is going. If necessary have a CPA verify the assets and cash flow and give you a Statement of Financial Condition.

Don't rely on the books alone. Ask the owner to let you sit in for a week to see how the business runs. Some businesses may look like they're not making any money until you notice that $5,000 or $6,000 a month is going to the owner as a salary or other compensation. Find out also how involved the owner is in the business. Is he or she doing 80 percent of the work? If you looked at my dad's books, they would look great. He does very well, but he and his wife do almost everything. That keeps their costs much lower than ours and improves their bottom line. Our bakery has a higher gross but its income as a percentage of gross is lower because of its higher overhead. Without my dad's skills, however, anyone who took over his bakery would have to hire an assistant baker, a bookkeeper, a salesperson . . . and suddenly that cash flow would disappear. On the other hand, I have a staff, and those expenses are covered. While I own a bakery and am an integral part in its success, it can run without me. My dad owns a bakery but he's it; without him the doors don't open. You need to analyze the business's structure to see if any cash flow is left after paying expenses you might otherwise overlook.

Buying a business is kind of a spy game. There's nothing wrong with being very nosy here. You want to find out all about the business from other people. Don't take the owner's word. Some owners are very motivated as sellers; they want to get out and when they show you the business they'll put the whipped cream and cherry on top. Find out who the bakery's main suppliers are. Contact them. Tell them that you're interested in buying and you want to know what kind of customer the bakery has been. Find out if it has always paid its bills on time and how much product it goes through in a week. Have its purchases have been declining? Try to provide for every eventuality.

When you get a copy of the applicable state health regulations and the new-business checklist from the health inspector, ask to see the bakery's past inspection reports to learn about any deficiencies. The owner will have copies but may not tell you. These records are available to the public and accessible at the local public or environmental health department. Before you draw any conclusions from the report, look at a few other bakeries' reports. Keep in mind that health inspectors don't go around to lavish praise on us. The best thing they can say is nothing at all. If you find your intended place has extraordinary problems and you have to spend $25,000 just to bring it up to code, you may be in a position to dicker. This information can be a bargaining chip or a reason to look elsewhere.

For some people the chance to pay a bargain price for a business that is doing poorly can be irresistible. Our place had fallen on hard times when we bought it, and as the Courthouse Bakery we've managed to turn it around. But you should look at the shop's whole history. Some places just can't get over a bad reputation. I've seen good restaurants and restaurateurs go into ostensibly good locations and do poorly. Usually a succession of failing establishments will have been there for many years. The place gets an unsavory history and you just can't change it. If you're from out of town, ask people how many businesses have been at your bargain location. If they say that in the last two years it had 12 places—all of them bad—yours will be the 13th, and people will think, "Well, here's another one." You may be able to improve a rundown shop, but see what caused its problems and make sure you can fix them.

If you decide to buy a going concern, you'll be buying tangible and intangible assets. The seller will want to value the tangible assets low in order to avoid depreciation recapture for taxes. You want them valued high so you can depreciate them. If the sale includes accounts receivable, review them for their age and credit standing. How successful was the previous owner in collecting them? Does a lender have a security interest in them?

When you buy a bakery like ours by purchasing corporate shares you get the assets and the liabilities. When you buy an unincorporated business you usually don't get its liabilities, but check for outstanding debts. Court and other official records will show if there are any lawsuits pending or any liens against the business. Check accounts payable and other liabilities for liens against the owner or the business. The Uniform Commercial Code (UCC) lets you file a Form UCC-3 with the Secretary of State to search for federal or state tax liens, attachment or judgment liens, and private encumbrances on the business's assets. Some liens are blanket encumbrances on all the business's assets, others apply to specific assets.

One contract protection for the buyer is a set of seller warranties that lets the buyer deduct the cost of any undisclosed debts or other shortages from the sale price. Other breaches may permit canceling the deal. The seller usually warrants good title to real and personal property, disclosure of all material facts and liabilities, the truth and accuracy of financial statements, and that there is no litigation or governmental proceeding against the business. You need to make sure all applicable taxes, including withholding, income, and unemployment have been paid. Clearance certificates from the proper agencies will cover them. Also notify the IRS of the sale, and be sure local taxes have been paid, and see that a bulk-sale transfer notice gets filed. Review the local master plan for potential new competition, new housing, large businesses that may change the character of the neighborhood, zoning changes, and code changes that will require a major upgrade of the premises.

Make sure you can assume any lease or get a new one on the kind of good terms mentioned above. Some leases are written in totally incomprehensible legalese. Even if yours is not, review it, write down any questions to discuss with a lawyer, and review it again with the lawyer.

Finally, check not only how much the bakery sells every week, but how much sales vary from season to season. Be sure to see what percentage wholesale and retail business the bakery does, and if it meshes with your plans. See how much the owner spent for maintenance, repair, and capital improvements, and whether these costs are constant, increasing or declining. Get a list of equipment, fixtures, furniture. You'll also want to have an inventory taken just before the transfer date. Purchasing a business is hard work and usually needs professional help. We recommend reading *The Complete Guide to Buying and Selling a Business*, by Arnold S. Goldstein. You probably won't end up doing it yourself, but you will be a better client for a business broker or lawyer who handles the deal.

HEALTH CODE COMPLIANCE

Before you close your deal on a lease or the purchase of a building or the whole business *go see the local health inspector*! The department is very, very strict when you first set up, and the inspector, who should know all the local businesses like yours, will issue the final approval of your premises. Take the inspector a copy of your proposed menu and product list, with a list of all the equipment now in the bakery and what you plan to install. You will have settled on your products and designed your kitchen to suit, but the inspector will determine the kind of equipment you need. You'll get a whole bunch of surprises. The inspector will tell you if your equipment is NSF-certified and whether you have overlooked things that the code requires for your menu. You want to find that out before you drag a 500-pound refrigerator or mixer into the kitchen and learn that you have to drag it out again. You also want to be sure everything you need will fit your kitchen and your budget. Then get an inspection date that won't delay your opening.

Seeing the inspector before you open can prevent very expensive problems later on. For example, things that you may think you can display at room temperature, for example, may need to be refrigerated or heated. If you plan to have pizza by the slice, be prepared to keep it 140 degrees or above, or chilled to 41 degrees or below. Everything considered to be a bacterial hazard—such as dairy products, meat products or soups—must be stored within those ranges. Anytime you expand or produce something outside the scope of what you were approved for, you'll be subject to new regulations, and they will cost you. Regulations in California for processing dairy products—including ice cream—are so complex that you need to set up a separate, very sanitary workroom. If you want a yoghurt machine you have to qualify for a permit and show that you can comply with all the federal bacteria laws. Never think about diversifying without making that preliminary trip to the health department.

You'll have to base dining capacity on fire and safety regulations. If the bakery has a parking lot, it's size will be based on the dining area's "official capacity."

EQUIPPING A KITCHEN

You should have a projected cost of equipment. I always price out equipment by making a table of what we need with its new and used prices. Then I go shopping and try to buy it at auctions or from other bakeries. You should be able to buy good used equipment for 50 to 60 percent off the cost new.

If you have time before opening the bakery, you can go to auctions to size up used equipment and selling prices. Two or three times a month we receive notices from two different auctioneers of sales from supermarkets, restaurants, or other food establishments that have gone out of business. The brochures tell what is for sale and when to show up to preview it. You buy as-is, and pay with cash or cashier's check.

Auctions are not the best place to learn what is available or to get a feeling for price. Go to auctions with an intention to buy and an awareness of new and used prices. Most cities have at least one used restaurant and bakery supply store. Poking around in them will give you an idea of prices. That will let you establish a maximum price that you're willing to spend. Then don't overbid it. If you can buy for that price, great; if not, do it later. Some auctions are really hot, and lots of buyers will bid on everything; so you won't get a very good deal. At other auctions you may be one of five bidders and get equipment at bargain-basement prices.

These auctions are huge operations. They might auction everything in a supermarket as big as a regional Safeway. Usually a few hours before the auction you have a chance to check the equipment. Purchase terms are usually as-is but, if there is a preview, use the opportunity to find out whether the item works. If you buy something expensive like a mixer, you want a guarantee that it is working at time of sale. If it breaks down shortly afterwards, it's your loss.

Buying used always carries a risk of unreliability. With some things it's more important than with others to buy new. We've bought our share of used refrigeration. It doesn't always pay. Inevitably, our bargain refrigerator needs a new compressor and labor to install it. It ends up costing about as much as a new unit, with the

We started corresponding with Alan Scott and exploring the possibility of building a brick oven here. We decided to go for it in the spring of '88. Then we had to go through this interminable process of applying for permission from the Historical Review Board. . . . And the Coastal Commission. Yeah, we filled out these forms about how many underground parking spaces we have [none], all this malarkey. It was just nuts. Anyway 13 months and 1300 dollars of application fees later we finally got permission to build this little 200-square-foot space and the oven.

—CHRISTOPHER KUMP
CAFE BEAUJOLAIS, THE BRICKERY

aggravation thrown in for free. Base your selection of used equipment on how much you have to rely on it and what is most visible to your customer—like showcases, which are one of your best sales tools. Even though you we've used old showcases and equipment, it's better to get "new-used," not "used-used."

We put together equipment for the home-improvement center by finding bakeries that were going out of business, upgrading, or changing their product line. They're easy to locate by word of mouth. You just tell salespeople you're interested in a new two-door freezer or an oven. The network among salespeople and their contacts is so huge that before you know it, you get a phone call from someone who says they want to sell what you're looking for.

For example, there was a bakery in Santa Rosa with a week left on its lease at a major shopping center. The landlord had offered $5,000 for all its equipment, which was easily worth $50,000 to $60,000 new. The owners had sold some of the mixers and hoped to get $20,000 to $25,000 for the rest, which would have been at a big loss, as it was. Rather than take the $5,000, they had decided to remove and store it. I had gone there on a salesman's tip to spend $2,000 to $3,000 for the sink and freezers. When I got there they had all this beautifully maintained, unsold bakery equipment. I didn't need it, but on seeing that they had a beautiful Baxter 12-pan revolving oven worth $20,000, I ended up offering $13,000 for everything—including the oven, the showcases, the refrigerators, the workbenches, the sinks. Eventually, we can use them all. It was an impulse-buy in the sense that if I didn't do it then, somebody else would have come by to pick up the pieces, and we would lose a very good deal. It was a good deal for the sellers who did not have to store it indefinitely and got more than the landlord offered.

The same thing happened when the bakery on the other side of the courthouse closed. Like many who sell a business, its owners had asked $30,000 for the business's goodwill and the value of its equipment; but when it finally closed there was no goodwill left to speak of. All that remained was the equipment, including dining room furniture, refrigeration, a stove and steam table, all of which went for $5,000.

Very often when someone wants to sell you a business for, say, $150,000, go in and look closely at the value of the equipment. That may be all you're buying. Often people bail out because there is no business or goodwill to sell. That's why a thorough inspection of the business is important. If you take on too much overhead to buy a bakery, you could end up just like the seller or worse.

First Steps

Decide where to locate the business

___Region or City

___Read statistical abstract,"Cities & Towns Rated," and other print sources for—

    ___Demographics

    ___Major employers

    ___Economic condition

    ___Proximity to suppliers

___Look at the places you select for—

    ___Economic conditions (again)

    ___Customer concentration and dispersion

    ___Your potential market share

    ___Labor pool

    ___Municipal services

    ___Zoning and planning departments

    ___Citizens groups

    ___Talk to people who will lead growth

___Street or Shopping Center

    ___Competition

    ___Volume of traffic

    ___Shop's visibility and potential "curb appeal"

    ___Convenience for shoppers

___Traffic and customer turnover

    ___Nearby retail attractions

    ___Sources of customers

    ___Peak business times

    ___Projected neighborhood growth/decline

Acquire real estate

___Persuade lessor to rent

    ___Business plan shows good projected income stream and stable tenancy

    ___Bakery's positive effect on area

___Get professional help to

___Lease or buy space

    ___Review contract terms

___Buy an existing bakery

    ___Inspect the business closely

    ___Talk to others

    ___Review contract terms

Shop for equipment

___Get catalogs and spec sheets

___Consult experienced bakers

___Get on the second-hand network

PLANT AND PROCESS

Let the number of bakers be always complete, and the place where they work always kept neat and clean.

—CHARLEMAGNE
A.D. 768-814

8

THE KITCHEN

A BAKERY is a very specialized kitchen, and kitchen design and construction will be your biggest challenge and expense. Even when you've acquired a knowledge of other bakeries, you'll still have a hundred decisions to make. Knowing what products you will start with and having a plan to grow into will set your present and anticipated equipment needs—you do need room to grow—but even then you won't find clear-cut answers about the best kitchen design for your needs. You could engage a qualified architect, engineer, or design consultant to help work things out, but a CAD (computer-assisted design) specialist who concentrates on food preparation services will be cheaper and better qualified to handle your special needs.

To find experienced assistance like this talk to restaurant owners or look in the Yellow Pages under Restaurant Equipment & Design. Large restaurant supply companies often have their own design teams. If you are buying $30,000 or $40,000 of new equipment, such a company can assign you a designer, often for only a nominal fee, if any. Sometimes the search requires getting on the phone and calling restaurant chains. They all use designers to one extent or another. Their branches are similar but have to fit into different sized and shaped buildings. They get CAD specialists to create the same environment over and over again with the stock equipment arranged in different ways.

COMPUTER-ASSISTED DESIGN

Hiring a CAD specialist isn't as expensive as you would think, and it's definitely cheaper to iron out the wrinkles on the computer screen than to wrestle equipment around later on. Also, it is comforting to know while the place is getting built that electrical outlets will be where they ought to be and that everything else will be within a half inch of perfect because that's how you and the CAD specialist arranged it. A good restaurant CAD specialist has software specs on every extant piece of equipment, can put your whole business on the screen, and will use every inch of space. If the distance between the door jamb and a wall is, say, 8 feet 10 inches, the designer will find equipment that fits in 8 feet 9½ inches. The designer can tell you exactly what size proof box you want. If you already have an oven, he or she can play with it on the computer to fit it into the best location. Before you know it, you have your kitchen on a piece of paper.

For our new place the designer and I reviewed our menu requirements and identified every piece of equipment we would need for it. Then on a computer screen we took the space available and moved the equipment around to where we thought it would work best. Everything we put in it is within an inch of not fitting. We ended up with a plan to submit to the health department that not only had all the specs on the equipment, but it was all NSF-approved. We just put our equipment in place, plugged it in, and went to work. And we're talking from the ground up. It's arranged now so that, if our equipment needs outgrow the current kitchen, we can move the wall out a little.

The advantage of having a CAD specialist is that you can then tell the contractor exactly where to put the walls around the kitchen. When the walls are already in place you could go in and take the measurements yourself, find out what kind of equipment you will to need, and decide where to put everything. That means first going out to learn what kind of equipment is available. Then you would use graph paper for the floor plan and either sketch or make cutouts of the equipment to move around on the floor plan. Ideally you would use several layouts and get opinions from other people in the business if you take that route. It takes more time and carries the risk of amateurs helping amateurs. You probably would not save enough this way to justify not getting a CAD specialist's expertise and experience. Even when the walls are in place it's worth hiring one to decide where to put the proper wiring, plumbing, and structural alterations suited to your equipment.

If you're remodeling, the building will determine what you can do. Its size and shape—square, rectangular, or irregular—will establish how you set up your equipment. If you're really constrained by space, you may have to arrange things a little less efficiently to fit it all in. While you would want your work flow to be from your mixing bowl, to your bench, to your proof box, and to your oven, the building's dimensions may force you to go bench, bench, proof box, oven—with your mixer on the opposite wall. You just deal with

CROISSANTS

Depending on whom you ask, the Ottoman Turks in the 16th (or 17th) Century once tried to sack Vienna (or Budapest) by tunneling beneath the city walls very early in the morning. Bakers were the only people awake at 3:00 a.m. (or thereabout) and, hearing the tunneling, alerted the city. The Turks were routed thanks to the bakers, who then created a pastry to commemorate the victory. It was shaped like the crescent in the Turkish flag for grateful Viennese (or Hungarians) to consume each morning. "Croissant"—accent on the first syllable (CRWAW'-sah[N])—is French for crescent.

things like that, especially if you don't own the building. The landlord is unlikely to let you tear down a wall or make many holes for plumbing.

Before you start laying out the equipment, have the architect or contractor you plan to work with survey the building's mechanical, plumbing, and electrical systems. If you have a stove or a donut fryer, you have to take the hood and its vent into consideration. You can't put a hood vent up through the ceiling where there may be electrical wiring or ducts in place, which is where the architect or contractor comes in. You need somebody to climb up and say, no you can't pierce the ceiling here.

WORKING WITH CONTRACTORS

We get most of our contractors and construction help by word-of-mouth, and I recommend it. When you go into a bakery or any commercial building that you know and like, ask who did the work. The owner will be happy to tell you about the whole experience whether it was terrific or terrible. The next best way is to check with the local building inspector to find out which contractors' jobs pass inspection without problems and with the lumber yard to learn which pay their bills on time, which is an important consideration.

If you work with an architect, he or she often likes to work with a particular a contractor. That can be helpful, but it's your choice. You're paying the bills. One thing to remember when remodeling is that it's not the architect's money or the contractor's money. The architect and contractor are working for you. They will know much more than you, so take it all in but don't let them make decisions for you. They may say that you can do one wall a certain way and it would turn out thus and so. Your response should be, that's fine but how much more would that cost than the original plan? You have to be skeptical, because before you know it you've turned a

$20,000 remodel into an $80,000 job. I got caught up in that for a while. And then I got the bill.

It's important to go through the bidding process with all your specifications stated in detail. Then contact five or six contractors. Make sure that they will all be using the same materials and processes, and bid the project out. Different bids on the same project can vary by thousands of dollars, even with the same materials and methods. Some contractors are cheaper. They may do all the work themselves and not hire a crew. Get back your bids in detail and make sure you are comparing the identical items in every bid. You don't always want to go with the cheapest bid, because the result may be inferior. So check on past customers' satisfaction.

Find out how your contractor wants to be paid. Will it be 80 percent of the project up front and 20 percent on completion? Local practice is to pay by 20-percent draws, holding back the last 10 percent until the job is finished to your satisfaction and the building inspector signs it off. You have to work payments into your budget as well. Try not to pay a contractor more than 50 percent up front, and also put your opening date in the agreement as a reference for the date of completion. Delays and at least 25-percent cost overruns are almost inevitable. If you are delayed past your planned opening, be up front. Tell the contractor quite honestly that you were supposed to be open a week ago, haven't made any money yet, and won't be able to pay him until you open. Better yet, insert a contract clause that for every day past the opening date, when you are not making any money, it will cost the contractor $200 a day, or whatever. Think of it as an incentive to finish on time. Otherwise, the contractor gets paid whether you do or not.

Make sure that the contractors and subcontractors working on your project are licensed. There are unscrupulous contractors and handymen who will be glad to do the project but are not licensed. They have no insurance. Then all of a sudden one of their workers buys it on the ladder in your building, and you're liable because the contractor wasn't insured. So make sure they have a current license, are insured, and carry workers' compensation.

Building new, and sometimes even when remodeling, pick a contractor with restaurant construction knowledge over one without, especially if you lack experience in food-service design and construction. Your contractor needs to know what your equipment requirements are if you don't. Do you need 220-volt electrical service in the wall? Do you need 110? Do you need one-inch pipe for water? Do you need half-inch pipe? You want to have all those decisions and everything worked out before they put the drywall up.

You want to know about electrical requirements in your building. Electricity will often dictate where you put equipment. If you have 220-volt service in some of the bakery, that's where you want to put your 220-volt equipment, unless you want to pay or have the

The recipes came with the business and that's another important thing, because you have to taste your product. It isn't always easy and it was one of the things I had to overcome— because I may detest a particular product, like my macaroon cookies. I'm the only one that makes them. I don't even like coconut, but everyone says how wonderful they are. The same went for our M&M cookies. They were not at all to my taste. In fact, I thought they were disgusting. But the kids bought them because they had M&Ms in them. I looked at the recipe and said this just does not look right to me. So I dropped one ingredient and added a little more of another ingredient, and it turned out to be a wonderful cookie.
—MURIEL GLAVE
THE LANDMARK BAKERY

landlord pay to extend 220 to that area. You'll also need numerous outlets around your workbenches for small 10-quart mixers, for fans, for cake decorating machines. You want to have enough outlets by your work space. Look also at the amperage. If the building has 100-amp service, and you go out and buy $50,000 worth of equipment that needs 200 amps to run it all, you're stuck, until you upgrade. And it is cheaper to install adequate service even during remodeling than to retrofit.

When we started, the bakery was on a 75-amp fuse box service. We just went pop pop pop! We were popping fuses from one end of the bakery to the other, and ended up having to upgrade to 200-amp service. It cost us $6,000 but we have adequate service now and we're on breakers. Gas and water require the same knowledge. Do you have all the lines for a gas oven or an electric oven? If you're running a dishwasher, a coffee machine, and sink, do you have enough water and water pressure to keep your dishwasher going? You also want proper ventilation and cooling in the kitchen with either a squirrel cage or pull fan at one end, and at least a swamp cooler so that there's some kind of cooling and a flow of air through the shop.

EFFICIENT WORKFLOW

Design for task efficiency, from mixing bowl to bench to proof box to oven to packaging. It affects every other step of the work process. Our bakery has a pair of sheer walls that we can't pierce. Our dish and sink area is behind one of these walls, and that's where our only water for mixing doughs is. I guarantee you it's an absolute nuisance for something as basic as water to be an extra 25 steps away. Life would be much easier if it were right next to the mixers. At my dad's bakery his water station is right there. You just turn from the scaling bench with the all the dry ingredients and add water. It makes work much more efficient. We plan to solve the problem by running a pipe around the wall, with a hose attached that has a control nozzle like those in filling stations but metered to let us measure water into mixing bowls. You'll have to find similar solutions if your space has problems like that.

Baking takes plenty of bench space. We have three thick maple work benches, an 8-footer, a 10-footer, and 12-footer. That's 30 feet of working bench space. You have to plan for that kind of space. We use them all; we could use more. It's great to have them because you can also store utensils below or on a shelf right above them. It makes all your ingredients, pans, and utensils very easy to grab and speeds up production.

You want to have a scaling bench where you weigh out your ingredients, and have all those ingredients—sugar, bread flour, bran, cake flour—all lined up under it, every one of them with a scoop in it. That's very important. If you have one scoop, you go crazy looking for it. And that scaling bench should have the water as near as possible. From there you want the mixers to be within a step or two of where you are scaling. You want to be able to scale the ingredients and dump them in the mixer without wasted motion. You don't necessarily need to have your work benches to the left or right of the mixer. They can be across the room. You simply pull the doughs off the mixer, take them to the bench, and work the dough, rounding it up, molding it, and so on.

The proof box should be as close as possible to the oven. If you wanted to design a kitchen and had three walls to work with—two long sides and a short one, with the fourth wall open to serve customers—refrigeration and a scaling bench could all be on one wall along with your mixers. On the opposite wall you could have your work benches with the proof box right next to the oven, which would be as close as possible to the packaging area. The packaging area would be near the service or retail area, so that the process went: scaling area, mixing area, workbenches, proof boxes, oven, and then, as you pulled product out of the oven, you would leave it there to be packaged and sent out front. That way you will have brought the aesthetic quality of the product up to the front.

AREA SELF-SUFFICIENCY

Some bakeries erect walls between their pastry department, their bread department, their mixing department, and their refrigeration department. Keeping departments in separate rooms is very helpful in a bakery of any size, because it keeps your personnel working exclusively in each department and not constantly running into each other trying to use the same bench. Ideally, you would designate each area for the activity to be carried out in it.

A good example is the deli operation. Deli people should work separately from bakery production. Gayle's Bakery in Capitola approaches this by designating different areas for different production purposes. Its deli area is probably no more than 100 or 150 square feet, but it is highly efficient, with a big chopping block table in its center and counters around all the walls. They do rotisserie chickens, prepare all their sauces, and get out a complete menu from that one area. The deli people never mix with bakery production. They can also work more efficiently because they don't have to wait for a stove or other equipment.

In our bakery we have a six-burner stove. We do two soups on it every day. Usually the pots are so big they cover up four burners. At the same time the bakers are trying do custards, chocolate dobosh or lemon filling on the same stove. It gets to be a tight squeeze. It's better to have a stove and refrigeration just for the deli, and in its own area. The easiest way to separate the deli department from the bakery, if you can't wall it off, is simply to use a large bench with high shelving on it to differentiate the areas. You try to

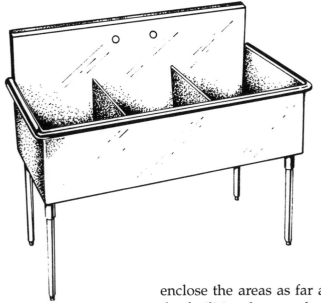

Here it is. . . the kitchen sink, in this case the regulation three-drop model that many public or environmental health departments now require of food-service businesses.

enclose the areas as far as possible, while giving them access to all the facilities they need.

Good Flow in the Area — Keep workbenches clear of tools and the last job's remnants. You'll accumulate what seems like a million different little tools. You should have a tool box, whether in a drawer underneath or above the bench, to store your pastry cutter, your donut cutter, and all those special devices. You'll appreciate having hooks or hangers for all your rolling pins and having them very close to where you work. You want a pail for all your scrapers.

Having your tools in the right place every time you work makes life much easier. When you have to look for something while you're in the midst of barreling along, work comes to a full stop. That's a real vexation. There has to be an ironclad rule for the staff that when they use something it goes right back where they got it if it doesn't need to be washed. We'll take that up later, but for now it means providing a place for every tool.

Organizing pots and pans is a necessity. Our building is very old with masonry party walls. We had a carpenter build a frame up against one wall. Then we wrapped the frame in sheet metal, and he screwed huge hooks through the sheet metal into the frame from which to hang our bowls. We can also hang up the dirty ones until they go to the dishwasher. That keeps them off the floor and accessible. It also helps keep things clean, which is surprisingly tough to do in a busy bakery. Just keeping things up on hooks makes cleanliness much easier.

There are also pans for use every day and those used only during the holidays. You have to designate areas to store them. You would keep your Christmas-tree pans, your pumpkin cake pans, and so on, in a low-use area like dry storage or a storage shed because you won't use them every day. You don't want to keep stumbling over them in the stack of the pans you use all the time. You should never throw away a sound pan. Whenever you order a specialty pan for a customer keep it for future use, even if you charge the customer for it. We charged for a Mickey Mouse pan, for example, and kept it. If that customer or another wants a Mickey Mouse cake in the future we have the pan and won't have to charge for it again. Finally, always put pans beneath the benches that are closest to the station where you use them. Most likely all your black baking pans will be under the bench that's closest to the oven. Your cake pans will be beneath the place where you scale your cake batter.

FOOD AND OTHER STORAGE

While it's a good idea to have at least one refrigerator nearby for often-used chilled ingredients, the ideal bakery would also have a refrigeration room or space to keep freezer and extra refrigerator storage out of the work area. It lets you put things aside and out of the way. If you can't afford the luxury of a cold-storage area, it's more logical to move freezer space, not refrigeration, out of the way. Refrigerators get used more often. You're always getting out your cream cheese, custards, creams and the like. But freezer space is where you store prepared doughs and pull them out for the next day. It doesn't have to be as close to your work space as the refrigerator.

When you're paying rent by the square foot, or have a mortgage based on a square-foot price, you usually end up with less than all the space you can use. You always need more. Refrigeration seems to be one place that feels the pinch, and you learn to use it very efficiently. Poor refrigeration, poor ventilation, and a hot work space advance spoilage dates and raise costs. If you have room for a big walk-in refrigerator, you might be able to store all you need. You could buy lettuce, fresh vegetables, dairy products, and meats by the case. Buying in volume from one supplier usually gets you a better deal. When you lack enough space, you have to order from two or three different suppliers that deliver on a different day of each week and buy a smaller amount from each one. That way you don't pay for larger cold storage. You have the convenience of multiple suppliers to store the food and keep it fresh for you, but you pay higher prices for smaller quantities. It's very important to figure out cold storage in this way as a cost of business.

Dry storage can be stuck just about anywhere out of the way. You can build shelves in the back corner of your bakery, or upstairs, or wherever there's room. We try to keep dry storage and canned goods in the same part of the bakery, which makes doing inventory easier. For broken-bulk dry goods consider metal flour bins. They're rectangular and fit side by side right under the bench.

For dish, utensil, and pot washing we have a small dish room where we hang all the pots and all the utensils such as paddles and

"It was a typical mid-life crisis," Bruce Hering, of Bruce Bread, explained. "I got divorced, quit my job, and moved to California. I had been a computer systems analyst and manager for a missile maker. I worked some of that time in finance. There wasn't a lot of career satisfaction in it. I decided I was not going to have any plans, so I lived with my daughter Diane, who baked bread. Not having an awful lot to do, I just got intrigued by it. I started baking and soon discovered I could bake bread better than anything I could buy."

As Hering baked more, and his surplus got around in the community, he got an offer: "Burt down at the Boont Berry Store said, I'd like to sell your bread but you can't bake at home and sell it; it's illegal. He said if he got a mixer and an oven, I could come down and bake and sell it right out of the store. I asked my daughter Ellen if she wanted to go into it with me. She said she would. Her only stipulation was that she wanted to make it a legal business. I was just going to be a guerrilla baker. But she said, no—follow the rules and she'd do it. I told her that's okay with me if she'd take care of all the dealings with the government, the taxes and all that stuff."

Bruce Bread
14111 Highway 128
Boonville, California

Hering is a partner in the wholesale bakery with two of his daughters, Ellen who manages the kitchen and Diane who manages the office. The company has risen on a loyal customer base, selling initially to natural food stores within the county. When business increased they rented space and bought a mixer and a pair of convection ovens.

"I didn't have the foggiest idea of how the bread business was run. I still don't. We have this customer base and they pried us into places like Safeway. I had to go down to the headquarters in Fremont. We were such a small deal they didn't want to talk to me. I said I couldn't do it big-time because I only wanted to deal with the stores in Mendocino County. The woman in charge said, 'Look, just deal with the managers directly. You're too small for us to mess around with.' That worked out pretty well. We got the Safeway in Willits, which is a big customer of ours, and then Fort Bragg and Ukiah.

"We've had pretty good relationships. The managers don't have a lot of freedom of movement. It's dictated by the main office. In our case they get a little leeway. They can deal with us and they like that.

"The manager in Ukiah once told us we couldn't sell bread there anymore, because we only delivered twice a week. The big companies deliver five, six days a week. I said, we don't have that kind of volume. Well, he says, you're outta here. A week later he called back and says, 'You know, you've got some pretty loyal customers; come back'. So we came back and they gave us, not a lot of shelf space, but enough. We have a niche in the market place."

"You hear all this talk about 'right livelihood,' and I kept thinking, well this is pretty good. People eat our bread and I like making it. It just seems right. We manage to have a family business without too many disagreements, and I have a chance to be around my grandchildren. We have a great life here."

mixing whips on the walls. They go right above the sinks where they can drip into the sink to drain.

You don't need or want much space for equipment storage. Unless you have space you haven't grown into, use every square foot for production. You can get a garage-size storage space outside the high-rent district and keep your unused or seldom-used equipment there. You can use it for dry storage and to keep machinery and furnishings you begin to assemble for future expansion.

You want a maintenance or broom closet for keeping cleansers that the health department considers hazardous. Technically it's called a chemical storage cabinet. You can't leave bleaches and disinfectants such as Simple Green around food, and a closet for mops, brooms, and other clean-up equipment is a good safe way to keep those chemicals separated from food. This storage could be in part of your dish-washing room.

For clean and dirty linen storage all you need is shelf space and a hamper. Try to keep it out of the way, near the dry goods. It's a good idea to allocate linen items to your personnel one at a time when they come in. Each employee gets one towel and one apron every day. Hand it over. Linen can get very expensive. Between the two places we spend about $300 a month on linen. Partly it's because people tend to be wasteful with it. They don't have to wash it; so someone will grab a towel to wipe up one simple spill then throw the towel in the hamper. If you can keep the linen behind locked doors—preferably in your office or with the manager—and allocate it, you can cut down the linen bill and the mess. If you leave linen out, free for all, the shelf will look like a clothes hamper in a messy home. People will take off their aprons and chuck 'em; there are clothes everywhere, like a teenager's bedroom.

DELIVERY SPACE

If, unlike us, you're lucky enough to have a back door, that is the best place for deliveries from your suppliers and pick-up for your own deliveries if you make them. You want to keep the area uncluttered so there is room for bread carts or anything else you use for pick up and delivery. You also want your dry-storage area closest to the back door. If your suppliers' drivers haul in 100-pound bags of flour, you don't want to make them come in and wheel all the way through your production area to pile their sacks at the far end. You want delivery right inside the back door. They come in, drop it off, and leave, without disturbing your people while they do it.

PARTS OF THE WHOLE

Lights, Lockers, Air—You need to have an employee personal-item area. It's a health department requirement. Employees' personal items can't be mixed in with dry storage or anything else. It can be in the same general area as dry storage but has to have a designated space. That is also where you will put your employee posters and information.

You want to have really bright lights in the kitchen, preferably fluorescent. First, they help keep things cleaner. Second, they use less energy. Third, they help keep the staff awake. It's better all around, in fact, to have a bright, shiny white work area. Nowadays fluorescents can replace incandescent bulbs in most fixtures in the front of the bakery. Try them out first, however, because the brightness ratings very often seem over-optimistic.

You want a good flow of ventilation, because hot air stands in a bakery. That means installing a swamp cooler or other air conditioner at one end of the space and an air-duct vacuum at the other to pull the air in, through, and out. As we mentioned before, you can use the ventilation with a duct system from the baking area out to the service area, so that when cookies come out of the oven your draw or squirrel cage on the roof pulls the air through the front and, on its way out, entices people with those wonderful aromas.

Floor Surfaces — For years ceramic tile was the floor surface of choice in commercial kitchens. Today you can use concrete if you put a food-grade sealer on it. For the new place we used a concrete sealer in front, but in the work area we put down a high-grade vinyl. Vinyl cleans up well and is very serviceable, provided you put all your equipment on wheels.

My recommendation for setting up to clean the bakery is to put everything on wheels. Every bit of refrigeration and storage, every appliance and work surface can be set on locking wheels that you can push up against a wall and lock in place. When it's time to clean underneath things simply unlock the wheels, roll everything out, and clean behind it. We have nothing on wheels in our downtown bakery. It's a chore to clean underneath things. At the new place with its vinyl floor we put everything on wheels. We just unplug, roll out, clean, mop, and roll it all back. It takes a fraction of the time and it gets cleaner.

Specialized Equipment — For our self-service coffee and tea station we run out fresh pots from behind the counter where the coffee, tea, and cappuccino machines are. The customers help themselves. You can set up beverages as self-service or for service from behind the counter. You can put coffee machines behind the lines and run out fresh pots of coffee in vacuum carafes to the counter or for custom-- ers to serve themselves. Or you can keep the machines behind the counter and pour coffee for the customers at that point.

Pot washing — There is no getting around the need for a three-drop sink in California and many other states now. The new standard is one sink each of soapy water, rinse water, and bleach water. The drain area must be as long and wide as your largest sink bowl. A dishwasher theoretically eliminates the need for the three-drop sink, provided it is big enough to wash your biggest pots and pans. Since that's unlikely, you still need the three-hole sink.

The hot water supply is very important. Dishwashers have a minimum temperature at which they run. There are high-, medium-, and low-temperature dishwashers. Lower temperature models need extra chemicals to run a little cooler. If your water heater can't keep up, you just change the chemicals you use. Your choice is between stronger chemicals and higher energy use.

You want easy dishwasher access where the bus tubs come in and go back out, with at least a swinging door between the dish room and the dining area so that people don't see the dish washing in progress. You also want a window in the door so people don't bump into each other when they go through it. A dish washing station located far from the dining room reduces the need for the door, but complicates bussing.

A hose to wash out the dishwasher makes clean-up much easier. A floor drain and a hose to wash the whole area down is an excellent idea. Otherwise you have to mop, scrub, and scrape everything.

Restrooms — Restroom requirements depend on whether you have a café on the premises. As mentioned elsewhere, ours is old, barely adequate, and grandfathered in for café use because of the building's age. Generally, a bakery without a café needs facilities in good repair for employees. Other requirements, whether for employees' or patrons' facilities, are set by local building and plumbing codes. You'll learn about them at plan check if not before.

THE BAKER'S OFFICE

I built a closed office in the back of the bakery. It actually has a door and its own ventilation. It's a place to keep records such as current invoices, insurance records, and other paperwork that may be needed at a moment's notice, in case of an accident or price change. If there's enough room you can keep them at the office, but inevitably there will be too much, and everything winds up going to your home or storage shed every few months. Having a quiet area is valuable for getting away from time to time and for conducting business either with salespeople or important customers. Whether you have a retail or wholesale business, there is nothing like an office in which to present yourself and your product.

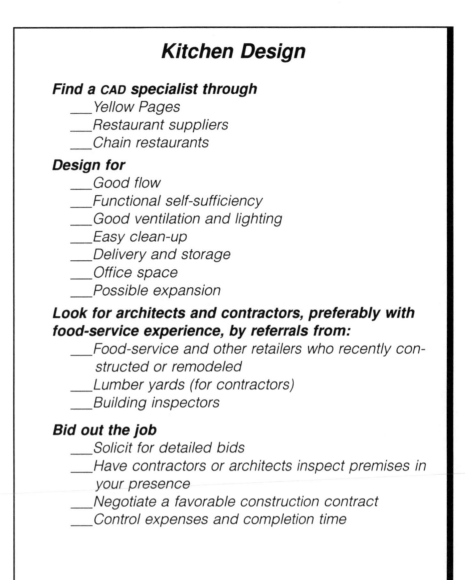

Kitchen Design

Find a CAD specialist through
___Yellow Pages
___Restaurant suppliers
___Chain restaurants

Design for
___Good flow
___Functional self-sufficiency
___Good ventilation and lighting
___Easy clean-up
___Delivery and storage
___Office space
___Possible expansion

Look for architects and contractors, preferably with food-service experience, by referrals from:
___Food-service and other retailers who recently constructed or remodeled
___Lumber yards (for contractors)
___Building inspectors

Bid out the job
___Solicit for detailed bids
___Have contractors or architects inspect premises in your presence
___Negotiate a favorable construction contract
___Control expenses and completion time

9

KEEPING IT CLEAN

CLEAN-UP AND MAINTENANCE are as much a part of running a bakery as rolling in, proofing, and baking doughs. You have to do it continuously and well. Bakeries are tough to keep clean because there are eggs splattering, and batter and bread dough spilling. Flour dust gets everywhere. Bread dough seems to turn into concrete once it dries on surfaces like walls or shelves.

Our practice has been to have a normal clean-up routine by department and supplement it on a walk-through basis: That is, in addition to our normal cleaning routines in each part of the bakery, I'll decide that today we do the stove and the proof box; the next day we'll do the outside of the oven and the inside of this refrigerator; two days later it will be the other refrigerator and that table. It takes a close watch and some diligence, but our bakery stays respectably clean for an old brick building. I don't entirely recommend the walk-through method. My problem—and I'm not alone in this—is to push production so much that clean-up goes on the back burner. Right now, however, we're developing a clean-up schedule and shifting those tasks to the schedule as part of organizing all the routines the business should have.

SCHEDULING FOR CLEAN-UP

Schedules make the job easier. You just check your worksheet and follow the list, no need to rely entirely on memory. For daily clean-up you don't need a list; it's part of the work and becomes automatic. The schedule is to help you keep up with the less frequent tasks. For example, every week you might have one day when you thoroughly clean one refrigerator or the shelves, or the oven, or one or two appliances. At different times—which you can mark on the calendar if need be—you could clean the freezers, vacuum the dust on refrigerator coils and vanes, mop and vacuum under and behind equipment, clean dishwasher nozzles, and wipe down walls. You have to work it into the production schedule. Some things—like refrigerators, shelving, and small appliances—are weekly tasks. Others may be monthly or sooner, depending on when they exceed the acceptable "grime-level." You have to build your schedule by trial and error. The local health inspectors will also be there to advise and prod you.

SIDE WORK

With or without a schedule, routine clean-up gets assigned to the staff as side work. A baker will be responsible for a certain amount of shelving, bins, and so forth. The same goes for the head cook and assistant cook. On closing, the service staff up front will clean the tables, the soft-drink dispenser, and display cases, wipe down the coffee maker and espresso machine, and turn off and clean the coffee machine and dump its filter—as well as clean the coffee carafes and coffee pots. It's easiest to divide the entire bakery into departments. Everybody is in a department and part of the job includes department clean up routines. It's just a task, part of the job: Joe does Department One today, Sue will do Department Two, and John Department Three. Then it's best to rotate your staff through departments so the same person doesn't do the same job over and over again. Department tasks can be in conjunction with a shift: Department one gets cleaned during the 8:00 to 11:00 o'clock shift, and so on. Clean-up depends on the business's peak times. Whoever works the 6:00 a.m. to 1:00 p.m. shift, which might encompass the peak business hours, should have a light clean-up load. Those on the slower 2:00 to 6:00 p.m. shift would have a heavier assignment.

Our dish washer picks up whatever cleaning is left. Other shops may use an outside clean-up crew. Janitorial services are all right, but it is hard to find a good one. The dish washer doubles as our all around clean-up crew. We seem to have fallen into using the term "dish dog" for our staunchest worker; it certainly isn't derogatory. There's an attitude, unfortunately, that it's all right to leave everything for the dish dog. You have watch out for this "clean-up crew will get it" outlook. As long as you assign everybody a job, you can keep it under control; but, if you ever relax, a bakery can look like a tornado hit it.

KITCHEN CLEAN-UP

Ideally we end the day with everything clean and ready for tomorrow's production. If the kitchen is a mess the next morning, and there are no clean bowls or dough hooks or scrapers, you lose much more production time than you can afford.

I used to get upset when I saw crumbs on the floor. But I began to realize that the more crumbs we had on the floor, the happier the customers were and the busier we were. If I go to sweep the floor in the middle of the day now and there's nothing there, I look at our cases and see it's because we haven't sold much. Getting into that was strange. The employees have gotten used to it, so when I say there are a lot of good crumbs on the floor they know what I'm talking about.

—MURIEL GLAVE
THE LANDMARK BAKERY

One clean-up aid for tools and utensils is a "clean drawer" for everything that's clean and a "dirty barrel" for whatever is dirty. That way you can tell at a glance if anything was left unwashed. When you arrive in the morning the dirty barrel should be empty and the clean drawer full. Our dirty barrel is an 80-quart mixing bowl with water in it. A big sink works, too. Whenever we finish for the day with a scraper, a gallon measure, or the like, we throw it in the 80-quart bowl. The water in it keeps any dough or batter on the tool moist and easier to clean. A large stainless-steel bus tub, our clean drawer, holds all the knives and scrapers. If they're still a little wet the tub won't rust.

It's a good idea to make sure before you leave each evening that you're set to go in the morning. Put all the mixing bowls on the mixer, make sure that the bins have scoops in them, then wash and put away whatever was missed. The morning is bake time, it's not for asking where is the scoop or where is the mixing bowl?

We scrape most of the big wood benches and dust them with flour in the course of the day. Don't use solvents on them between doughs because the taste might get in the dough. Also you don't need to do it. You want a floury bench. If you're working on the bench rolling in a croissant dough, and next you will be rolling in a puff paste, you clean your bench before starting again. Even though they are similar doughs you clean the bench. You absolutely do not want a build-up of residue from old jobs, so cleaning between jobs is essential. At the end of the day, our dishwasher scrapes the benches with a metal scrub pad dipped in very light bleachy water that will dissipate by the next day. We seal the working surfaces with mineral oil at least monthly, which also hardens the wood.

When you change from cutting cheese to turkey on the slicer, or from one to any other food product, the health code requires you to remove and clean the slicer. You should do the same for every appliance. Cleaning the working surfaces keeps them more healthful and nicer to use, and it assures the result you want.

A good way to clean some things, such as racks, is to take them to the car wash and blow them out with a high-pressure hose. It's asking a lot to take your rack into the dish room and expect the dish washer to scrub the whole thing. At the car wash you can blast it with the power nozzle and bring it back clean. We cleaned all the used equipment for the home-improvement center shop by renting a power washer. We power-washed the old paint right off some of the equipment, then sanded and repainted it.

RETAIL AREA CLEAN-UP

Tap water and a little vinegar in a spray bottle work for wiping down the glass on our tables out front. Commercial window cleaners smell like solvents. You don't want to use them where people may drop something off a plate and pick it up to eat it. Vinegar cleans glass just fine.

A local baker claims that carpets put her customers on their good behavior and helps keep a cleaner customer area. My own experience is that vinyl, concrete, wood, or ceramic floors stay cleaner, although these things may vary from market to market. We have a carpet runner from the front door to the display cases because our vinyl floor gets very slippery in wet weather. Vacuuming keeps it reasonably clean, and when it gets crummy we toss it. We vacuum the vinyl floor every day, and strip and wax it every two weeks to keep it looking fresh. Certain heavily traveled floor areas need scraping, because in the course of a week or two vacuuming or sweeping doesn't pick up everything. Sometimes a damp cloth is enough to supplement sweeping.

As mentioned, the service staff wipes down the cases at least once every day with a water-and-vinegar solution. A little hand-held vacuum gets all the crumbs out of the showcases' gaps and cracks. Every appliance has its own cleaning instructions. The cappuccino machine gets cleaned a certain way. The coffee machine gets wiped down either with a soft or coarse pad. Don't use steel wool on stainless steel. . . . All this side work is part of the closing list.

RESTROOMS

If, unlike the Courthouse Bakery, you have public restrooms and get a chance to design them, they should be up to code, well lighted, and homey. Clean-up materials are the same as you use at home, and you should clean them at least daily.

SPRING CLEANING

Every bakery needs a thorough clean-up at least once a year, and every one gets cleaned the same way, with minor variations. We aim for a deep cleaning three times a year but don't always make it. Drafting a to-do list precedes the work. The list is divided into each of the bakery's departments. Then we try to get volunteers by seeing how many staff people can work on a Sunday. Whoever comes in on that Sunday gets overtime if it's their sixth day. Otherwise, we pay them for extra hours. Every dish dog and janitor on the staff gets scheduled to work that Sunday. Usually that's two extra dish washers. Everybody has a department. We all come in at the same time and try to make it a party atmosphere. We turn on the good music nice and loud, the bakery provides lunch and soft drinks, and we lock the front door.

Spring cleaning means pulling all the picture frames and decorative pots and pans off the walls. It means cleaning all the baseboards and the bases of all the tables. As we move toward the back, it's cleaning the top of all the refrigerators. Over the course of the year the refrigerator tops become like shelves; everybody just sticks stuff

At La Farine, where my boss the Swiss-German Lily used soap and bleach together, we called it 'Swiss perfume.' We cleaned everything with it. Bleach is a good cleaner because it oxidizes in the air so that there's no residue. We had to clean the bakery ourselves every Sunday. That was part of our job at La Farine. There was no janitor; we were the janitors, and it was very, very clean. Every Sunday after we closed the bakery at, I think, 1:00 p.m. then we cleaned until 3:00. It was a good experience. We didn't do the production at La Farine that we do here. I have somebody clean every night because there's flour everywhere. You can dust and it's dusty two hours later because somebody's in the back putzing flour.

—Jacquie Lee
The Garden Bakery

up there. We clean off the tops of all the refrigerators, all the outsides, and the door jambs on the inside. We use scouring brushes and fine combs for the refrigeration condensing units. You can't use anything too coarse, because if you break a tube you're into it for a hundred bucks.

Simple Green works well for cleaning up front, and we clean the stove hood and other hard preparation surfaces with it too, then wipe them off with a bleachy towel. You need an intervening non-work day to use chlorine bleach, because it takes about a day for the smell to dissipate.

Spring cleaning is also a good time to rearrange equipment to increase your shop's efficiency. As long as everything is pulled out from the walls and you have your work crew assembled, you can decide, for example, that if this bench and mixer go over there, and that mixer or bench goes over here, we can get a better flow. This time we completely rearranged the bakery's layout by moving all of our heavy bulk supplies of flour, sugar, shortening and so forth closer to the production area. For as long as we've had the bakery they were stored in the very back room. Now we don't have to walk all the way back there to get our heaviest supplies, anymore. It's amazing what you learn to live with.

This is a good time, too, to go through every single product and decide whether or not to use it anymore. For example, you may have thought you were going to make something in quantity and ordered 10 cases of a special ingredient. Predicting the market is one of those gambles. If you've never used up that ingredient, this is the time to dump it or give it to Food Bank. Over the course of five years we had absorbed the cost of those items, so it was time to clear them out and recover the space. The result was as if we had suddenly created 80 square feet more shelf space in the back room.

We filled up a long-bed pickup twice with things that we finally decided we would never use. Much of it involved utensils or parts like old whips and paddles for an obsolete 120-quart mixer that has been gone for two years. It also was time to get rid of all the old paint cans and other hazardous materials that somehow accumulate. You paint shelves, lube equipment, and use solvents. They all have to go to the hazardous waste site, the Hazmobile as our local disposal people call it.

It was a huge project, but with five people cleaning all day it's amazing how much gets accomplished. The payroll costs for that day—about $250—were well worth it because of the difference a deep cleaning makes in production efficiency. If we had scheduled re-sealing our hardwood production-area floor and benches, it would have been a two-day job. It also lets you get the cleaning crew up to a new standard. You can say, "Gee, this is nice clean. Let's wipe it down or do a scrape job on it once a week from now on." It also helps set up the department rotation schedule we mentioned. All that could have made it better would have been for the health inspector to show up the next day—because for a week it's great.

MAINTENANCE

Maintenance also deserves a schedule. You can have an expert come in to sharpen the knives every two weeks, and another can maintain such things as the oven, the mixers, or anything else you'd feel better about giving to an expert. All refrigeration and air conditioning are best put on a maintenance service program with a local company. Our service comes in monthly and cleans the exterior working parts, checks the refrigeration levels and temperatures, and changes the filters. It even looks at our mixers to see that the lubrication points are well oiled or greased. It's a justifiable cost because you pay for someone else's time, not yours, to do it. Also, if you waited for an emergency and had to call it on a weekend or after hours, the charge would be double. Finally, it's reassuring to know that when the health inspector comes your refrigeration temperatures will be just right. It's peace of mind that comes directly from a maintenance program.

TRASH

Outside the back door is the right place for a big trash dumpster. Although we don't have a back entry, there's a door next to us in front that opens onto a long hallway parallel to our retail area. That's where we fill up trash cans and bags. Produce, flour, and paper supplies come in big cardboard boxes that create enormous bulky waste. We run it to the landfill or recycling center ourselves. The baker around the corner has slightly smaller production than we do and is able to stack trash in an industrial rack on wheels beside her storefront on collection day.

RODENT AND VERMIN CONTROL

Rodent control is harder in some places than others. If you're next to a field, you will always have problems. Some neighborhoods have endemic rodents. They multiply fast, and you've got to jump at the first sign of them and be all over the problem. We had one episode with mice where they just took off. We brought in a pest control service, used traps, and were rid of them within a month. Once gone, it's necessary to keep them out with traps, rodent bait, and the pest service once a month. If you have rodents in the food business, you're in serious trouble. Besides being a health problem, they can literally eat up profits. If they chew through a bag of flour, you've got to throw the whole bag away. Hardware cloth around small openings is a good idea if you have a somewhat porous perimeter. You can't take any chances, and it's something to watch out for when you're shopping for space.

Vermin like roaches, ants, and flour weevils are a nightmare. While you can control flour weevils by keeping limited flour supplies tightly seealed, you will need professional assistance if other insects appear in your shop. That unfortunately usually means introducing all kinds of poisons onto the premises. It forces you to choose the least of several evils.

Professionals will seldom ever tell you that simple boric acid, is lethal to insects in amounts completely harmless to warm-blooded animals. A dilute solution makes a good safe eyewash for humans. A third to quarter teaspoon of it per pint of a homemade sugar syrup—also harmless to pets and people—in small bottles laid on their sides where ants travel will wipe them out in a few weeks. Never trifle with anything you intend as a poison, however, and take every precaution with this syrup! The ants must take the solution to the queen. If they die in the bottle the solution is too strong. If they keep coming it's too weak. Before you employ a pest controller ask if the company knows about boric acid. I've used it; it works. Roaches are also susceptible to boric acid. We have never had them as a problem, so I can't recommend how to use boric acid to exterminate them. See if you can find a professional who knows.

Clean-Up

___Start every day clean
___Have a kitchen clean drawer and dirty barrel
___Assign each employee departmental clean-up tasks
   ___Employee with lighter shift cleans more
   ___Follow-up all cleaning
___Have one person like the dish washer assigned general janitorial duties
___Schedule longer-range cleaning on a calendar
___Deep clean at least once a year
   ___List all departments
   ___Use all janitorial workers and ask other staff to volunteer
   ___Make it a party
   ___Rearrange equipment as seems suitable
   ___Review products and equipment for weeding
___Routinize trash pick up
___Have a maintenance routine
___Consider professional maintenance service
___Consider professional vermin control service

10

SUPPLIERS AND SUPPLIES

ROOKIES in the business are often unsure where to find supplies—flours, fresh produce, paper, and dry goods. It's easiest just to sign up with a local purveyor. Usually that won't bring the economies of scale that regional suppliers offer. Even the biggest local firm may charge far more than the regional companies. So look before you sign up. Ask owners of restaurants and other bakeries where they buy. If you don't have the benefit of family experience or long-time involvement in another bakery—with those bits of knowledge that filter down practically without noticing—go find a retired baker. Advice from an older baker is the best way to learn how to deal with salespeople and suppliers.

SELECTING SUPPLIERS

If you've been in the business awhile, you'll recognize the companies' names as soon as you start asking around. Then just telephone and ask the companies if they service your area and, if so, will they send a salesperson? When the salesperson shows up ask for a product list and prices. Or give the salesperson a list of the products you will use and ask to get it back with the company's best prices. Hand your list out to every supplier and ask the salesperson to get it back to you in a week or whatever is reasonable. When you get them back you've got a file of competitive product prices.

Many companies will come in low on some items when they want your business. Then before long the price has shot back up to where you're giving them a pretty good profit. Also be sure to check each one's prices as a whole. While one company may sell cheese for 10 cents a pound less than everybody else, every other price in its list might be 20 cents higher. Many vendors will carry the exact same item. Most will be pretty close on price, but they can be way out of line on few items; so you have to read the lists carefully.

Nearly all companies will give you their product-list guides. These are printouts with blank spaces for orders. It's best to have one from every supplier you use. The lists are huge. They can be 200 pages thick and look very intimidating, but they can also be great references, because they show everything a company carries. Often they give each item's price from single units to case lots. Frequently, however, they do not carry prices because many items are commodities whose prices fluctuate continuously. You can use the guides as a starting point for items to put on your product list. Even now that we have all the product lists we need, I look through them and find tempting buys. It's the old Sears-Roebuck appeal. For instance, one company carries pre-shaved chocolate so you don't have to order the bars and shave it yourself.

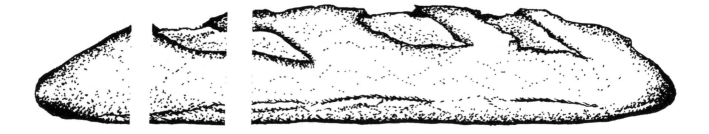

Next find out what each supplier's minimum order is. They're all different. We have one supplier that requires a minimum order of $250. Another has a $150 minimum. If you want to do business with one company but you can't meet its minimum order price, try to order every two weeks instead of weekly. If that company is the only one that carries an essential item, you may have to scratch and scramble to find other things to get that one item every two weeks.

If you're close enough, you should try to visit the suppliers you're considering, preferably before you order. Look at the size of their warehouses and try to gauge how well-run they are. Big is not always better. We use a few suppliers that are small one-person operations but often are cheapest because they have low overhead and can compete head-to-head with the big guys. Usually the big ones are cheaper because they buy at heavily discounted wholesaler prices. The middle ground often includes companies that probably can't compete as well on price as the small guys or the big compan-

MONTAGU'S FARE

John Montagu (1718-1792) is notable for his bad reputation and a culinary landmark. As Great Britain's First Lord of the Admiralty he indirectly aided the American Revolution by keeping much of the fleet at home for fear of a French attack. His administration on the whole was disastrous, and he was criticized for inadequate naval supply and preparedness.

Inclined to advance his own and his party's interests, he was also accused of taking bribes and selling patronage. As Secretary of State for England's Northern Department, he joined in prosecu-

ting his former friend John Wilkes, thus earning the nickname "Jemmy Twitcher," after a snitch in John Gay's BEGGAR'S OPERA. Montagu was probably held in more contempt than any man in 18th Century England, partly because of his "excessively immoral" personal life.

An inveterate card player, his table manners also were considered atrocious. Montagu was the Fourth Earl of Sandwich. Whether or not he invented the dish, he gave us a name by which to call it when, during a 24-hour card game in 1762, he ate nothing but meat between slices of bread.

---

ies but that specialize in hard-to-find items. You have to shop around carefully.

When we establish a history with the company I like to get the profile sheet that the salesperson uses for us. It shows everything we ordered from the company. As a printed history it can show items we haven't ordered in a year but may have to order again soon. It may show a change in market tastes. Usually, the supplier will purge items you haven't ordered from them in 30 days. We'll ask the company not to purge our profile sheet of those items if their computer program allows it. The complete list is a useful reminder. We know from experience that we won't need pumpkin till the holidays. As I go down the list and see "On hand: zero," it usually signals a need to order something, but when I see pumpkin, which normally we don't need, I ignore it until it's October or November. All of a sudden it rings a bell, and we order some. Everything you use should be on every list. If you kept separate "rarely ordered items" lists, you would probably rarely find them and might end up forgetting to order them when you had to.

WAREHOUSING SUPPLIES

If you have limited refrigeration, of course, you should arrange to have two or three different produce deliveries and get one delivery early in the week and one later on. As mentioned, it saves having to "warehouse" all your supplies all week long. Prices are usually close enough to permit that. Our bakery suppliers deliver every two weeks. Luckily for us, one delivers one week and the other the next week; so they warehouse the supplies for us. We always know what we will order from whom and we keep the orders constant. Every week we get a bakery delivery. There is always some overlap with the other order so that we don't run out of anything.

You'd think you could always order dry goods in volume to take advantage of lower prices, but it's important to place some volume orders according to the season. While you can stock up on flour in the winter when it's too cold for insects, summer is the worst time, because flour weevils can run rampant then and devastate your flour supplies. So during the warm season, buy the bare minimum and keep lids on all your flour and similar ingredients. Otherwise, if you get a bad infestation of flour weevils, you'll have to discard that huge stockpile.

When you're small you can't demand deliveries at a certain time, and delivery times may determine which supplier you use. For a deli or café Friday is the busiest day of the week, with the busiest lunch trade. Even if you live in an out-of-the-way place, and the company delivers in your area only at noon on Friday, you will have to look around for whoever delivers at another day and time.

Always order to get quality goods delivered on time. Once you accommodate your routine to a company's delivery schedule you have to be firm. If the company says the truck will be there Tuesday by 10 o'clock and it's not there, you have to say, "Look, I won't have any turkey on Tuesday because I'm going to run out on Monday. I'm doing business with you to get food supplies on time." You have to work with your suppliers, especially if you're a small guy, but, if delivery is late too often, all you can do is change companies.

SHOPPING AROUND

Suppliers routinely provide you with an invoice sheet for your order. When an order you placed arrives, double check it. Whoever checks the invoice—and *you* should do it starting out—must compare it to everything on the order form. Be sure that what you ordered is on the invoice. Often you get so tied up with "what did we order from A and what did we order from B?" that you may not remember what you ordered in the current shipment from company X. Also compare the order with the prices you paid in the past and with what the salesperson said you would pay. For us, when something comes through 20 cents a pound higher—say for 80 pounds of cheese—and we weren't told about it, that's real money. The supplier will hear about it.

We could probably get everything we need from one company, but we like using two to provide a back-up as much as anything. Things happen. Your suppliers get all of their products by a contract they sign with another company. If something goes wrong with their contract, and their prices go out of sight, or they lose the contract, they may no longer have an item. That's why you have Supplier Number Two for a back up.

I want to see what's going into my products. . . . I want good ingredients. If I don't get good ingredients I let the suppliers know about it.

—MURIEL GLAVE
THE LANDMARK BAKERY

In most regions there are plenty of vendors to choose from, but try to deal with no more than half a dozen—although a maximum of three or four is better. That will cover everything: all your baking ingredients, dry goods, meats, cheeses, dairy products, and fresh produce. You could have as many as are available to meet your needs, but you need to keep comparing each one's prices to use them to best advantage. Use a list of all your ingredients to cross-compare each company's prices. We place an order with the company with the lowest price for each item. Right now we have the two bakery suppliers, two meat and cheese suppliers, and two paper companies. That gives us two of everything from which we can break out and compare prices. We also compare among different kinds of suppliers. Sometimes the meat and cheese supplier will offer ingredients such as flour at a special promotional price a few dollars a sack below my regular supplier's price. We'll give our business to the meat and cheese guy until his price goes up. Suppliers are always trying to get your business and, when they do you, take advantage of it. When the promotion ends you switch back.

You have to watch every supplier. I was going through some invoices at my brother's bakery recently and saw the price he paid for honey. Honey had just gone through the roof, and everybody was playing it up. We paid $68 for a five-gallon drum of honey. My brother was paying $91 and had no idea he could buy it cheaper. The company had no reason to charge him $91 a drum. It was just a matter of taking advantage of a buyer who didn't watch his invoices or compare prices very diligently. You want to be as friendly as possible with all of your suppliers' representatives but you also want to make clear that you know what's going on in your business. Even if it's an increase of only a few cents on one item, you want to point out that cheese, for example, had been $1.50 and now it's $1.55. Most likely the salesperson will say the company's price has gone up and it had to pass along the increase. Usually that's true, but it's not a bad idea to check and see if another company is selling at the old price. Most salespeople are trustworthy and straightforward but the ones who aren't will nick you for a tidy sum if you're careless.

SPECIALTY SUPPLIES

Some companies specialize, but a few larger outfits do it all. They offer bakery supplies, restaurant equipment and supplies, dry goods—you name it. Big multi-purpose companies know a little about a lot of things, but the smaller suppliers know more about their specialized markets. We order bakery supplies from our baking purveyors, because we can deal with a party—either the salesperson or the company—that has been in or involved with the baking business for a long time. These specialists usually offer the best prices,

PRODUCT	W=WESTCO		D=DAWN					
DATE								
					WK1	WK2	WK3	WK4
			UNIT	PAR	OH/O	OH/O	OH/O	OH/O
CREAM CAKE					/	/	/	/
MOIST MUFFIN					/	/	/	/
CHOC CREAM CAKE					/	/	/	/
SPREAD-N-GLOSS					/	/	/	/
LOWFAT BRAN MUFFIN MIX					/	/	/	/
NON-FAT MUFFIN MIX					/	/	/	/
WHOLE EGGS					/	/	/	/
PASTRY PRIDE (WHIP. CREAM)					/	/	/	/
LG CULT. BLUEBERRIES					/	/	/	/
LG CULT. BOYSENBERRIES					/	/	/	/
CHERRIES					/	/	/	/
APRICOTS					/	/	/	/
EGG WHITES					/	/	/	/
DIAMOND HIGH GLUTEN					/	/	/	/
CAMEO PASTRY FLOWER					/	/	/	/
SOFTASILK CAKE FLOWER					/	/	/	/
WHEAT ALAX					/	/	/	/
RICE FLOUR					/	/	/	/
TABLE WHEAT BERRIES					/	/	/	/
000 RYE FLOWER					/	/	/	/
MED. RYE MEAL PUMPERNICKEL					/	/	/	/
BAKERS BRAN					/	/	/	/
9-GRAIN CEREAL					/	/	/	/
REG. ROLLED OATS					/	/	/	/
HIGH-HEAT MILK POWDER					/	/	/	/
C&H GRAN. SUGAR					/	/	/	/
C&H POWDER SUGAR					/	/	/	/
C&H GOLD-C					/	/	/	/
C&H CONFECTIONS SUGAR					/	/	/	/

Many suppliers provide order sheets like this (though not always with the same spelling). You enter par for your stock of supplies on the left, and each week enter "On Hand" to determine how much to "Order."

and their experience counts. They can inform you of trends and savings the big guys will miss.

Linen — Linen supply companies are hardest to deal with because typically they want you to sign a contract for a year. We've walked away from a few such contracts because we weren't happy with the service. If you're a fifty-dollar customer they won't chase you too hard to hold you to the contract. We started out by doing all our own linen. We bought all our own towels and aprons, and washed them ourselves. When you're small that's worth considering if you have a washer and dryer at home. Linen supply companies are expensive. If you lose one of their towels or aprons, the replacement cost can bring on real sticker shock. You might consider getting your own stock of linen and sending it to a good laundry. You will probably have to sacrifice the convenience of pick up and delivery, but the price break may justify it.

Cleaning and Maintenance Supplies—Often your purveyor for paper goods or dry goods will carry cleaning and maintenance materials. The big companies like Allied Sysco and Ritz Food in our area are full-line companies that carry everything, including paper goods and cleaning supplies.

Printed Materials and Paper Products—Go to a local office supply and set up an account for printed materials. Order paper from a paper purveyor. Paper goods are something else to watch closely. All paper fluctuates in price from month to month, and it's a good idea to have two sources of paper products. If you're dealing with only one, the salesperson may not tell you that pink boxes came down $10 a case, because when you signed on paper prices were high and a case of pink boxes cost $30. When prices come down, the salesperson may think, This guy's not buying from anybody else, so I'll keep his prices high. Paper is not perishable. If you have storage space, it's worth stocking up when prices fall.

THE SALES REPRESENTATIVE

Get to know the supplier's salesperson and try to deal with the same one all the time. The sales representative is your link to the company. The reason we dropped some of the larger suppliers is that their salespeople were impersonal and seemed programmed to follow the corporate script. It's been far easier to deal with salespeople who come across as working hard like the rest of us to make a living. They represent their company well, and they'll talk frankly about it and say things like, "We're high this week, you'd better find somebody else," or the next week say, "We're low now, you'd better buy." You can make very good friends with reps like that. It makes buying easier because usually if you have a good personal relationship with somebody, they'll be on the up and up with you. But even at that you have to check prices every once in a while, just so they know you're on top of your business.

When you get a sales representative ask questions about the company. You want to find out what the minimum order is. Is there a broken-case charge? That is, if they break a case of six one-gallon containers to give you a gallon of mayonnaise, will that one gallon cost you $2.00 more per unit than if you bought the whole case?

Ask the rep what the company's credit terms are. Do they discount, say, net-less-two-percent if you pay within a certain time of the invoice date? The discount period may be seven days; sometimes it's 14, or 30. Habitually, we paid for each order as soon as it came in, because the companies gave a percentage break for prompt cash payment. If they had to finance us for a few days, it was money out of their pocket. One of our bakery companies gave us a two-percent break for payment on the delivery day. When it stopped offering the break we started paying a week later. We get to use the money for a week and keep it earning interest. If the company goes back to a discount for cash, we'll pay on delivery again.

THE ORDERING ROUTINE

Organizing the business means routinizing everything, including supplies. All our order sheets hang from a clipboard in my office. When we order we take an order sheet off the clipboard and inventory what we have. It's important to label your shelves so that everything is always in the same place. We also group items together in categories: tomato paste, ketchup, tomato filets, pizza sauce, and so on. That makes it easier to see what we have, regardless of how the order sheet is arranged.

Relax when salespeople come in; remember you're their customer. They will walk back and ask how things are going. They generally avoid your peak hours. They know that if you don't have time to chat they won't have a chance to sell you something new. They don't just walk in to fill the ordinary order. They'll have a "special of the month" sheet. It's what they do: sell. So they'll try to come around when you're least busy. If we're very busy, I'll ask them to come back a little later or check back in the morning. Or I may tell them we don't have the order ready and to take a look around. It's best to develop a weekly routine when the salesperson comes in at the same time each week. Having the order ready speeds up the process, but sometimes a hectic schedule won't let you. Always make salespeople welcome. I like those we deal with. I always feed them or give them loaves of bread. . . . Well, no. First I give them a hard time then I give them bread.

The sales rep will usually come in at least two days before the delivery date. The order goes to the customer-service agent at the company. Then that service agent's typed invoice goes to the warehouse where the order is filled. If the company can't supply an item, the invoice comes back to customer service marked "out of stock." By that time your order is on the truck, and you're not getting it. With so short a lead time you won't be able to cover unless the company contacts you about the shortages. Usually they will substitute a like item for what's short.

Also, because of the short turnaround time, you can't expect the salesperson to get an item you overlooked onto the truck. The trucks are usually loaded 24 hours in advance. If your sales rep comes in on Tuesday and your delivery day is Thursday, don't expect to call Wednesday night and ask the company to toss whatever you forgot on the truck. If you forgot to order flour and it doesn't show up, then it's you who has to explain it to the customer. If the company messed up, you may be able to insist on delivery but don't count on it. Try to develop a local emergency supplier, even a large supermarket, from which you can borrow supplies.

Until recently, travelers driving to the redwoods up California's Highway 101 passed an enormous red and white store-front sign just north of Ukiah: MRS. DENSON'S COOKIES. The store was immense for an ordinary roadside stop. Mike Bielenberg's father—part of a wave of urban emigrants from the 1960s—opened Mrs. Denson's Cookies to sell to tourists. His father's wife added a gift shop.

As it turned out, Mendocino County's low labor and overhead costs, and its direct access to urban markets, also provided an opportunity to develop a wholesale supplement to the highway trade. Wholesale production soon grew into the bakery's major activity, and the little shop by the side of the road began to expand. When Mike Bielenberg took over the company in 1982 one of his first acts was to reduce the size of the gift shop. The gift shop, he said, represented $20,000 of capital that would better serve the wholesale business; by then even retail bakery sales provided only a minor part of the business's income. In the early 1990s retail sales declined more after a four-lane freeway replaced the old road. The next logical step was a shift entirely to wholesale production.

In 1994 Bielenberg moved the company to an industrial site within the city limits of Ukiah. Despite the rural parcel's lower ground costs, the move cut ex-

Mrs. Denson's Cookies
120 Brush Street
Ukiah, California

penses by giving access to municipal water, gas, and electricity—as well as proximity to the region's major labor pool. The bakery now occupies a large steel building about a block east of the city's main commercial artery. A discreet sign identifies the company; otherwise, there is no clue from the large tractor-trailers and pallets in the yard about what goes on inside. The overwhelming sensation on entering Mrs. Denson's, however, is a wonderful and abiding aroma of fresh-baked cookies.

Mrs. Denson's regularly runs its tractor-trailers to San Francisco, Sacramento, and Los Angeles to deliver cookies and haul back supplies and ingredients. It now employs 47 people, including two production shifts that bake cookies on a 3-foot-wide, 250-foot-long steel conveyor that transports the product through the oven and delivers them for sorting and packaging. The company now ships 60,000 pounds a week, which is about 1½ million of its excellent cookies.

Bielenberg explains that Mrs. Denson's does not and cannot compete head-to-head with Nabisco, any more than Keebler or Sunshine can. Instead it has targeted and developed sales of natural-ingredient cookies to the health-food market—mainly supermarkets and natural-food chain stores on the East and West coasts. It sells most of them under a variety of other companies' labels.

Like many small concerns, its every change had been in response to shifting market and supply conditions. Now, according to Bielenberg, the company has reached a size that requires advance planning in order to stay competitive. That can be as simple as replacing an old, declining product line with an attractive new one. More materially, Mrs. Denson's is adding a second band oven to increase production 45 percent, and it plans to expand sales into all 50 states by packaging cookies under its own label and contracting with distributors to place them outside its traditional markets.

I happen to enjoy haggling and I recommend it. It's like a game. The first thing I like to do, especially whenever I see a bakery sales rep come in is say, "Whaddaya mean sugar came through at $20.50 this week? Last week it was $19. What's going on?" And then I like watching them back up: "Oh, it came through at $20.50? That was a mistake," or "Oh yeah, prices went up." You catch them a little off guard and you start talking about prices. One major problem is that, while all these commodities fluctuate, you sometimes don't find out until the order arrives. When you're using a thousand pounds of sugar a week, it's important to know if the price goes up five cents a pound. If you're only using five pounds of caraway seeds a week, a nickel-a-pound's increase hardly matters. When sales reps don't tell me while I'm ordering that a major ingredient will have to come through at a dollar or two per bag higher than last time, I'll insist that we get it for the last price, because that was our reasonable understanding of the deal.

Similarly, you will often buy a certain grade of ham or some other item at, say, $2.50 a pound. Then two days later, the order arrives without your $2.50-a-pound ham or whatever but with a grade that costs $3.50 a pound because the $2.50 ham was out of stock. When that happens we insist that they sell it to us for $2.50 a pound, because that's what we ordered. These things can't always be helped. But if the salesperson orders it, and two days pass without a phone call or other notice—then 80 pounds of it show up at a dollar more a pound—we'll send the invoice back and demand a credit. It isn't our fault that they ran out of the ham. If they had told us ahead of time, we could make an adjustment by requesting a different grade or ordering from a different company.

PICK UPS AND BACK HAULS

If we were closer to the San Francisco Bay Area, I would go to the General Mills warehouse or to the Giusto's warehouse and pick up our own flour. By using your own truck you can get flour at better than wholesale prices, probably 20 or 50 cents a bag cheaper. When we lived in southern California my dad used to drive his van to Los Angeles once a week and pick up 2,000 pounds of flour or 1,000 pounds of sugar and haul it back. It was a big saving. If you live near a port or major production or warehousing area, it's worth having a business truck to go directly to the company—to C&H Sugar, General Mills, Giusto's, or the like—to buy for less than a distributor's wholesale prices.

You can also look for a large commercial baker in your area. Mrs. Denson's Cookies is a large local operation that runs two semi's down to the Bay Area. It's located in the industrial part of town and produces and sells cookies all over the country under different names. It "back hauls" all of its own supplies and sometimes hauls for us. If we want a pallet of flour, they'll back haul it—since they're coming back anyway—for 10 cents a bag over cost. If they make 10 cents a bag off us, that's 10 cents more than they would have made if they didn't bring it back.

Occasionally I go to Denson's warehouse and shop. A large bakery like this can be your safety net in case you forget to order something or it didn't come in. We can almost always go there and find raisins, walnuts, and most of what we need. If you have a good working relationship with such a company, you may be able to buy from it for less than you usually pay, because often it buys at much lower prices than small bakeries can. The potential savings, however, may not justify picking up from a warehouse or large bakery. You have to weigh the time and inconvenience of having to go to get an item at the warehouse, unstack it, load it into the truck, and unload it and stack it at your bakery. When you buy from a supplier, it shows up at your doorstep. The delivery person unloads it, stacks it, and will often rotate it. That's what you pay for.

DELIVERY

Never give delivery people a hard time, because they have no say in the ordering of supplies, the loading of the truck, or anything. All they're doing is delivering. So if something doesn't show up, they had nothing to do with it. Those guys work hard. Always offer them a cup of coffee and something to eat. They also get around, and when they mention your place to other people you want them to say good things.

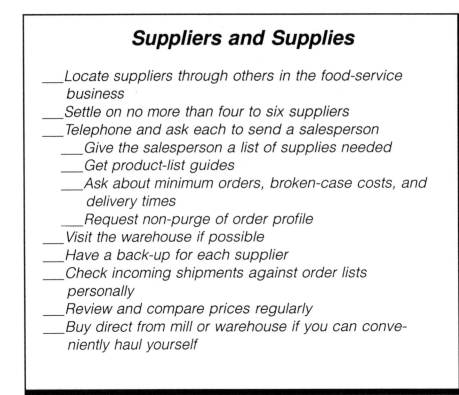

Suppliers and Supplies

___Locate suppliers through others in the food-service business

___Settle on no more than four to six suppliers

___Telephone and ask each to send a salesperson

   ___Give the salesperson a list of supplies needed

   ___Get product-list guides

   ___Ask about minimum orders, broken-case costs, and delivery times

   ___Request non-purge of order profile

___Visit the warehouse if possible

___Have a back-up for each supplier

___Check incoming shipments against order lists personally

___Review and compare prices regularly

___Buy direct from mill or warehouse if you can conveniently haul yourself

MANAGEMENT AND OPERATIONS

"Qu'ils mangent de la brioche."
("Let them eat cake.")

Attributed to Marie Antoinette on being told her people had no bread, but in fact a common saying that Rousseau had noted in 1740 in his CONFESSIONS

"No bread! Then bring me some toast."

PUNCH, 1845

11

CO-WORKERS: YOUR ABLE STAFF

STEPPING BACK from doing the work to managing it is harder than you might think. It involves hiring help, training them, and learning to work with them. When you stand by and watch someone else do your work, your first impulse may be to think, I can do that twice as fast, lemme at it! But when you manage you need to let your employees' become efficient by holding back and letting them learn to do the job the way you want it done. As an employer the rule is hands off but also hands on. Hands off the product, but hands on by teaching people how to do things. That way you provide guidance in area A then step over and help out in area B. You multiply your own efficiency and give yourself freedom. You don't want to work seven days a week all the time; you want to make a living and have a life. Hiring employees can give you that freedom.

HIRING

Most of our hiring is through help-wanted ads in the newspaper. We also post notices at the Employment Development Department (that's the Unemployment Office in many states) and the college employment office. Relying on word-of-mouth, especially among people who already work for you, is one of the best ways to hire and also the cheapest. If you put the word out among your staff, almost every one of them has a friend or acquaintance who wants to work. But always ask how good a friend it is. We avoid best friends, because then there gets to be altogether too much socializing on the job. We do want our people to know the referral at least well enough to confirm that the new hire will be a good worker. There's always a temptation to set someone up with a job, even without being able to recommend that person as a good worker. I can vouch for that as a former student employee myself, and offer it as a warning to other potential employers.

We also use a network of students who worked for us while at the local community college then transferred to a four-year school. When they're home on vacations, which are usually our busy times, or for the summer we try to bring them back into the system because it doesn't cost anything to train them. Students fit in very well, especially for odd-hour shifts, those two- or three-hour spots during the day when you need to cover certain positions. If you're open later in the evening, that works even better for many students. Always talk to them before hiring about their schedules and what will work for them. You probably won't get anyone *except* students to work a two-hour shift. In fact, it ruins most people's day.

Avoid hiring your friends. It can be hard to cut the old ties when you work with somebody you know. When you hire a friend you have to communicate to them on a level you've never used before. While you may think you can go into the relationship on strictly a professional level, more often than not it just doesn't work out. The same can be true of family, although many successful businesses are family affairs. It probably depends on how much bickering they can tolerate.

THE APPLICATION FORM

Be sure you use an employment application form that complies with federal Equal Employment Opportunities laws. Usually you can find them at office supply stores. A simple form that asks only for name, address, telephone and Social Security numbers, experience, and references is all you need for bakery work. We've adapted our form by adding a questionnaire that asks things such as, Would you object to having short hair if it was a requirement at this bakery? Not that it is, but we like to see what people's answers are and what kinds of attitudes they have. We ask questions such as, "What do you think is the single most important aspect of the job at Schat's Bakery?" When we get answers like, "It's helping the customers in an efficient and friendly manner," we know we're on the right track. Look out for the applicant who says, "The most important aspect is what time I take my lunch break." We even put a few simple math questions on it as well. Many people come across as reasonably intelligent, but give them a simple problem such as, "If somebody buys a muffin for 85¢ and a danish for $1.00, what is the grand total, and what kind of change would you give them from a $20 bill?" We'll give them a calculator if they want, but some of the answers are amazing.

You want to hire good honest people who can communicate, so you need to see how they do it on paper. It reflects a person's attitude. Someone who hasn't made much effort in school, probably won't take much more interest in a job. That's a general rule; there

We have about 25 employees, and by far and away the most challenging part of running the business is managing 25 people. On any given day, there are going to be five or 10 soap operas going on. You become a family, and I get drawn into every one of those soap operas or personal dilemmas. And it's always changing. It can be anything you can imagine, and anything you can't imagine. It was the least expected part of the job for me.
—PAUL LEVITAN
THE CHEESECAKE LADY

JOB APPLICATION & APPLICANT QUESTIONS

Name_____

Address_____

Social Security No._____

Phone No._____

Of all positions available at Schat's Bakery, which do you see yourself likeliest to fill: Counter sales ... Prep. Cook ... Dishwasher/janitor ... Management training. (Circle one.)

How would your experience, either working or academic, help you succeed at your desired job at Schat's Bakery?

Describe your customer service skills in your own words.

Would you be comfortable with a dress code? No visible body piercing?

Tell what you think it means to have a work ethic.

If a customer order comes to $4.44 and he/she gives you a $20.00 bill, how much change would you return?

What's 10% of $16.00?   What's 20% of $8.00?

If you found yourself with no customers to help or no obvious work, what would you do?

Finally, What do you think is our number one priority in this bakery?

Date you can start training for work:

Do you have any schedule restraints?   What are they?

Our employees must be able to work Saturdays and Sundays. Is that a problem?

Signed_____

Employer comments:

A food-service business needs only basic employee information, but a brief pre-employment quiz is a good idea.

are exceptions. We've employed people who could hardly spell their name but were great workers.

The only position that doesn't require much past experience is dish washing, which is an entry level job. Even there, you should check to see if the applicant has done some kind of grubby work as a preparation. For kitchen help find out if they've been either a prep cook or have cooked elsewhere, and whether they prepared food from fresh ingredients or just put together mixes and frozen products in a fast-food chain. For counter help see if they've worked at least one other retail spot and had experience at a cash register and with people. Personality can overcome a lack of experience. If we interview or talk to an applicant who has a great personality but has only packed pears, we'll let personality prevail: This may be a great retail person who hasn't had the job yet. The interview is where you'll decide whether to hire. We rarely hire off the application and I'm sure we've missed good people for lack of an adequate background.

TRAINING

Training can be tough when your staff has shrunken to a skeleton crew, and suddenly you're in the busy season. By then you've waited too long, you're understaffed, and you just need a warm body. That's when you'll hire anybody who will stand up and say "Hi, there, how're you doing?" Plan ahead to avoid this pitfall. When we hire, our training period lasts for three shifts. Those first shifts are not the new employees' own. They simply shadow someone else. On the first day they don't even touch anything but just follow their mentor around. It looks foolish and no doubt irritates customers, who can't understand what's going on: Trainee-A is watching Trainer-B make a mocha, and there's a line all the way to the door. The customer must think, "Why doesn't the silly drone come over here and help me?" But you have to give the new hire two or three days to get comfortable with the place. A well-trained employee can make a customer's experience much more enjoyable than can one who is still learning.

You want to be firm on points like product knowledge. We send new counter help home with a product list. You won't give a test or anything, but after a person has worked for about three days, go up and ask if they know what certain items are and what they cost individually and by the dozen. Do it in the spirit of a game, informally and without pressure. It's a good way to build up product familiarity. If you do it right, it helps relax new people and build their confidence.

TURNOVER

Your highest staffing turnover will probably be in counter help. Counter help might stay longer if they made tips from table service. With a straight salary you pay them just as you pay the dish washer, but they have to deal with the public every day, which is hard work. That means you'll be training new people up front continually to keep it staffed. High turnover in dish washing is well known, but some people take to it and last a long time. At that, the dish washer might last only six months—or a year at most—although that isn't high turnover in a retail bakery.

DRESS AND DEMEANOR

When we were small, the job interview included telling applicants what we wanted from them. Once we decided to hire, we would lay out the details of the work. Since then we've set up job descriptions, which work much better. If you hand somebody a written job description, there's no coming back later and saying, I didn't know this was part of my job. You have to be very specific and put in even things you would assume, like showing up to work looking neat, with hair pulled back and wearing jeans without holes in them. It would probably never occur to you to go to work in jeans with holes in them, but some people will. You have to let new employees know what you expect on an appearance level, on an attitude level, and for the job itself.

If you don't have a dress code, there should be some discussion at the time of hiring about what is appropriate and what's not, such as neat denim shorts as opposed to cut-off shorts. If there are company shirts, wear company shirts, and so on. If you give your staff a sartorial carte blanche, you could end up with Madonna look-alikes on the job. What you aim for is simple, clean, attractive dress. For bakers the job dictates dress, and they just show up in whites.

TEAM PLAY

Many businesses now approach staffing as a team idea. The home-improvement center calls every employee a team member and has team-member meetings. In a small shop you may not do that in just so many words, but things do run more smoothly with a staff that works together as a team or group of teams, usually led by what you could call captains. When the managers of the different groups get along well together the people who work under them also seem to pull together.

There are times when the team theory doesn't work because of conflicting personalities: people who can't or won't cooperate. Often it's just one person. Ten people working for the good of the bakery won't overcome that one bad personality. Personnel management on this level is one of the most difficult tasks in small business. You have to get involved in people's personal problems and settle them to everyone's satisfaction. It takes a great deal of diplomacy, patience, and perseverance. Most of us are unprepared for it, but it's a skill you'll have to acquire if you plan to have employees. You can learn it. Sometimes the local college gives courses on personnel management, or mediating conflicts. There are a few books on this subject that we suggest in the Appendix. Ultimately, you will have to develop your own techniques and reflexes for keeping your staff happy and productive. In the meantime, do all you can to learn.

One way to try to limit this problem is to look up past history on job applications and make a few phone calls to confirm it. You can never tell at the interview how a new hire will work out in six months. The main thing is to get a sense of how people got along with their fellow workers. You want to hear from former bosses that your applicant works well with other people. Listen also to what is not said, because some employers are wary of giving a bad report.

Sometimes you hire people who are excited about working for you at just what they want to do. That's great, and you should nurture it as much as you can, but at the same time you must make sure they take care of their job duties and don't just engage in flights of imagination. If somebody has a good idea and you implement it, however, it does wonders for morale. Almost nothing makes an employee feel better than seeing his or her idea have an impact on how you do things at work.

There's one exception where baking is concerned. Our family has made some items in its bakeries in a certain way for years. They've been fine tuned; so I'm highly averse to improvisations or attempts to "improve" them. Where it concerns a *new* product or method that somebody thinks can be improved, we'll try it and, if it's better, we'll do it like that. Improvisations that are simply shortcuts are also suspect. A shortcut is a way to do something quicker, and quicker in baking is generally not better.

It hardly seems worth saying that counter staff has to be attentive, helpful, and friendly to customers, but that doesn't always just happen. You the owner will be everything on that list because you'll have a vested interest in doing it. Most counter staff are attentive and helpful, too. But we have had help that just doesn't get it. You try to teach them and to make them understand that service is as much a part of our business as a good product. Sometimes you just can't teach it no matter how you try. A good bakery owner will normally try to lead by example at the counter, but in the end all you can do is let the difficult help know that you are concerned about their customer skills and that you do arrange to monitor staff to assure good service. Either you can see how they address the customers or ask a friend whom nobody knows to come in and look for certain things. It's what you call a spotter. You ask your spotter, How did the help greet you? How did they say their farewell? Were they pleasant? In big cities you can hire spotter services. Ultimately, for help that can't get a grip on good customer service, you just have to let them go.

KITCHEN STAFF

Kitchen help is the core of the business, and ours is busiest at lunch time. We have two full-time kitchens: the deli kitchen with its help, and the bakery kitchen with two full-time bakers, a pastry chef, and a part-time baker who comes in occasionally to shorten the full-time bakers' shift.

WONDERFUL BUSINESS . . . GREAT PRODUCT

The Cheesecake Lady became a $1-million-a-year business in 1995. Its founder, a relative of the current owner, had baked her first cheesecakes in Philadelphia to great reviews but had to close owing to a want of business skills. She started again in Mendocino County in 1982.

She first rented space from midnight to 6:00 a.m. from a wholesale baker, Mrs. Denson's Cookies. She did all her prep work, baking, and packaging during its otherwise idle graveyard shift. Then, after an hour or two of sleep, she climbed into her van to deliver and sell. Business began to build within the county, especially on the Coast during the summer months. But after the first summer, when the tourist season ended, she pursued accounts in San Francisco and the Bay Area to keep the business going. Hyatt Hotels were the first to order from the company. Eventually she also placed orders with other exclusive hotels and restaurants, including the famed Tadich Grill, in San Francisco. The company moved to an interim space in Ukiah, then opened at its present location on the main street of Hopland (pop. 817) in 1985.

In early 1991 she telephoned the current owner, Paul Levitan, and said, I've got a business that's been growing every year for nine years; I'm about to have a baby; I can't handle it all. You're in business school, what should I do?

**The Cheesecake Lady
13325 South Highway 101
Hopland, California**

Levitan said he was in love with the company's cakes. He came to look it over and saw a wonderful business with a great product and loyal customers, but no computers and no sales force. He raised enough money to buy it. He has since built the sales force and, through the mail-order division, now sells cheesecakes in all 50 states and seven countries. The café provides 10 percent of the income, but the bakery chiefly sells wholesale in 20 states.

Walk-in retail trade—from people out either wine-tasting or traveling—is substantial on weekends, especially during good weather when lines go out the front door. Until recently the Cheesecake Lady seemed to have the only espresso machine on Highway 101, from San Francisco to the Oregon border, and loyal customers still pull off the highway for a double espresso.

The company employs 25 people in a 6,000-square-foot commercial space. On average it ships 300 to 400 cakes a day. In the peak mid-November through Christmas season the bakery runs 24 hours a day, loading Federal Express, UPS, and company trucks to ship all over the country. Its mail orders are through Bloomingdale's in New York and Horchow in Texas. It has also sold via the QVC channel. For mail order it freezes and places the cake with an ice pack in a special polyfoam container. The cake thaws partially in shipping but stays below 45 degrees.

"We're cheesecake snobs," Levitan explains. All the Cheesecake Lady's cakes are handmade—the original is from an old family recipe—using the best pure ingredients. The company's latest triumph is a line of individual 3-inch round cheesecakes, which other bakeries have copied, much to Levitan's delight. These led to a 3-inch individual "Mendocino Mud Puddle"—a rich, moist chocolate cake dipped in chocolate, then chocolate-iced—and a "Peanut Butter Mud Puddle" with a peanut-butter mousse filling.

Certain days of the week, Saturdays for example, are pretty relaxed. There's not nearly as much prep work, because our main shop is closed on Sunday. Saturday's atmosphere is lighter and easier even on a big special-order day. During the week we always have to think ahead for the next day. There's a popular belief that tension makes people work harder and produce more, but there's a flip side and a risk to that. The tension can become entirely too great, and things will just bomb.

A bakery's pleasant, relaxed atmosphere can vanish when weekday activity shifts to fast-forward. That's when your staff must be able to get down to work and let the boss—I hate to use the word "order"—let's say instruct them without adding "please" to every direction, as in, "Hey, we need to have these cookies mixed. . . . I need five extra pounds of flour in that." And you must have employees who can do more than one thing at a time—like having something in the oven, something on the mixer, and something on the bench all at once. You'll need a staff you can "instruct" in the middle of a bake to "pull that out of the oven." They have to run over, pull it out of the oven, and go back to what they were mixing without forgetting where they left off. People like that are hard to come by and deserve more appreciation they seem to get. Everyone in the business should remember that while you need to assure your product's quality, you should do it by positively reinforcing your staff's successes and rather than criticizing mistakes.

COMPUTING STAFF COSTS

How many employees it takes to handle your volume of business isn't as important as how many hours you can afford to staff your shop. If you staff simply by demand you'll have no control over labor costs. We've approached the problem by taking the percentage of gross sales that we want to allot to labor—let's say it's 25 percent—and, if we know how much money we'll take in a day, we convert the percentage into how many hours of staff time we can afford, that is, how many hours of labor at $7-an-hour per employee to schedule within the budget. You may conclude, for example, that 25 percent of your daily gross will cover 50 hours of work a day. If you know that 16 hours of work a day must be in the kitchen and will take two eight-hour shifts, you can break it down. You might need one eight-hour dish washing and clean-up shift, which leaves 26 hours for staffing the counter.

You do need to consider the "demand" side of the equation. If you know or you've projected your daily volume of business, you must calculate how many employees it takes to handle it throughout the day. The staffing budget often must stretch, at least a little, to meet this demand. If you plan to be open for 12 hours a day and stay within your budget, you can staff the counter with two eight-hour shifts, two four-hour shifts, and a two-hour shift for the busy lunch time. It also allows enough flexibility to cover busier days of the week and absences.

If you haven't hired anybody yet, you start looking at job applications to see whether this applicant wants to work full time or part time, and you start filling the gaps. It's a direct way to calculate how many people you'll need to fill the hours. Also take into account the dependability of the people working for you. That usually calls for an extra part-time person who can cover a shift on a moment's notice.

If you target the percentage of gross income you want to use for payroll you can go from there. If you find you're under-staffed, you adjust by either asking people to work more hours or hiring a new person. If you have too many people, you let somebody go. Usually, allocating 25 percent of gross with competitive prices means everyone will work pretty hard and stay busy. Past a certain point, if you hire more people, you encounter Parkinson's Law: "Work expands to fill the time in which do to it." The same work gets divided up and done less efficiently than at a higher cost. Don't hire more than enough to do the job.

I should add that we've stretched these rules enormously to accommodate the routine outlined in Chapter 2. Right now we could certainly take on a little more staff. Once things are back to normal we'll hire by the book. I might add also that it's much easier to schedule help for a self-service deli or café. You simply calculate how long it will take two people in an eight-hour shift to prepare everything for the showcase. With a serve-at-table lunch business you may serve 200 lunches one day and 100 the next. You would still have to employ servers for 200 if that's your busiest day; but when only 100 customers come in it leaves half your people standing around with nothing to do.

To figure out what rate to pay for wages, start by looking at the market. In Santa Barbara, say, we would have to pay more per hour because there are more better-paying jobs competing for employees. In our region not even white-collar jobs pay very well. You definitely take the local economy into account and peg your wages commensurately. You don't want to pay $1 and $2 an hour more than the competition, because it raises your overhead and thins your profit—if it doesn't erase it entirely. And if you let your prices reflect the higher wages you'll have a tough time selling your product.

Most of the time our help-wanted ad or job description, will say, "Counter help. Starting pay $5.00 an hour, maximum pay scale $8.50 an hour." The applicant knows up front that pay for the job will never rise to more than $8.50 an hour. That's all we can feasibly pay unless the employee becomes a manager or skilled baker. You use the starting pay figure for somebody without much experience, a student or other young person. If you find someone who's really sharp and has had good retail experience, you might start them in the middle at $6.50 an hour. Often you can get better people that way if you're competing with places like yours that starts them off at $5.00 an hour. Better paid people have a greater vested interest in the job and generally work harder.

Even so, if your new hires understand that $8.50 is about as high as the job pays, they will leave eventually. The minimum-wage people are where the turnover is; that's where you can afford turnover and where you should expect it. What hurts you is when you invest time and effort to train someone, and they move up the pay scale to $7.00 an hour. They've settled into the job and they've got a niche—then they quit because they found $7.50-an-hour a job. That costs you not only the services of your skilled employee, but forces you to incur the delay and expense of finding and training a replacement.

ACCOUNTING FOR THE HELP

Employees mean bundles of paperwork. Just to cover the subject without going into too much detail, here briefly, is what payroll accounting involves.

When you plan to become an employer contact the IRS for Form SS-4 to get an Employer Identification Number (EIN). Also get W-4 forms for employee tax withholding and, while you are at it, a supply of W-2 forms. Before January 31 of the following year you must send one W-2 to the Social Security Administration, keep one for your records, and give the employee three copies. Somewhere along the line you will have to buy the standard set of employee informational posters that cover the minimum wage, Occupational Safety and Health Administration (OSHA) requirements, and all manner of discrimination rules. Then you post them where every employee can see them. Usually they end up in the restroom, unless the company has a regular employee space.

You will need to set up a payroll sheet for the employee and to comply with all the state and federal laws, rules, and regulations that apply to employers. This means carrying workers' compensation, either through your state or a private insurer, and complying with Occupational Safety and Health Administration (OSHA) regulations, with the Immigration Reform and Control Act (IRCA), and with the Fair Labor Standards Act (FLSA). You will have to pay for unemployment insurance and for half of your employees' Social Security.

- *OSHA.* To maintain safe working conditions, the Occupational Safety and Health Administration, a division of the U.S. Department of Labor, publishes minimum standards for each industry and inspects workplaces. It is highly unlikely an OSHA inspector will ever come calling on a bakery, but that is no reason to get careless and invite trouble.

FLOUR: WHITE, WHEAT AND GRAHAM

Flour is the fine, clean product of bolting (sifting) meal that comes from milled whole grains. Wheat's gluten, which gives its doughs and batters their unmatched texture, strength, and character, is a dingy, gummy chain of proteins left over if the starch is washed out of the flour.

The baking quality of different wheat flours' depends on the kind and amount of gluten they contain. And that depends on the kind of wheat from which the flour is milled and how it is milled. On this continent, the "strongest" or "hardest" flours grow chiefly between the Rocky Mountains and the Mississippi Valley, principally north and west of Missouri. Less glutinous wheats grown between the more humid Great Plains and Atlantic Coast and along the Pacific Coast are "softer" or "weaker." Wheat's endosperm controls hardness, harder kernels being more difficult to break during milling. A stronger or harder flour with more gluten and less starch is preferable in bread, while weak flours from soft wheat are best for cakes and pastries. Durum wheat is very hard with a very high gluten content and makes a tough, yellow or grayish flour. Soft wheat has a white, starchy endosperm that yields a pleasing flour color. Dur-

um, although sometimes blended with other flours, is darker and would produce a grimy looking bread; it is normally used to manufacture pasta which requires a very elastic dough.

Most wheat bran—the brown, fibrous byproduct of milling—is made into animal feed. Although it is rich in minerals and vitamins, people digest it less completely than the rest of the kernel. As it stimulates peristalsis, it may move food through the digestive tract too quickly for us to absorb its nutrients fully. Bran's chief value in modern diets is its laxative property when used in limited amounts. Of the minerals and vitamins in wheat—especially iron, Vitamin B, and Vitamin G—most are in the bran and germ which milling for white flour removes. Either may be sold separately. Graham flour is unbolted wheat meal, while commercial "whole-wheat" flour may be steel-ground white flour to which bran and wheat germ are added then further milled. Graham flour contains all, and whole-wheat flour at least part, of wheat's natural constituents. Their baking strengths are lower, they keep less well, and their dietary benefits have not gone unquestioned.

- *IRCA.* You and every employee you hire must fill out an INS Form I-9. The federal Immigration and Naturalization Act permits you to hire only U.S. citizens and aliens who are permitted to work here. For compliance with the Act you must review documents like birth certificates, drivers' licenses, Social Security cards, passports, visas, naturalization papers, and green cards. You must decide whether the documents are genuine and then record the evidence of your compliance on Form I-9. The form's instructions take you through the steps of filling it out. Each employee's Form I-9 must remain in your records for at least three years, or one year after a longer term employee leaves. Contact the nearest INS office or telephone 1-800-777-7700 for publication M274, its *Handbook for Employers.*
- *FLSA.* The Fair Labor Standards Act sets the minimum wage and the standard work week, and determines overtime pay. There is no restriction on anyone over 16 years of age working more than

40 hours a week, but the act requires compensating at time and one half for work exceeding the standard work week. What exceeds the standard work week is fairly complicated. It is all right for you to work 90 hours a week, but your employee can't unless you pay him or her one and one half times his or her usual pay for the excess.

- *FUTA*. You must also pay federal unemployment tax on each employee and file it with an IRS Form 940 or 940EZ if: (1) you paid $1,500 or more in wages in any quarter of a year or (2) had (a) at least one employee for (b) part of at least one day of (c) 20 different weeks in a year. The tax is calculated on the employee's first $7,000 of wages during the year, and any state unemployment tax is credited to your federal tax liability.
- *FICA*. You pay your portion of your employees' Social Security taxes directly and withhold the employees' equivalent portion from their gross pay. These are reported on Form 941.
- *Workers' Compensation*. All states require employers to carry workers' compensation insurance. I discussed some of this under insurance as something you should shop around for. The laws vary from state to state, and you should contact your state agency for details. You could not cover yourself with workers' compensation as a sole proprietor, but a partnership or corporation may elect to provide you with coverage as a partner of the partnership or officer of the corporation.

The best thing to do with all of this is to give it to your bookkeeper. The problem is that even many bookkeepers and accountants dislike it. So, when you shop for a bookkeeper or accountant see if they handle payroll or will arrange to contract it out to take it off your hands for a reasonable fee.

WHO DOES WHAT

Work is a kind totem pole. People at the top of the pole get the tasks they like to do. People at the bottom have to do what nobody likes. If it's a tedious task, try to divide it: Joe gets it one day and Jane gets it the next. But all work is a matter of perspective. When an employee comes in at the entry level, they get jobs that the veterans don't have to do anymore. These are not always the sweetest tasks, but if you convince the employee that it is all just work, they will get in and do it. That's what we try to tell new people. Even if it's the least desirable job in the bakery—say, cleaning out the drain at the bottom of the dishwasher or cleaning the bathroom—it's just work, like baking bread or decorating cakes. It's just a whole lot less glamorous. The job will take either 10 minutes to finish off or half an hour to complain about, but the first way is faster and less painful. It means trying to change people's attitudes. You can't do it with everyone, which is one reason why some people don't work out.

We went to the Wedding Show in Mendocino, and that's how we sold our wedding cakes on the coast. People liked the taste of our cake. We sell fewer here in town. I think a lot of people sell them from their homes. My prices are low compared to the Bay Area, but I can't compete with their prices because they don't have to pay my overhead. Wedding cakes are always nightmares, though, because something always goes wrong. They're big and they're heavy. Frequently the butter cream cracks when you're moving them just because of the engineering. You have to put supports inside the cake, wooden pillars to hold the layers up. A friend uses bamboo skewers to travel with a stacked cake so the layers don't slide. You always take a bag of butter cream and a patch kit when you're delivering. The ones that we delivered yesterday touched, so we had to do a little repair. I'm so casual about it now, nothing would bother me unless the cake fell on the floor. Other than that, everything else is manageable.

—JACQUIE LEE
THE GARDEN BAKERY

Our bakers usually move up through the ranks. They come from either the deli line or the dish room. There are dish washers who love their work and want to stay there because they don't want the responsibility of baking everything off. They'll reject the chance to become assistant bakers because they prefer to do their everyday job, which they know exactly and like. Occasionally you acquire a good dish washer who wants to become a baker. The problem then is that when you're lucky enough to find a reliable dish washer who likes the work and does the job well, you'd rather not have to try and find a replacement. But when you want to reward the dish washer, you'll be reluctant to offer a promotion since it's a hard position to fill. On the other hand, you can't offer a big raise and skew the pay schedule too far. It's a Catch 22.

THE HAPPY SHOP

Everyone needs a station with the necessary tools at hand. You don't want the cake decorator to come in and have to pull tools out of boxes everyday. It's inefficient and it won't please your staff. We handle the work-station routine mainly by shifts. Lacking all the room in the world, we have the pastry baker come in five or six hours after the bread baker in order to have a bench available just for pastries.

Our ironclad rule, that staff puts a tool right back where they got it if it doesn't have to be washed, is basic to an efficient work station. If a tool needs to be washed, whoever uses it has to make sure that the dish washer, or whoever is washing, washes it and brings it right back to that spot. Most important, each and every morning when you start, everything must be in its regular place, because searching for tools at the outset can put you way behind schedule. If it takes you 15 minutes to find a scraper in the morning, you're ready to do mayhem.

Besides putting away tools, you always want your benches to be clear and clean after every product. First, dough that gets stuck to the bench surface will cause later doughs to tear, and second it seems much easier to work when your benches are clean. It's like having a clean canvas for painting. You start a new project on a clean canvas, and when you're done you scrape it down and start another one with a clean canvas.

For regular eight-hour shifts, lunch and breaks are the law. Many of the part-time help won't get that opportunity. If people don't take the benefit of a whole half-hour clock-out, they may just take an extended ten-minute break and eat fast. It's their choice; however, it does feel good to get away from work for a while, and I encourage it.

One easy benefit to provide for your help is to throw a party once in a while. Not only at Christmas time. Just say, We're having an employee party, it will be at my house, we'll have some beers, I'll supply the dinner, and we'll all relax. . . . If you can build friendships with everybody that works with you, it makes the atmosphere more pleasant and improves relationships on the job.

We hold a staff meeting for managers about once a month, and for our entire crew about once every two months. If it were easier to get the entire crew together, we'd probably do it more often. Because of the turnover you'll find yourself going over the same things in every meeting. Staff who have been with you for one or two years will get pretty bored with meetings. It's a good idea, however, to reiterate the principles of customer service, which is on every meeting's agenda, and to cover points of policy you might like to change.

It's also helpful to bring people together to get their ideas. At the end of every meeting I call for a few suggestions about what people think will help. It's just like the classroom. Everybody's got something to say but for some reason doesn't say it. Then, when the meeting's over, everyone walks up afterwards with all these great ideas. It's just like school, unbelievable.

THE PERSONNEL MANUAL

Upon hiring you should communicate your employment policies orally, but I recommend having a personnel manual that includes job descriptions for every position in the bakery and sets out the business's procedures and rules. Ours stays up by the front counter so everyone can look at it at any time. Keep it simple, just a few pages of major points that you can add to as questions arise. The advantage is that it sets out procedures in black and white for everyone to refer to. We have included a sample personnel manual in the Appendix. It's not what we use. It's a generic set of suggestions that can be adapted to different situations. You should look at a variety of personnel manuals to learn what different managers consider important for personal relationships on the job.

QUITTING AND DISMISSAL

California is an at-will employment state, which we make clear when we first hire. We even use an at-will agreement. It simply states that you have the right to quit when you like, and we have the right to dismiss you from work whenever we like. This is legal in California, unless there's an employer-employee contract that states otherwise.

If you have to discharge someone, however, be careful. Lawyers have found out about lawsuits for wrongful termination, and even small employers can face expensive litigation if they're careless. Before firing someone who has been with you a long time, be sure that you have a good reason to do it, that it is clear you hired the employee for an "at will" position, and that you never made any promises or suggestions about tenure. If you have to fire a long-time employee, meeting these standards becomes very difficult. You may want to see a lawyer first.

If you run into a bad apple, use written warnings and try to get the employee to improve. The first time he or she does something, write it up. Part of our policy is that if you receive three write-ups, you lose your job. We stick to that and write everybody up for the same things. With a third write-up we dismiss. That way we've given the employee ample opportunity to keep the job, and when he or she applies to get unemployment benefits we simply tell the unemployment office that we had to write the employee up three times. That keeps our unemployment insurance payments lower than if we just walked up to somebody and said, you're fired. We've had to do it; and then, of course, the employee is entitled to all unemployment insurance benefits. That can get expensive. If somebody is a real problem, we may engineer a quit. Part of the write-up may involve losing a shift or two. Then the person will either change to get back the full-time employment or quit. Firing is tough. It's not easy to fire someone, even when you can't avoid it. It's always easier to fire someone in the heat of the moment, which is inadvisable because you don't have full control of the problem. On the other hand, it's very difficult to fire someone who is not expecting it. I don't like to do it, but you have to remember that it's for the good of the business and then deal with it.

Staff

___*Calculate how much staff you can afford*

___*Decide who does what, and draft job descriptions and personnel manual*

___*Learn and comply with all government regulations*

___*Hire through classified ads, employment oiifces, word-of-mouth, network of friends and current employees*

___*Limit application form to name, address, telephone, Social Security Number and include a brief quiz*

___*At interview ask about experience, and discuss appropriate dress and punctuality*

___*Check references*

___*Hire and train counter staff*

    ___*Teach prices and product descriptions*

    ___*Discuss safety and sanitation, general quality standards, right to day-olds and surplus product, and write-up and dismissal policies*

12

MARKETING THE BAKERY

M ARKETING is only as successful as the product or service behind it. That's a given in this or any other business. When you first start out you can use marketing to get people in once to try your goods or services. But after that, if their experience is negative, all the advertising and promotion in the world won't bring them back. The rule is to give people a good product at a good price, with good service in a pleasant environment. Beyond that you need to create a strategy to keep your bakery in the public awareness and your products on its tables. Don't let the terms "marketing strategy" or "marketing plan" scare you off. It is mainly common sense and it just happens in the course of running the business.

Our bakery's greatest marketing success has come less from advertising than word-of-mouth, and that arose directly from the product and service. When we opened at the home-improvement center we saturated the market with radio and newspaper ads to generate interest and curiosity, but, as the initial push ended, our products and service carried the business there, as in the original shop.

PUBLICITY

The first step in marketing your bakery is generating publicity or public awareness of it, and for a bakery that's the easiest thing in the world. Just have the bakery smell like a bakery. When the morning crowd is coming in you want the items coming out of the oven to be the kind that will get people to buy. You don't want to take out cream puff and éclair shells or puff pastries—products that don't have a pronounced aroma. You want cinnamon rolls, danish, and cookies to come out, because they're strong sensory items. We're just down the street from the post office annex, and all the mail carriers and clerks up the street come in every morning and say, "Oh man, I can smell it; I had to come down and get a hot roll or bear claw." That's what you want.

And you definitely want the front of the building to be inviting. If you remember driving down the street of an unfamiliar town when you were hungry, you probably saw a place and thought it looked neat and inviting. You were more likely to go there to eat than to some plain but probably just as good place. So we've put as attractive a façade on the building as we can. It has a new awning, designed so that the sides facing the two cross streets say "bakery, pastries, coffee." You want people who drive by to see that. The front of it has our name on it. There is a bench and table with two chairs in front, and a couple of hanging plants. Don't hesitate to put advertising on the building, including the windows. Let people know what you have; don't make them drive by and wonder.

Ideally, the bakery would incorporate the front windows into its showcase displays. For example, our windows face north so that, except for a brief time in the evening, there would be no direct sunlight to dry out the product, and we could light up the windows so the bread stood out in the shade. As customers drove by they would see stacks of fresh bread in the window and the product stretching all the way back along that side of the store.

At some point, while you're setting up and thinking about façades and other visual attractions, you should come up with a company logo. Luckily we inherited a family trademark. It has a western rope—a lariat or lasso—encircling a tulip. The tulip identifies Schat's bakeries as Dutch and the rope places us out west. Every business benefits from having a logo for instant recognition. You can work with a printer or graphic designer, or you can brainstorm one with the people you work with. It's cheaper, more fun, and it gives the staff a sense of involvement and shared interest. Then put your logo on your shirts, on your business cards and menus, on bags and cartons, even printed on cups, plates, and saucers. Pretty soon people begin to identify the logo with the bakery, and whenever they see it they think of the bakery.

The next step in getting publicity takes more work. Contact the local newspapers with human interest events. We've had good coverage in the local paper, in part from being bakers for five generations, but I think there's a story in everybody. For example, Don Pittman, who is our pastry chef now, once worked in insurance before coming here. There was a nice background story in how he turned his life around at the age of 48 to go from insurance executive to pastry chef. In a way his story—a first-time baker at age 48—was just the opposite of ours. If you think of some original characteristic about you or your staff or even the bakery building itself, you can probably get a story out of it. The baker around the corner

For my Christmas display in the window we did sugar-cube houses. I wanted to do a sugar-cube castle and I thought it would be nice for the school to be involved and let the kids make the rest of it for me. That way it brought the parents and the kids down. It was good advertising. All it used was sugar cubes and butter cream, and we had a tremendous amount of fun with it.

—MURIEL GLAVE
THE LANDMARK BAKERY

occasionally publishes an article in a food magazine and gets good coverage out of that. We got a good story on our 8-foot pumpkin pie for the local Pumpkin Fest. Use a little imagination to think about newsworthy events, and people will find out about your bakery at no cost to you.

Usually it takes more than a telephone call to get a reporter into your shop. Most media have business reporters who are eager to write up commercial events. Learn who it is for each of your local media. You don't have to be a writer; just send the appropriate reporter or editor a succinct, factual account of an event or new development. The item should tell *who* did or will do *what, when, where, why,* and *how.* It should have something to hook people's interest and shouldn't be an overt pitch for your shop. Newspeople want an "inverted pyramid" style of writing, with the most significant fact first, trailed by those of decreasing importance. If you ask, some media will give you a press-release kit to help you frame your story. Have a friend read your copy for grammar and spelling. You could send a brief, pleasant letter about you and the bakery with your first press release. A follow-up telephone call can help gauge interest in the event. Don't push; just be pleasant and become a person, not just a name. If the press does pay a visit, give them a good cup of coffee and a sample of your baked goods.

Don't be shy about trying for the coverage you want. Build the story up while the paper is doing it. It's good for the paper and good for you. The newspaper decided to run a photo of Don in the bakery holding one of his cakes. But there was nothing behind him. So we got every basket of pastry from every case in the store and stacked it up as a backdrop. That made sense. We liked it, the newspaper liked it, and best of all our customers loved it.

Don't forget about people who are just passing through; they have to eat, too. Ukiah is on a tourist highway from the San Francisco Bay Area to the redwood forests and Oregon Coast. It is not itself a destination, but tourists do stay here overnight. We've arranged to place an announcement in a "What to do in Ukiah" brochure that will be in all the motels. Motels, large service stations and rest stops often have racks of brochures that travelers love to pick up. If you don't have a brochure, the rack would be a good place to leave your menus instead. This is more in the way of advertising than publicity. It's a good idea to keep clear about what is publicity and what is advertising, and when to use each.

News items are almost always better than ads, because people actually read them. An advertising agency's survey once estimated that the average reader spends about eight seconds on the average ad. That probably means that people don't read most of them. Not that we never advertise. Publicity is much more effective than advertising—for what publicity does—but only advertising can keep your company's name before the public. You will never get as many news items about your business as you can buy ads for it.

ADVERTISING

Advertising should start before you open. It builds up interest in the bakery. Locally, a place called the Coffee Critic did a record job of that. It took them three years to put the project put together, with ads and publicity running off and on the whole time. It's a good idea to place signage and advertising on the storefront right away, even while you're putting your shop together; so is a "Coming Soon" ad in the newspaper. Advertising like that before you open can help create interest and really pump it up. Then, on your opening day, whether you plan to do $10 or $1,000 of business, put out enough product for a $1,000 day—even if you end up having to donate most of it. You want your place to look completely stuffed with good things.

Copy writing and design for ads call for specialized skills, and you may want to consider hiring an agency to write and design your advertising. A successful agency will tell you that if you do your own ad it will probably look like everyone else's and get lost in the crowd. If you live where agencies produce most of the advertising, shop around for a good one by getting references as you would for any other service. Or you can find out which agency designed particularly effective advertising that you like and has stood the test of time by being around for awhile.

We don't use an advertising agency. The *Ukiah Daily Journal*, our local press, has its own advertising department, which makes up local ads. Most newspapers have ad departments that can do that. Usually you get to keep the "slick" and re-use it in different media like high school baseball and football game programs. It's important to keep a file of all your old ads and ad slicks. By keeping those the paper has set up in the past, you can often run them again with a few changes. A Yellow-Page display ad is expensive but a necessity. Always review your ads before they appear in print, whether in the newspaper or Yellow Pages. You'll have to wait a year to correct an erroneous Yellow-Page ad. You can also advertise effectively on local cable TV for a reasonable cost these days, and it's worth investigating.

Since we're on a tourist route we had a billboard set up three years ago at about a 15-minute drive south of us. It cost $4,000 a year but the response paid for it well within that time. It was very visible and attractive, and just far enough ahead of town to give people time to think about our baked goods and get hungry. You wouldn't want a sign a quarter mile before the turn off; signs seem to work best with at least a five-mile lead.

THOROUGHLY MODERN MILLING

In 1878 fire caused an explosion in Washburn's Flour Mill in Minneapolis. It destroyed the mill and killed almost the entire work shift. Minnesota's governor ordered the mill when rebuilt to use the new Hungarian roller-mill process for "the whitest bread the world has ever seen." Hungary's development of roller milling—which began with sketches from the 1820s—could not be perfected until the development of reliable steam power and the Bessemer process for making grooved steel rollers to replace the original ceramic rods. By first removing the bran and germ, roller milling can produce flours from pure white to fortified with any proportion of bran and germ desired.

The holidays are the year's busiest time and the best time to try out something new. If you plan to add a new line like preserves or to introduce a catering service that's when to do it. It might seem like a hectic time to expand your product line or services, but it gives the best exposure. And if you can handle the extra business during the holidays, you can do it any time. It's also a great opportunity to advertise. For example: "When you come to [YOUR BAKERY] to get your Thanksgiving dinner rolls try our new homemade preserves." Or "Have us bake your turkey golden brown." And so on.

Coupons are a good idea if used judiciously, especially when starting out, but don't run them all the time. It brings people who come in just for coupon specials, and you can't afford to give goods away on coupons all the time. It's a great way to build business but a bad basis for running one. Perhaps a leading bad example is a popular franchise steak restaurant. It seems to have been built on coupons. I always went there when I had a $5.99 coupon, but never ate a meal there without one because it never seemed worth the regular price. Every once in a while we also run a special on the back of a raffle ticket or a likely handbill.

Always have an expiration date on the coupon. We once made the mistake of putting an ad in the local high school paper which just said redeem this coupon for one free mocha. There was no need even to buy anything. You want the customer to buy something with a coupon—the first item with the second one free—or to get a discounted price. We didn't put an expiration date on the coupon either, and these high-school kids grabbed every newspaper they could find and cut out our coupons. They had enough coupons for six months of free mocha with no expiration date. Kids have no shame, of course. They got me. We were serving free mocha all day long that whole six months to the same bright shining faces.

We haven't tracked advertising on a regular basis. Often you go into stores and they ask where you heard about them, but in a shop like this with repeat customer business it would be absurd to ask people every time. By all means get feedback on your advertising.

If you run a 30-second spot on the radio for three months and not one person mentions hearing it, don't do it again.

We ask new customers how they found the place, and they may say, for example, that they asked at the gas station where the best place in town to get lunch was. That kind of thing is great for the morale, and it's where word-of-mouth pays for all your efforts. The Chamber of Commerce will also refer people when they ask for a good place to eat lunch. I have heard of people driving through town who will roll down the window and ask the car next to them where to eat. That's where name recognition is important. We're lucky because our family name is all over the state, and four of our shops are in this county. You may not be able to build up name recognition in the same way, but the tools are available for anyone in business and you should use them.

A recent mailer we received claimed that people pick out their bakery—the place where they hang out and have coffee— within the first 30 days of moving to a new town. It may be worth providing flyers to real estate companies or arranging for a coupon that goes out with the first utility bill to a new homeowner. Or you can offer a special through Welcome Wagon. You want to introduce your products and services early and get the customer in the habit of coming to your bakery. The heart of your business is in return customers. Even in a tourist area try get return vacationers to patronize your place every time they're in town. It can make a big difference in how much money you take in each year.

Finally, since there is only one other full-range bakery in town and our markets don't overlap much, we have little need to advertise competitively. If you were in a situation where there were three or four other bakeries competing for much of the same market, then newspaper ads with special deals, Dollar Days, and "buy one, get one free" promotions would probably be worth trying. We've run a few in the paper and they work for us by bringing people through the door. It's a way to get people who may be routinely shop at another bakery to try yours.

PUBLIC RELATIONS

Public relations involves getting your name known in association with public activities and building a good reputation. That sounds simple enough, but you have to work at it. Any bakery will donate to nearly every local group that needs baked products. Think about the public relations you're already engaged in and how you can make them better. At the front counter you try to make your place one that people will think well of and want to come back to. You'll also want it to be known as one that's involved in the community. It may seem like a big order on top of everything else, but, like much of marketing, it must be part of the business. If a good product is the bedrock of marketing, good public relations are the fertile

Another problem in a big town: You advertise your bakery. Let's say there are 10 or 12 of them. When you advertise your little bakery, you're advertising for the whole city, which is not your market. Your market is the area right around you. Under those conditions advertising is astronomically expensive. You're wasting most of your advertising dollars. The same is true for rent. Your customer base is going to come from a small part of the town. But you're going to pay for the location as though it was the whole town.

—KEN MOORE
MOORE'S FLOUR MILL, BAKERY
& DELI

soil—because no amount of publicity or advertising can overcome a selfish or rude attitude, or a bad reputation.

I don't participate in service clubs like Lions, Rotary, Kiwanis, or the like, not because I don't want to, but because their breakfast and luncheon meetings are during our busiest time. We do cater their events and donate to their fund raisers. If the police or fire department does something local, like the firemen's barbecue, or the Police Activities League (PAL) we like to help by offering gift certificates. But you have to be wary of organizations that claim to be "associated" with the local police and fire departments. Watch out for out-of-area outfits that purport to call for the local departments but are just commercial promoters. You'll get phone calls all the time, all day long. You'll reach the point where you just have to say no.

We belong to the Chamber of Commerce. It helps the downtown by keeping up on what's happening in the state legislature, where they are active, and trying to represent the interests of business owners. It also gives an opportunity to rub shoulders with other business owners who are not in your immediate neighborhood. You will already know all the business owners in your area and probably belong to a downtown merchants association. But at a Chamber of Commerce mixer you might meet the owner of a major manufacturer or retailer whom you wouldn't otherwise meet.

Public relations include ordinary day-to-day practice. If you make a mistake and irritate a customer, everybody will learn about it soon enough. We all love to bad-mouth, and the news is full of it, because negative things make a story. For a business, however, they go miles deep and they're very hard to repair.

When you err—and you will—the first rule is don't make a big deal out of it. Sometimes my staff or I will make a mistake and we'll worry more about how we did it than about just taking care of the customer. If there is a problem—as when you serve lunch and miss somebody's order, leaving them sitting there with no lunch—that person will come up and ask where the sandwich is. Then five people begin to run around yelling, "Where is the order? Where is the order?" *Don't!* Make the sandwich; get the customer happy. Give the customer a free lunch. After it's all over with, then worry about where that order went astray. The customer doesn't care about how your procedure works or doesn't work. Always take care of the customer first. If you make a mistake like that or any kind, there should be no problem giving away a free sandwich or free lunch for two, or even sending a half a dozen cookies to the table. If you do that, it's good PR and it's very good business.

LOCAL CELEBRATIONS

More tons of pears per acre grow in the 3,000 acres devoted to the crop around here than anywhere else in the country. That's 57 percent of national production, and nearly nobody knows about it.

The bakery recently hosted a "first annual" pear cook-off sponsored by civic leaders, packers, and growers to help put local production on the map. The winning recipe was featured in the bakery. We also get involved in downtown events, such as the "Pumpkin Fest," for which we baked the 8-foot pumpkin pie, and the Iron Car Show, for which we sponsor a trophy. Things like that, and soccer and little league sponsorship tax a business but that's part of its obligation to give back to the community. It's another judgment call: a good idea, but one you shouldn't overdo or it will break your bank.

The pear cook-off, which took place during the Iron Car Show, got us plenty of good response and brought people into the bakery.

MORE HELP

This chapter is a very brief survey of a pretty complicated set of skills. If you want to read the most enjoyable and helpful books there are on the subject, check out Jay Levinson's *Guerrilla Marketing* series, a few of which we list in the appendix. Levinson was a vice president of a big Madison Avenue firm and now consults with *Fortune* 500 companies and small businesses. You can hire him as a consultant for the price of a free public library card.

Marketing

___Create start-up and permanent marketing plans with
   ___Publicity
   ___Advertising
   ___Public relations
___Settle on a signature product, product line, or at least a style to identify your bakery
___Create a company logo, stationery, menus, and packaging
___Design bakery for visibility and appeal to passersby
___Start pre-opening advertising and follow up with opening-day promotions.
___Get local press coverage
   ___Make notes of who covers business and human interest in your local media
   ___Contact about human interest events (e.g., opening)
   ___Draft press releases and send with a brief cover letter about you, your bakery and the event.
   ___Follow with a phone call to establish a personal relationship
   ___Keep trying
___Appeal to travelers
___Use coupons, introductory offers, sales promotions
___Track publicity, public relations, and advertising results
___Put customers first
   ___Be pleasant always
   ___Have a clear, logically priced menu
   ___Keep the premises clean
   ___Watch customer response closely
   ___Evaluate to perfect your service and product
   ___**NEVER, NEVER** argue with any customer
   ___Be sure all your staff knows the above
___Participate in the community
   ___Donations
   ___Local events
   ___Youth activities

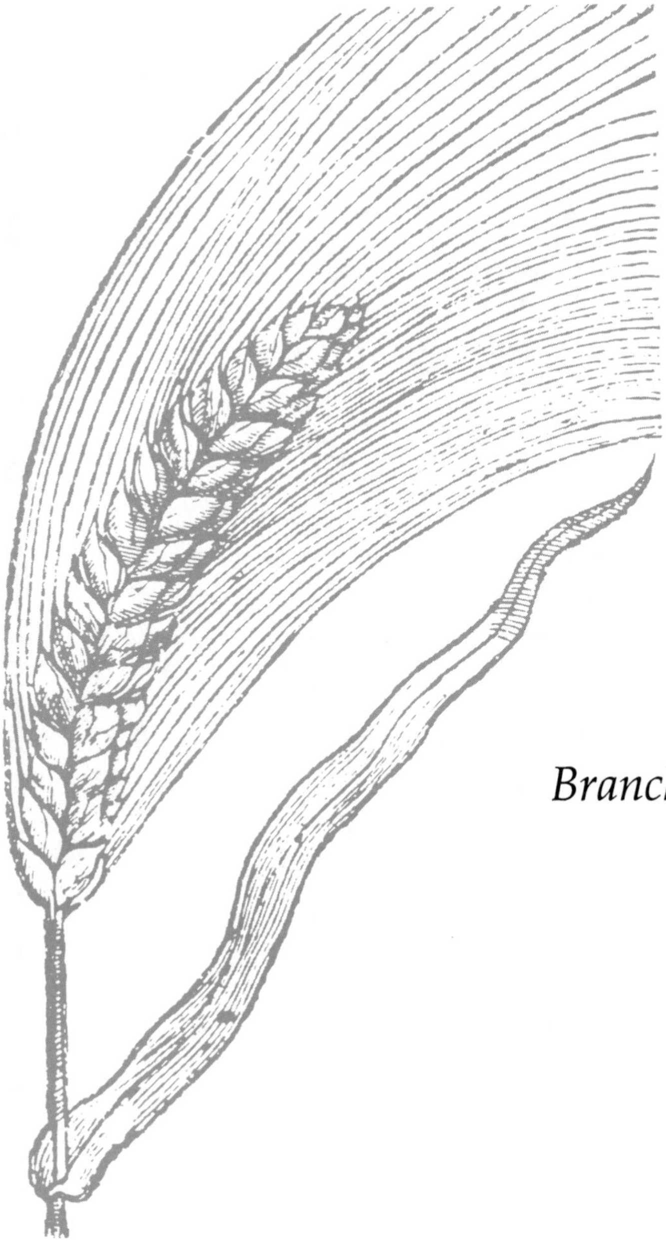

13

ADDING TO THE MIX

DDING A CAFÉ to the bakery, if it didn't start with one, is about diversifying—so is adding any new product line or service. There's no limit to how you can customize and refine your business, but it should grow naturally out of what you're doing, when you do it right. You might, for example, add a line of fruit jams and preserves, dairy items, or coffees. We probably captured a good portion of our lunch business with full-sheet pizza breads. It wasn't a bakery item and it wasn't a café item; it was a combination of the two, just something we tried out. Now we can hardly make enough of them.

DIVERSIFYING

If you start as solely a bakery, a good way to ease into a wider market would be to put out a few tables and chairs to serve coffee and rolls. People may start to ask you to put eggs on their bagel or in their croissant, and before you know it you're in the café business. It's a natural progression that could take you as far as you want.

Retail food service is an evolving business right now. Many dual-income families often lack the time to cook meals at home from scratch. They could come by our bakery to get everything for a caesar salad—the dressing, the croutons, the cheese, and vegetables—all as a package to take home and make for dinner. A bakery that was set up for it could diversify to provide all kinds of ready-to-go foods. It wouldn't put the product together completely but would provide items for the consumer to take home and finish. Another approach for some places has been to stock a limited line of grocery items, so the customer can pick up a loaf of bread, a quart of milk, and a jar of pickles, and the like. This would combine well with

Schat's Bakery and Deli at Friedman Bros.

1255A Airport Park Blvd.
Ukiah, CA 95482
(707) 468-5850

Lunch order for: _____

No. of Items ordered: _____

☐ **For Here**   ☐ **To Go**

Pick-up time: _____

We've Also Located In Downtown Ukiah Across From The Courthouse

See Reverse Side for Many Other House Specialties

Quick Breakfast Ideas *(Breakfast Served Until 11:00am Daily)*

☐ **Breakfast Burritos** $2.50
scrambled eggs, cheese, seasoned potatoes, with salsa on the side
Add your choice of meat:
☐ Ham   ☐ Sausage   ☐ Bacon or   ☐ Chorizo for .... 75¢

☐ **Filled Croissants** $1.95
fresh baked croissant filled with cheese and your choice of meat:
☐ Ham   ☐ Turkey
Add Scrambled Eggs inside for .... 80¢

☐ **Breakfast Tostada** $2.50
scrambled eggs, cheese, mild green chilis, with salsa on the side
Add your choice of meat:
☐ Ham   ☐ Sausage   ☐ Bacon or   ☐ Chorizo for .... 75¢

☐ **Breakfast Bagels** $1.50
Fresh bagel filled with scrambled eggs and melted cheese
Add your choice of meat: ☐ Ham ☐ Bacon or ☐ Chorizo for ... 75¢

Don't Forget Our Fresh Baked Goodies and Slices of Quiche!

Special Sandwiches

☐ **Check Out The Cold Case For Quick Grab Sandwiches**

☐ **2 X 4** $4.25
*Turkey, ham, pastrami, roast beef, jack & cheddar cheese, lettuce,
tomato, mayo & mustard served on a fresh multi-grain bread*

☐ **Sub-Contractor** $4.25
*thin sliced salami, ham, turkey, onions, olives, provolone cheese
tomatoes & lettuce with Italian pesto sauce served on a french
roll*

☐ **Tool Time Tuna** $3.95
fresh croissant with tuna tomatoes & sprouts

☐ **The Arc Welder** $4.00
*Louisiana hot sausage on a french roll heated with pepperoncinis
& jack cheese*

☐ **The Green House** $4.00
*avocado, sprouts, onion cucumber, tomatoes, spinach carrots &
jack cheese with special sauce on multi-grain bread*

☐ **1/2 Sandwich** $2.50

☐ **1/2 Sandwich** *with a bowl of soup or side salad* $4.75
with side caesar add .25¢

☐ **Friedman Bros. Classic** $4.25
*heated lean New York style pastrami topped with cool cole slaw
on a french roll with dijon mustard–Give it a try!*

Or... Build Your Own Sandwich

☐ **Full Sandwiches** $4.00
☐ **1/2 Sandwich** $2.50

Breads:	Meats:	Cheeses:
☐ Multi-Grain	☐ Turkey	☐ Cheddar
☐ Sliced Sourdough	☐ Ham	☐ Swiss
☐ French Roll	☐ Pastrami	☐ Jalapeno Jack
☐ Croissant (50¢)	☐ Roast Beef	☐ Smoky Cheddar
☐ Sour Rye	☐ Tuna	☐ Jack
☐ Sheepherders	☐ Salami	☐ Provolone
☐ Skquaw Bread		☐ Mozzarella

Condiments:	Fixer Uppers:
☐ Lettuce	☐ Carrots (35¢)
☐ Tomato	☐ Cucmbers (35¢)
☐ Mayonnaise	☐ Avocado (50¢)
☐ Mustard	☐ Pepperoncini (50¢)
☐ Dijon	☐ Sliced Jalepenos (50¢)
☐ Onion	
☐ Sprouts	
☐ Pickle	
	☐ Potato Salad ($1.25)

Lunch Specials

☐ **Special of the day** *(check the chalk board)*

_____

☐ **Pizza by The Slice** *with green salad* $3.50
☐ *with caesar salad* $3.75

☐ **Homemade Quiche** $4.95
with dinner roll and green salad ☐ *with side caesar add .25¢*

Large quiches made to order!

We Do Box Lunches For Large Get Togethers–Ask Us!

Our deli order sheet/menu works with a few changes at the home-improvement center shop.

ready-to-go food. We're unlikely to go into the grocery business, but it could work in the right location.

Nowadays you'll see good bakeries with sufficient shelf space sell their own preserves, or they may contract with somebody who makes them locally. While you wouldn't stock and sell just a commercial brand, you might know of someone with a small business or who makes food specialties at home but who lacks retail exposure and would be glad to let you provide it. In our area we can sell Mendocino Root Beer, for example. There are probably homegrown foods that define your region or your bakery's theme and have customer appeal. Then you can stock and sell any number of specialties as part of your retail business. You don't have to limit

MILLING WHEAT FLOUR

Until recently, wheat was ground between two large flat stones that revolved upon each other. Stone grinding is cooler and preserves most of the kernel's nutrients, but it provides no good way to separate the starchy endosperm from the bran and germ. While whole grain stores fairly well, whole-grain flours spoil quickly because the germ's fat content soon turns the flour rancid. Stone-ground flour has to be used quickly after milling.

Steel milling first strips off the grain's outer coatings and germ then crushes the starchy, glutinous endosperm with a complex system of successively reduced steel rollers. For a truly white flour some of the outer endosperm must be removed with the bran, so only about 70 percent of the wheat kernel becomes white flour. The bran usually accounts for 14 percent of the loss. The rest of it—the germ and remaining bran with endosperm attached—forms a byproduct called shorts. The wheat kernel's protein level decreases toward its center, so that the whitest flours contain the least gluten. The remaining gluten is better quality, however, and that is where the best baking flours are.

After being cleaned at the mill by washing or blowing, wheat grain is "scoured" to remove part of the outer coat by friction in a large cylinder with beaters that force the kernels against the casing while air streams blow away the bran fragments. To keep soft wheat from crumbling, it is tempered with steam or water after a few scourings. Milling begins by passing the wheat through the first "break rolls," which crack the kernel open to make granular semolina or middlings. This is sifted, and the coarse pieces proceed to a second break roll. There are at least five breaks, with successive rollers set closer and closer together. Sifters are flat, framed sieves of nylon or wire cloth—up to 26 of them—across which the meal travels from "head" to "tail." "Throughs" pass through the sieves, and what falls off the tail are "tailings." Sifting is also called "bolting."

To remove dirt and bran specks, the flour is finally treated in a "dresser" that removes coarse material and lumps. It may then be bleached. Flour will bleach naturally over time, but mills hasten the process with a variety of chemicals, including chlorine. Bleach chemicals destroy the vitamins in flour that the heat of milling has not already removed; by federal law they must then be replaced to enrich the flour artificially. Bleached flour is better for high-speed mechanical dough mixing, but otherwise bleaching is unnecessary. Some countries—notably France—prohibit it. The finished flour is then blended with flour from other wheats for a uniform product.

---

your stock to food items. My uncle sells blue Delft ware from Holland in his bakery in Bishop. He lines the whole bakery with it. It's attractive, it fits, and people buy it.

Diversification can involve looking for other outlets like mail order, chain stores, frozen food distribution. Except for mail order, however, all of that means getting into big business. Chain stores and frozen food distribution require having warehouses and freezer capacity. Frozen food is one of the toughest markets to crack. The mail-order business is an inviting possibility. The Cheesecake Lady, a bakery in Hopland twelve miles south of us, has built its success on very significant mail-order sales. Its business by mail is much greater than through its retail outlet, which enjoys a good tourist trade. We list two good books on running a mail-order business in the Appendix, in case it appeals to you later on. And here is a secret about doing business in an economically distressed region like ours. The companies that make the most money in it, and create jobs and taxes for it, use its cheap resources, including labor and rent, to sell outside it where the money is. It's called export. That's what tourist and mail-order businesses are built on. If you can capitalize on that secret, you will multiply the results of your efforts enormously.

No matter what market you pursue, however, always remember to take *all* the formal steps necessary—no matter whom you deal with—and be sure to have all the business systems in place before you expand. There was a terrific baker in the next county who had a frozen chocolate-chip cookie dough that she had every reason to expect would sweep the market. It involved a new way to cream the sugar and butter so that freezing the dough improved it dramatically. She took all the right steps to make it a big success by taking business courses at the local college, hiring design teams, getting local wholesale accounts, and retailing the cookies from a storefront. She worked as hard as you must to succeed, and business started to take off.

Then a family friend who wholesaled food offered to service her existing accounts and promote the cookies through a regional frozen-food warehouse. Since the frozen-food market is so tough to get into, she accepted and stepped up production. A few months later her old customers began to ask why she wasn't shipping cookies any more. Checking into it, she found that the family friend had done nothing to market her product or even to service her old accounts. All her existing business went down the drain and she went so deeply in debt that she had to wind up the company. Worst of all, there was no way to recover from the family friend because she did not have a written agreement with him. The lesson here is that it's critical at every stage of your venture to prepare carefully for expansion and never to omit the formalities for *any* reason.

If a new product or service takes off, the business may experience a snowball effect—not an unmixed blessing. You'll start catering for people you serve lunch to, or make ice cream in an annex, or roast coffee in the old store room. Until you coördinate all the parts, there will be growing pains, but in our experience they'll be worth it.

BRANCHING OUT AND EXPANDING

If your shop experiences explosive growth consider branching out or expanding the existing location. But be careful not to spread yourself too thin, especially within the same community. When we opened the new place, it was far enough away not to compete with the original shop and it had better parking. We got not only a new clientele but also many of the old customers we'd missed at the old place for lack of good parking. So it's worth considering your limitations as reasons to branch out. If you're busy but you could be

The next step—when we feel like we have maximized the capacity of the oven and our bakers—would be to create a whole second shift. We'd have to hire new bakers and train them, and they would start baking at 1:00 in the afternoon. It would be even harder to find someone willing to start baking at 11:00 at night and work a real graveyard shift. But short of building a new oven, those are the limiting factors. If you look at a 24-hour clock and say, okay, we're baking eight of those hours right now, we could triple what we do now but, we'd literally have three shifts baking around the clock. It's a little bit of a dance where you have to try to gauge the potential for expansion and get set up to expand before you can actually sell the extra bread.
—CHRISTOPHER KUMP
CAFE BEAUJOLAIS, THE BRICKERY

IN A BAKER'S GARDEN

Cooking and baking have always been important to Jacquie Lee; and flowers, herbs and produce fresh from the garden are central to her cooking and baking.

"I love gardens, I love vegetables, and I love to garden. When someone mentioned that you could put a garden here," she says of her shop, "I got hooked on this place. . . . Gardens go with food."

The bakery gets its strawberries, lettuce, and other seasonal produce from a grower in nearby Redwood Valley. The grower takes back the bakery's kitchen parings. "It's a cycle—which I love. He gets all our scraps, puts them in his compost pile, and grows us strawberries."

A graduate of the two-year culinary arts program under Kenneth Wolf at Contra Costa Community College, she worked as a sous-chef at Berkeley's Chez Panisse for four years and at Lily Lecocq's La Farine, a top-rated bakery in Oakland, California. Then she left to run a lodge in the Sierras. A brief spell of setting up kitchens for resort hotels after leaving the lodge took her eventually to Hopland, 12 miles south of the bakery's present location. For four years she baked in Hopland for Fetzer Vineyards.

"I like to use the best of ingredients—organic flour, imported chocolate, local produce. Everything we do here is made from scratch. I make the jam. We buy nothing packaged. . . . The only thing we use vegetable shortening in is the pie and tart dough, and that's five ounces of shortening to 25 ounces of butter to give the crust elasticity. That's how we use it. When you read the ingredient label on my bread it's flour, water and salt— and in some instances (not all) yeast. If you read the bread label at some places there are 20 things in it. It's sort of scary."

**The Garden Bakery
210 South Main Street
Ukiah, California**

Like many others of its size, the Garden Bakery serves a wholesale as well as retail market. "Fetzer Wines is a large account. . . . When they closed the tasting room on the highway, they moved it to where they are now [at Oak Valley Farms] and put in a nice deli. They buy baguettes from us and fougasse and focaccia. This morning they got cinnamon rolls and coffee cake and scones, enough to round out the day."

The bakery's garden is not only a pleasant setting for outdoor diners, but also provides fruits for jams and items like fresh fig tarts with pastry cream. "Kate Frey who put in the garden takes care of it. We took out 38 truckloads of stuff just to get down to where we could level it and lay the brick. And then we brought in five yards of mushroom compost for the garden. That's why everything likes it. We have some tomatoes coming up. They grow up on the trellis and they're like hanging berries. People like it and I like it. It's a nice little secret garden. Kate's the one who picked everything. I'll eventually finish that corner over there where the lattice is. It's always a matter of time and energy and finances."

About her work, she says, "The hours I keep are tiring, but I can't think of anything else I'd rather do. I also have talented people working for me who give me ideas and feedback. I could do better if I had a financial and business manager standing over me. But as far as the creative end goes I love to do it."

busier, what's holding you back? It could be a basis for deciding whether and where to open a new shop. A new location with ample parking, for example, may absorb your automotive overflow and perhaps relieve the first shop of too frenzied an atmosphere. Opening in a different community or neighborhood, also depends on the market's size, socioeconomic makeup, and consumption habits. You have to decide whether a customer base that wants your mix of products and services is there.

Another problem with opening a branch, if you're a small-time bakery like us, is transferring the original shop's atmosphere—those fresh-baked goods and the bustle of on-premises baking—to the new location. You may end up having all your production at the first location and taking it to the other one. An outlet or a satellite operation will lack the home shop's vitality when all the baking is done off-site. That doesn't mean it won't succeed. It's just that you have to anticipate the difference and adjust the new shop's operation and attractions to make up for the difference.

We would like to have expanded next door, but unfortunately the landlord's lease with an adjoining tenant, a small coffee shop, barred him from renting to another food establishment in that series of buildings. On the other hand, there is something appealing about a small, quaint shop that's busy all the time. By expanding you could lose that feeling. People might walk into the bigger premises during a slow time and feel they were in a huge bakery with nobody in it. If you do decide to expand, or need to, try to sense what more space will do for the mood of your place and hire a designer if necessary to make up for the greater size.

DRAWING THE LINE

Expansion and diversification can have other drawbacks. I spoke recently to my cousin who has a bakery in Mammoth Lakes, California. It's a 3,000-square-foot shop like ours but quite a bit fancier in a prosperous tourist area. He had just added another 3,000 square feet and put in a restaurant. He found that it was too much work to run both; so he sublet it to tenants who call the restaurant Café Vermeer. So far, so good, he tells me.

You'll find some of these principles for helping to decide about expansion or diversification scattered through the rest of the book. The main thing is to do what works best and most profitably, and not to become burdened with work you don't want. And, aside from that mandatory prior trip to the local public health department, there are no rules. Food service, which includes bakeries, is changing rapidly. Restaurants are hiring in-house bakers and bakeries are adding cafés and delis. What the business consists of, as noted in Chapter 1, is retail and/or wholesale manufacturing and service. Until fairly recently it was limited to baked goods, but the old definitions are out the window. It's your call and almost anything goes.

MONEY MATTERS

*Two things limit the Roman peo-
ple's anxious longings—bread
and the games of the circus.*
　　　　　　　　—Juvenal
　　　　　　　　SATIRES

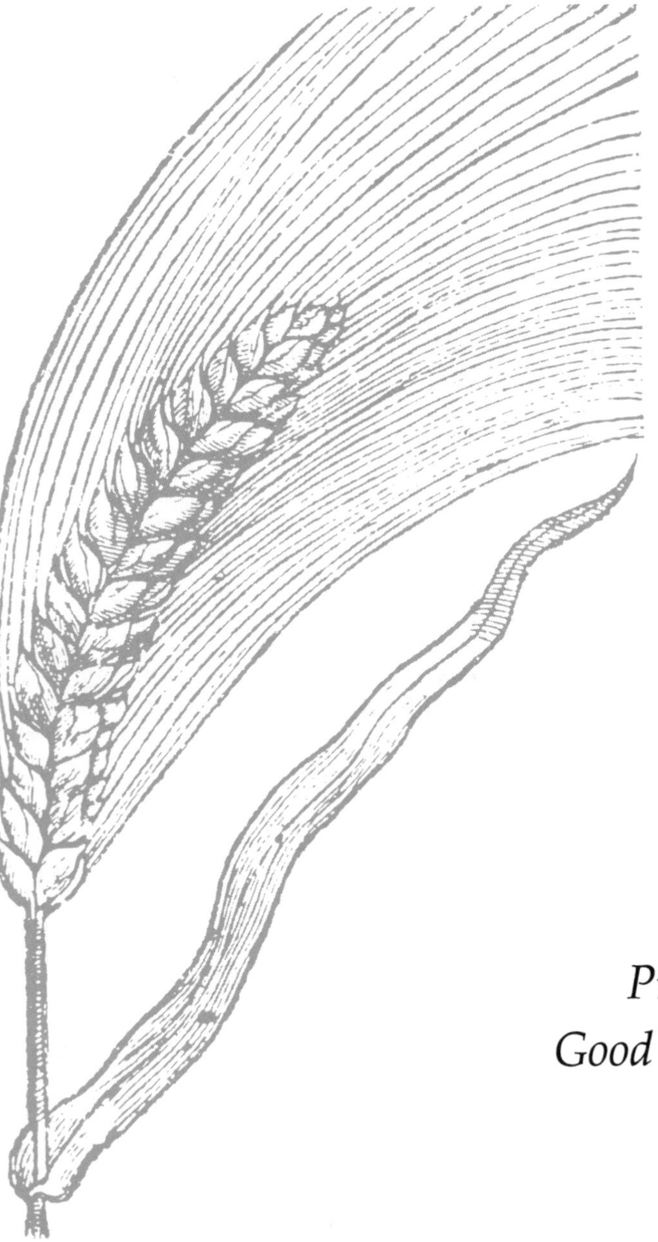

14

PRICES AND PROFIT

N O MATTER how much you sell day in and day out, if the prices of your bread, cakes, bagels, pastries, and so on don't cover their share of expenses—including a salary that puts bread on *your* table—your bakery will lose money and you'll have to pour more into it to keep it going. You don't want to do that, and you probably couldn't do it for very long if you chose to. So you'd better learn about pricing and make sure you price each item to cover costs and profit and to be competitive.

Having grown up in bakeries and never been far from the market, I use very little if any technical analysis to price our product. My pricing philosophy is simply to sell a good product at a fair price, and our prices seem to be roughly what the public will pay. After a while in the business, any baker will acquire a fairly automatic sense of pricing to the market and the bakery's needs. There are technical rules that control pricing and, consciously or not, you will follow the rules. Anyone can learn them. Three major ones are: Each item has to pay its way and meet the profit target; it has to be competitive within its market; and the price has to be adjusted fairly often.

First, competitive pricing means setting prices "at the market," or according to what the competition charges. Sometimes it's called charging "the going rate." You can learn the going rate pretty informally by dropping into a competitor's bakery to see what a bear claw or croissant brings. For example, if the same pastry is smaller and more expensive than yours, consider raising your prices. If the market won't pay much more than the competition already charges, no matter how big a bear claw you sell, you might make it a little smaller and raise the price a little, while still offering a better deal than the competition. Competitive prices should reflect not only size, but also the quality of the product. Quality includes not only how much better your bear claws are but also takes account of creative merchandising, product selection, management style and effectiveness, and so-called "customer-creation" strategies. Customer creation refers to any excitement you can generate to get paying customers into your shop. Variations from the market price also depend on special features such as customers' buying habits and differences in location or service.

Prices change, too. You'll have to price or re-price at the following times: when you introduce a new product or line; when you test for the best price; when you decide to develop a new market; when other bakeries change their prices; when there is inflation or deflation; or when you change your marketing strategy.

A good example of marketing strategy is "demand pricing." Demand pricing isn't really a pricing method but reflects the relationship of volume to costs and earnings. We all know that a greater volume lets you buy at lower costs and take a lower return per item. It's Price-Costco pricing versus the neighborhood hardware store's. It's what you'd do if you shifted to high-volume wholesale production or scaled back to an exclusive retail line. Aiming for a larger or smaller volume is perhaps the most obvious of the changes in marketing strategy that call for re-pricing your product. Differences in quality and product mix are more subtle strategies. They have a less obvious but just as real an impact on prices.

CALCULATING RAW COSTS

Before you can price your product you have to calculate its costs and cover them. Calculating raw costs for each item is the most detailed and lengthy but most accurate way to price. Since bakery products are merchandise manufactured by the baker, each product can be costed out to make a profit wholesale, retail, or both. If you sell to both markets, the important point is to keep your calculations for wholesale and retail pricing entirely separate.

Breaking Out Costs — The first of the raw costs to deal with are those of all the materials and other direct contributions, mainly labor. For us, payroll and ingredients are the two biggest costs. When we were small and I was more involved in production we managed to run a payroll of about 18 to 20 percent of gross. We had about a 30-percent profit margin. Now that we've gotten bigger our profit has shrunk and payroll has gone up. In this business payroll should be between 22 and 25 percent. We can't overemphasize that these industry averages are the best gauges of whether your costs and income are on track.

The next stage is to calculate overhead or indirect costs, which may or may not yield gross profit, depending on the formula you use. We'll get to the formulas in a minute. Remember that costs are either fixed or variable. Fixed costs—such as leases, loan repayments, cost recovery (depreciation), salaried employees, professional and janitorial services, and insurance—go on regardless of whether you do any work. Variable costs—such as wages, materials, freight charges, inventory, utilities, advertising and promotion, and delivery vehicle maintenance—increase and decrease depending on how busy you are. You also have to account for what you could call "frictional" or miscellaneous costs like over-production, stales, shoplifting, and other shrinkage, as well as seasonal business variations.

Once you have all the items' costs, you could multiply them by your pricing factor, or add your markup or profit margin. Prices must fall between break-even—enough to cover all costs and keep you solvent—and the most your market will pay. Again, remember

that your salary is *not* the profit; it's another expense. Profit is what you want the business to earn to compensate you for the risks of being in business. It gets socked away for expansion and modernization, against rainy days, or for your retirement. That means that to arrive at a price you must allow for a reasonable profit. Profit is adjustable down to zero, but you should aim for one that adequately compensates for risk—even if you have to go back and see where you can modify costs (while maintaining quality) in order to reach your target profit.

A Simple Instance — Here's an example of raw cost analysis. You would select a standard batch based on how many items of a certain size you usually make per batch, like six dozen danish fruit pockets. You would list all the materials and the amount of each material for the batch of fruit pockets. You would also consider what alternative production methods and comparable ingredients you can use. Sometimes an ingredient is unavailable or its price is noncompetitive. Next calculate the labor you need to make the six dozen pastries, including preparation and clean up time. That is, how much would you pay yourself or someone else to produce the batch? Be careful, because faulty labor costs can ruin you.

Estimate the portion of indirect costs to assign to the batch by adding up all your monthly overhead and dividing it by the hours per month you are open. Assigning variable costs as a part of overhead will require estimates based on your level of activity. Many, like labor vary directly with the product; you must estimate others. Next, multiply the hourly overhead by the batch's production time. At that point you have the cost for the entire batch of six dozen and can estimate how much to price each item. Just divide by 72 and apply your pricing factor or profit margin, or top the result with your standard markup. Since bakeries traditionally sell many items by the dozen, you might divide by the number of dozens to reach a fair markup for a dozen of the item. The price of singles would then be less closely related to your markup calculations, but if you sell enough singles at a competitive rate, it could let you lower your markup on dozens.

Sometimes the costing formula shows you can't produce an item to sell at a competitive price. Then you might think about modifying costs or adjusting your profit. That is, is the item so high-priced that you can still make a good return on a lower per-item profit? Sometimes you can analyze and adjust production techniques. A baker in Los Angeles managed to cut the cost of making chocolate chip cookies without affecting their quality by slicing the dough from a pre-chilled log, rather than dropping it with a scoop. When the price of vanilla went out of sight, he found rum was a good substitute for some items.

A retirement community may sound like a good market but that's deceptive; it's probably an average community. A lot of retired people don't have a whole lot of money. That's why they moved to some little town somewhere. They knew their fixed income was going to go farther there than it would in San Francisco.
—KEN MOORE
MOORE'S FLOUR MILL, BAKERY
& DELI

Raw Costs in Perspective — Whether you produce for retail or wholesale, you still have to cost out labor, materials, and overhead, then figure profit. Generally, the only costing difference for wholesale and retail is that the per-unit profit will be lower than for retail production, so your costs and prices must be lower. But the method doesn't change, and either way the price must support your business and be competitive.

Prices for everything change all the time. Theoretically, a change in the price of any ingredient would require a complete revision of your cost estimate per item. The rule of thumb for price changes has been to review costs of materials and labor about every six months or so, and adjust prices if necessary. Don't get stuck on six-month changes. The main thing is to increase prices gradually in frequent small steps. And don't hesitate to raise prices when the alternative is to lower quality. You could introduce a lower-priced item to pick up lost sales of more expensive items, but definitely maintain the quality of what you sell.

As we said, raw cost analysis is the most detailed and lengthy way to calculate price, and you may find that a few shortcut methods will get you close enough to the mark. After a while you may rely more on a feel for the market than a rigorous cost analysis. This is one place where you could even tolerate a shortcut as long as it keeps the business profitable. Before you get too far along in your pricing methods and too cozy with shortcuts, however, start thinking about using computer programs to work out prices for you. Once you key in the raw costs, analysis is a snap, and you could probably use the computer to price to the penny every day if you thought it would help. We will go over a few of the popular bakery computer programs at the end of the chapter.

COST + PROFIT = PRICE

Common pricing methods add profit by factoring, cost-plus, markup, and margin. All of them take into account your cost of materials and labor, but all of them do not initially include overhead figures in the formula. "Factoring" applies a standard multiplier to costs but not usually overhead, as when, for example, you sell a loaf of bread for 2.5 times cost. You can apply the factor to your final unit price or to the batch price, which you would then divide by the number of items. You might apply the same factor to most of your standard products but not to a very rich cake, because the price could wind up out of sight by multiplying its costs two and a half times.

Cost Plus — "Cost-plus" pricing covers all your costs, including overhead. Profit—say you want 15 percent—is the "plus." Here is an easy example:

Cost of materials	$0.60	
Cost of labor	0.45	
Other overhead	0.25	
Total cost	$1.30	
Plus desired net profit of 15%:	0.20	
Required sale price:	$1.50	

MARKUP AND MARGIN

Cost-plus pricing uses a profit markup. You will hear talk about "markup" and "margin." These are simple but easily confused notions. The difference between markup and margin is the same as the difference between a number *added to* 100 percent of costs (markup) and the same number viewed as a *portion of* their sum (margin). If you add 25 percent (the markup) to 100 percent, you get 125 percent. When you extract the last 25 percent (as a margin) from the 125 percent, you're considering one-fifth or 20 percent of it. Similarly, by adding a 25 percent *markup* to an item that costs $1.00, in order to sell it at $1.25, you have a 20 percent *margin*. Consider them "before and after the price" terms. Here's a simple example but one worth getting down pat:

Cost:	$1.00	100%
Markup:	.25	25% (before, i.e., 25¢ ÷ $1.00)
Price:	$1.25	
Less cost:	1.00	
Margin:	$ .25	20% (after, i.e., 25¢ ÷ $1.25)

This is a fairly simple relationship but it can tie you up in arithmetical knots. Books on small-business management often provide tables that correlate markup and margin percentages. You can find them in basic texts. It never hurts to get familiar with these terms and relations because somebody is always asking you, What's your markup? What's your margin? You might want to work through a few examples to give you an idea of your markup and margin.

Usually, "markup" pricing is based on cost of goods without calculating overhead costs. If you find that a 40 percent markup on the labor and materials for all your baked goods gives you a good enough return, you would charge $1.40 for a baguette that costs you $1.00 in materials.

A "cost of goods sold" calculation gives you a "gross margin" after you subtract the total cost from total sales. Cost of goods sold is sometimes called "cost of sales." Cost of goods refers to material and labor costs but not operating expenses. Accountants include freight charges in cost of goods sold and they like the formula because it lets them—and you—compare gross profit margin with the cost of the raw goods. That cost should fall within a narrow margin for any industry, including bakeries. Here's another simple example:

Total goods sold:	$1,000
Cost of goods:	425
Margin:	$ 575

This margin is your Gross Profit Margin sometimes called your "gross." The gross doesn't mean much unless you live and work in a magical kingdom with no operating expenses. None of us do. In the above example, your margin or gross would be $575 ÷ $1,000 (57.5 percent). Your net profit, or simply "net," is what matters, and net depends on operating expenses. (Watch out.) Now that you have a gross you can compute your net:

Shop	No. 1	No. 2
Sales:	100%	100%
Cost of Goods (or Sales):	57.5	60
Gross Profit Margin:	42.5	40
Operating Expenses:	25	20
Net Profit:	17.5%	20%

Breaking out the net can show how important it is to hold down operating expenses. Remember that it is easier to use a standard markup for all your goods as a way to assure that you will cover costs and profits than to cost out and price each item individually. As mentioned earlier, standard markups won't work for very expensive or very cheap products, but they are fine for the majority of goods you bake.

REAL-LIFE PRICING

There are a few real-life benchmarks to watch when pricing. You need to bring the price into line with a living wage. You need to create a product mix with a range of popular high- to low-priced items, and build a pricing structure on it. Customers must buy your product for quality, and be willing and able to pay for it. Ideally, you would consider all the above tools and theories when pricing— demand, raw cost analysis, cost-plus, factoring, markup and margin, and cost of goods sold—whenever you introduced a new product. You would never forget labor costs and competition prices. You would re-price about every six months, and your prices would always be fair to yourself and your customers. Doing all this in real life this would never leave you any time for baking, and no one would ever open a bakery. I wouldn't. But today you can actually do all or most of these calculations with the computer programs we referred to above and will discuss below.

PRICES AS A START-UP TOOL

As stated in Chapter 5 on start-up finances, once you know your product mix, costs, and prices, you can figure how much of each item you have to sell for the year to break even and make a profit. That much is straight math. Creating a product mix, based on your expected market, is as much a part of the formula as calculating prices, and, as noted, finding the right mix is a matter of trial and error once you open your doors. Still, you have to decide on the most likely items before you start and have enough flexibility from then on to shift with the market.

In making an annual projection you can't count on the same output every day. There's a little less science than art in deciding how much to make each day. You never know how many people will come in tomorrow, but you have to develop a feel for it and make a guess, especially when you serve fresh items every day. Shelf-life is short. If we anticipate a slow day, such as the day after a holiday—or a on "semi-holiday" like President's Day should we decide to open—we'll cut the bake by a third or a half.

If you have a café or deli, one more variable to toss into your projection is the number of tables you have and the daily number of anticipated customers per table. You have to isolate these sales from walk-in bakery sales but you must also estimate how many diners will take home a loaf of bread or a pastry. You project weekly, monthly and yearly gross, as follows. With 20 tables that are used five times a day, for example, each table producing $7.50 in sales per turn (but an average 75¢ of which may be take-out bakery sales), you would estimate income as follows: 20 tables x 5 turns/day x $6.75/turn = $675/day; $675 x 6 days/week = $4,050; $4,050 x 52 weeks = $210,600 yearly gross. You could include diners' take-out sales in these calculations. Just don't count them twice.

GOOD BUY, MR. SILICON CHIPS

If you do your homework and estimate conservatively, you'll be able to project how solid a business your bakery can be. That can be hard work, but with the right tools you can do it. Those tools are a computer and the right software. Every business in the country these days, no matter how small, can almost certainly run better with a computer. In fact, the smaller you are the more you will probably need a computer to stay competitive. If you don't use one now, just grit your teeth, get one, and learn to use it. It isn't that hard. A computer with a good printer will handle your faxes and

Over the last six or seven years I've seen bakeries start because someone will say, Oh, it's a great recipe, you should do it. Within a year or two they're not around anymore. A handful will survive. They do a good product, they're consistent, and build an enduring company. Robin [The Cheesecake Lady] had started her first bakery in Philadelphia. It didn't survive but it was a very valuable lesson in the business side. She made great cheesecake, one of the best in Philadelphia, PHILADELPHIA MAGAZINE said, but the important lesson was she also had to run a business. If a restaurant calls up, it doesn't make sense to put one cake in the oven and run it over to the restaurant. You need to know how much the cake is costing you and how much it will earn.

—PAUL LEVITAN
THE CHEESECAKE LADY

correspondence. It will keep all your accounts. With new desktop publishing programs it will make up good looking menus and flyers even if your talents do not lie in that direction. And it will manage the bakery's inventory, prices, ordering, and recipes through specialized programs for retail and wholesale operations.

Several companies publish business software for bakeries. You can contact any of them and request their demonstration disks (demos). The demos are easy to run. Usually you just slide them into the floppy drive, switch to that drive, type "demo," and keep pressing one key to get a "slide show" of the system. They will show you an able and agreeable partner that won't make any mistakes (unless you do). They will also show that you don't need much experience to run a computer.

*Baker's Choice** software was developed in 1988 as a productivity and costing tool for large supermarkets. It was modified to include production planning, accounting, nutrition analysis, and label printing for scratch bakeries and bake-off shops, whether retail or wholesale and whether in-store or centralized. The demo disk is a limited duplicate of the actual program to let you try before you buy. The system, which listed for about $200 when we went to press, has an inventory control module for any number of ingredients, and lets you key in formulas, labor, overhead, and packaging items. You can write formulas from inventory items, and each formula can be used within other formulas. The program permits formula and product costing, as well as a "what if" analysis of retail prices based on desired gross profit margins, sales and discount pricing, and other marketing decisions. It will generate a detailed profit and loss report, with percent-of-sales analysis. It permits planning production for any specific day, by showing products on order, and reducing inventory as you use up on-hand items.

The nutrition add-on, including a Vendor Nutrition Library, can calculate a USDA nutrition analysis of every ingredient used in a product, including those you key in, and can print the product's label with nutritional facts so they comply with the Federal Nutrition Labeling and Education Act (FNLEA) on a specialized adhesive-label printer. The printers run from $1,000 to $2,000. The accounting add-on is an order-entry and billing system that tracks customers' orders and account balances, compiles sales histories, and prints a variety of reports to help control cash flow. It does not appear to interface with stand-alone accounting software. The *Baker's Choice* manual listed for $29. There was an annual technical support fee of

* Computer Services Co., 2602 West Silver Spring Drive, Milwaukee, WI 53209-4220; telephone (414) 461-6006, fax, (414) 461-6912.

$200 and with options available, including an Internet Web Page ad for $100 per quarter.

The *Datapax Bakery & Food Processing System** offers a basic module for wholesale and retail bakeries free of charge. It charges for any add-on modules you select. A password option provides security against unauthorized users in order to protect secret recipes and formulas. The modules let you configure the system to a wide range of retail and wholesale operations.

The basic module lets you enter information for up to 1,000 more ingredients than are already in the system. Ingredients would include such made-in-house items as doughs and creams. Formula management, product specifications, and labor and overhead, let you cost out formulas and products, then estimate optimum prices. All ingredients can be priced and quantified for inventory. Recipes you enter in the program automatically offer alternate measures for conversion, and you can scale a recipe or formula for any number of items. The system lets you list up to 5,000 finished products. It will calculate cost to produce from primary or secondary recipes and check the effect of new supply costs. It keys price increases and decreases with up and down arrows, and you can run a what-if analysis for the effect of any changes on all products' costs. It adds packaging costs and services like slicing and bagging. Finally, you can compute prices for your required profit margins.

The retail module permits production and purchasing control, inventory control, and profitability reports. It helps manage retail order taking, it gives a sales/production history, analysis, and forecast, and it lets you analyze stales and overall profitability. It can network the host and remote computers with the cash register, work stations and the printer. Its point-of-sale cash-register segment can be programmed with special functions, including bar-code reading. Another option is a custom-cake module that reminds you of anniversaries, suggests a price based on ingredients, and computes the number of servings per cake. It can retrieve customer information by telephone number and save it to a diary. Yet more options include mail orders, thermal label printing, and nutritional analysis. It interfaces with advanced stand-alone accounting software and at time of printing was to work with *QuickBooks Pro,* but not yet with other popular bookkeeping software as of our publication date.

You can prepare production schedules based on customer orders. The system will print a bake sheet and add finished products to inventory, as it enters reductions in the ingredient list and tips you off

---

*　Datapax, Inc., 5125 North 16th Street, Suite A210, Phoenix, AZ 85016; (602) 274-1321; fax, (602) 274-1476.

COMMERCIAL BREAD BY THE "CONTINUOUS" METHOD

Until about 40 years ago, breads from large commercial bakeries were started by kneading either a very wet mixture called a "sponge" or a fully mixed dough in horizontal dough mixers that processed about 2,000 pounds at a time. Subsequent steps copied hand baking on a much larger scale. Commercial baking was not fully automated until introduction of the "continuous mix" system in about 1955. This method cut out workers who trundled troughs of dough between mixers, proofing areas, and rounder-dividers. A continuous mix machine runs without interruption and adds ingredients by reading the baker's formula into a controller that injects each ingredient at various stages of the process.

Most of the flavor in continuous-mix breads comes from a pre-fermentation brew—the "broth" or "liquid sponge"—which contains water, yeast, sugar, flour and other ingredients such as skim milk powder, oils, and yeast foods. These are fermented for few hours before being thickened into the dough. Oxidizers such as potassium iodate and (more rarely today) potassium bromate may be added because the process is low on oxygen. To speed fermentation, dough conditioners based on whey and cystine (an animal protein derivative) may feed the mix.

The fermented broth eventually flows to a "developer" that kneads the thickening dough to get the right gluten structure and gas-retentiveness. The process may aerate the dough, while the yeast merely flavors it—hence the term "balloon bread." Developers can process 100 pounds of mix every 90 seconds, changing the batter from a soup to a smooth, elastic dough. The dough then moves to a metering device that extrudes it and chops off loaf-sized pieces into passing pans. Following a brief pan-proof the product is baked. Continuous-mix bread has a small grained texture and a very uniform look. Its blander flavor seems to have had little effect on sales. Nutritionist Dr. Jean Mayer once referred to slices of it as "edible napkins."

to any low stocks. Then it saves all this information for daily and periodic reports and, to help restock, it automatically prepares purchase orders from the data. It assists in periodic physical inventory of finished products, add-ons, and records stales for comparison with cash-register sales. It keeps recipe and product maintenance records and you can adjust them to raise production and profitability. This is a very flexible and powerful program. The modules are not cheap, but once you get familiar with the basic program, you can judge whether to buy them or not. The free basic system may be enough.

SweetWARE* offers two modules called its *stockCoster* for inventory control, and *nutraCoster* for formula costing and nutrition analysis. By entering formulas with each ingredient's purchase cost into *nutracoster*, the program calculates the product cost, including labor, and nutrition content for any size batch. Recipes can be expressed

---

*   SweetWARE, 1906B Alameda Avenue, Alameda, CA 94501; (510)814-8800; fax (510) 814-8844; order number, (800) 526-7900.

as an ingredient in other recipes, so that batters and doughs can be calculated in more than one product. Recipes can be scaled to calculate ingredient and cost requirements for any sized batch. Instructions of any length can be entered for each process step, and you can account for moisture loss and other production shrinkage.

The system lets you work out labor costs by breaking production into individual steps. Set-up time is constant for any size batch and assembly time is proportional to size. You assign one or more workers to each step, assign each worker to a class, and assign a labor cost to each class.

nutraCoster comes with an ingredient database of nutrition information for some 4,000 ingredients, with optional ingredient libraries available that are keyed to name brand products from hundreds of companies, and you can add any amount of ingredients into the database. The program then calculates nutrition content for each product and will print nutrition labels that comply with the FNLEA. The labels can be printed on a laser printer and, if you use the Windows version, viewed on screen. The program generates reports including labor and materials per batch, gross margin or target selling price for each product. It notes products that deviate from the target cost, where ingredients are used, lists of recipes, and the nutrition content for any size batch.

You can use *stockCoster* as a perpetual inventory control system. Your available hard disk space is the only limit on how many ingredients, finished products, and transactions you can enter. It removes ingredients from stock based on *nutraCoster* formula use, adds completed production to stock, and removes sold or shipped products from stock. It also tracks ingredients' and finished products' shelf life, and calculates the cost of expired items. It identifies shortages, warns which must be reordered, and prints lists sorted by stock location. Reports include quotes for items from vendors and a history of vendor prices that lists which vendors supply each item. It costs out stock on hand using actual cost, last cost, average cost, and standard cost. It reports on any item's inventory and production requirement history for any period, and an inventory aging report that warns if ingredients or products have expired or will expire soon. It will also print lists of vendors, vendors for each item, quotes for selected items, and quotes from vendors.

Both *nutraCoster* and *stockCoster* run on DOS or Windows and come with unlimited toll-call telephone support. They are priced at $149 and $99 at press time, with a free 45-day trial period. Four considerations should control what software you use: (1) how complex a system you need, (2) what kind of return the software investment helps you generate, (3) how easy the program is to use, and (4) price. You can't tell which has the best payback without careful comparison. Sometime in the year before start-up, when you

UNIMAGINED FREEDOM

The ready smile of doughnut maker Sunny Poeng would never reveal his traumatic start in life nor his journey to settle in a small town in rural Northern California. Poeng, 39, and his wife, Lynn, 37, are celebrating their 10th year in the doughnut business.

The Poengs, refugees from Cambodia, met and were married while in a United Nations Red Cross refugee camp in Thailand for a year and a half. Sunny had escaped Cambodia twice, only to be caught by Thai soldiers and returned. In his successful third attempt over a mountain he survived on water and watched others ahead and beside him being blown apart by land mines. "That time in my life seems a million years ago. When crossing the mine fields, I would watch where people put their feet and try to put mine exactly where they had put theirs. . . . Each time I was caught trying to escape it only made me stronger to want to try again to leave."

"To us America meant freedom. . . . Being here is more than I could imagine freedom meant."

The couple has worked hard since coming to America in the early 1980s. Their first stop was Bridgeport, Connecticut. Jobs for people who didn't speak English paid only the minimum wage. When they finally saved enough to buy a house, Sunny decided to travel to Southern California where a friend invited

Sunny's Donuts
628 South State Street
Ukiah, California

him to come learn how to make doughnuts. He decided not to return to Connecticut and moved his family to Los Angeles. They bought a house and six months later were able to sell it at a profit when the city chose to build on the site. Investigating business farther north, they settled in Ukiah in 1987, with their first doughnut store. Two years later they sold it to acquire one closer to the central business district and moved it to its present location across from the Safeway and near the movie theater.

Work goes on six days and nights a week. The couple takes Sundays off and attends First Presbyterian Church, where they donate doughnuts every week for the church's coffee hour. They also give leftover doughnuts to Plowshares Monday through Friday. Sunny starts making yeast dough about 10:30 p.m. Then he starts in on the old-fashioned and cake doughnut mixes. He makes about 70 apple fritters and about 100 dozen of all kinds of doughnuts a night, using about 50 pounds of flour and 50 pounds of sugar to do it.

"My favorite thing to make is apple fritters," he laughs, "because chop, chop, chop—it helps to energize me and keep me awake." The work requires non-stop movement. He is economical in every step and movement, not wasting a moment. His kitchen is clean as a whistle and he's never been "red tagged" by the health department. "I like everything to be clean all the time so I never have a problem with inspectors."

"I want my children to have higher education. I want them to be good children. I remind them when we're together about my past, and how I didn't have food. I want them to be thankful to the Lord for His blessings, for His bringing us to this country, and for the health God has blessed us with so we could work hard."

—Carole Hester
THE UKIAH DAILY JOURNAL

have more time and can write off expenses, you should get the computer you need and take the production software for a spin. Ask each publisher if it can refer you to current users for their experience with the programs. That's the time to figure what cost savings each program will generate, regardless of price. It may even assist you in setting up a business plan.

ABOUT COMPUTERS

And while we are on computers, here are a few personal observations for what they're worth. First, get a PC—the Windows/Intel kind. Business is dominated by PCs. Apple Macintoshes are getting squeezed and there isn't as much software for them. None of the above programs run on a Mac. Computer prices are all over the map, mostly highly discounted. The cheapest are sold mail-order but you usually won't get technical support beyond what comes over the telephone line. You need hands-on technical support. Go to a business computer store; you don't need the multimedia frills. You will pay more than you would mail-order, but, with a good service contract, computer down-time won't tie up your business as long.

Walter Mossberg wrote some reliable specs in the *Wall Street Journal* in April 1997 for a computer that he predicted wouldn't become a horse and buggy in the next three years. First, you'll want at least a 166-Mhz processor chip. Current programs are memory hogs and new ones probably won't be on diets. So you should have 16 megabytes of random access memory—RAM, the temporary kind that turns on and off with the machine. Even better, pay for an extra 16 and get 32 megabytes of RAM. Your hard disk should be at least the 2-gigabyte size, larger if you can afford it.

Many programs come on CD-ROMs, and you can get by with an 8X drive, which runs eight times faster than the original drives. The computer's internal video circuit should have two megabytes of video memory. A bigger monitor is easier on the eyes if more expensive. Get a non-interlaced screen, with no greater than a .28mm dot pitch. Smaller is better here.

Cache memory is where parts of your programs are shunted temporarily during operation; the larger the cache, the faster the program runs. Get 512k (512 kilobytes) of "burst cache" memory.

You will need a modem to fax things or use the Internet. Get one that runs at 33.6 kilobits per second and can be upgraded to a new 56-kilobit standard. There are two incompatible 56-kilobit standards, so make sure yours works with your on-line or Internet provider. Computers in April 1997 were only mediocre answering machines or stereo systems. Mossberg suggested forgetting that and installing a couple of the new "USB" ports which make it easier to connect peripheral equipment to the computer. And even though the writer gave these standards a three-year life expectancy, like everything in print about computers it was all out of date as soon as Mossberg's ink dried. Still, we hope it provides a starting point or a basis for finding a good used model.

A good computer should cost about $2,000. If you shop around and stick to the essentials, you might find one for less. It's like going to a new car sales room. Don't let the salespeople push you into glitzy add-ons. Set up your computer in as a clean spot as you have; dust and grime are its mortal foes.

To find local technical support, talk to every business person you know. If you have to look in the Yellow Pages for computer consultants or suppliers, ask them for references. Talk to all of the references and ask embarrassing questions. Are they satisfied with prices and service? Did they switch from a service they were dissatisfied with? Which one? How reliable and prompt is the service? How good is it? If the service also sells computers, is there a good choice of equipment and software? How about mixing and matching with non-house brands? Is the service more interested in selling high-priced equipment and software than getting its customers the best deal? Does the service provider speak your language or computerese? Is the provider intimidating? If this service quit business tomorrow, could another firm take over the contract without any changes in your equipment?

Buy a name brand such as Hewlett-Packard, IBM, Compaq or Dell. They have good reputations for support and the companies will probably be around long after the local guys who make the supercharged dirt-track models have folded their tents and departed.

These days printers of choice are laser printers and ink bubble printers. They put out products of roughly equal quality, but bubble-printer ink is water soluble, has to dry, and will run if it gets wet. If those are problems, you may want to spend more for a laser printer. Make sure your computer technical-support team can service your printer.

15

RECORDS, BUDGETS, TAXES

HIGH on your start-up priority list should be: Who will your book-keeping and tax professional be and how will that person want you to keep your records? Before you open your doors or even think about your books, you should set up an initial consultation with the accountant or bookkeeper you found as recommended in Chapter 6. Your books are a job that absolutely requires professional assistance. You should deal only with the raw numbers while your professional refines them and gets you your best tax deal. When we started this bakery I knew no more about bookkeeping than what my dad's wife told me. Then my first bookkeeper took over most of the work and gave me a cash-report form that is still the heart of our system. It was one of the best start-up bargains we made. I recommend a pre-opening meeting with your numbers person, because it makes both your jobs easier right from the start.

Your bookkeeper or accountant can set up accounts receivable to ease your cash flow and set up accounts payable to let you benefit from any early-payment savings. He or she may give you a tax payment calendar and establish a separate tax account in which to keep tax payments, so you don't invade them for everyday expenses. And you will get monthly reports that give you a clear idea of the business's financial health. That initial consultation is the best and cheapest way to organize your record-keeping, to learn all your tax responsibilities, and to profit from tax planning—all before you ever take a pan out of the oven.

Even if a bookkeeper or accountant handles your books, however, you should know how to interpret and, if necessary, do them yourself. Unless you understand and stay up on the books, your business's financial health will be a total mystery and you'll have to rely entirely on your professional to explain the numbers.

This chapter won't go into detail on keeping your records and doing your taxes. That's why there are no illustrations of sample balance sheets and journal pages, or any introduction to individual, partnership, and corporate taxes here. If you wanted to learn how to manage your own records, you would need a whole separate book to learn it well. Fortunately, the book already exists. There is no better or enjoyable way to learn about bookkeeping and taxes than from Bernard Kamoroff's *Small Time Operator*. Kamoroff is a certified public accountant with a great sense of humor whose book is in its fifth edition. It will repay its $18.95 purchase price many times over. If you don't already know about bookkeeping, you will find his book the easiest and most readable introduction on the market to the intricacies of small-business financial management and income taxes. If nothing else, it is the best way to help you understand the tables and analyses you will need for a good business plan. You *could* use it to learn how to do your own books—but you could never do them as well as a hired professional without taking hours away from your primary job, which is to juggle everything else necessary to run a successful bakery.

Once *Small Time Operator* teaches you the basic skills, you should still go out and hire the best number cruncher you can find. The book will at least help you judge who will serve your needs best and let you explain exactly what you want. You will also always know what your expert is up to, and bookkeeping won't cut into production, management, and sales time more than necessary.

Keep your part of the books as simple as possible and limit them to just the records you need. We restrict ours to a few essentials: the daily sales or cash report for each place, the payroll, and ordering. Those three things keep us on top of the bakery's cash-flow. Turning the numbers into meaningful reports and figuring the government's share are the accountant's or bookkeeper's jobs.

If you acquired a computer, and we recommend it, you could check about running a bookkeeping program on it such as *Quickbooks, MYOB, One Write Plus, Peachtree Accounting* or whatever your bookkeeper or accountant recommends. I know of a very good bookkeeper in the next county who uses *QuickBooks Pro* to handle all of his business-clients' accounts. One limitation is that bakery management programs, if you use one, won't interface with every home-computer oriented accounting program. Datapax reported that its program would soon interface with the new version of *Quick-Books Pro*. At this date we aren't sure what other simple bookkeeping programs it or the other bakery-software companies plan to work with. If you let a professional do your books, an accounting program on your computer might serve only as a daily reminder and you may not need it. So think it over.

Diane has got our receivables tightened up. That was a big problem. When I went into this I didn't have any real firm commitments from people about when they were going to pay. We've been stung a few times. We deal with these health food stores. They're the people I like to deal with, but boy they don't have much money. They go out of business, and there we are holding the bag. Once you get in with the big outfits, like Safeway and Raley's, and once you lean on them enough and you get into their system where they've got to pay you every two weeks, or whatever, you can count on them. You don't have to worry about it after that.

—BRUCE HERING
BRUCE BREAD

```
┌────────────────────────────────────────────────────────────────┐
│                                                                  │
│             SCHAT'S Courthouse Bakery and Cafe                   │
│                     113 West Perkins                             │
│                   Ukiah, California 95482                        │
│                                                                  │
│                                                                  │
│                   DAILY CASH REPORT                              │
│                                                                  │
│      DATE: _____                                        │
│      SALES (Cash Register Total)              $_____        │
│      LESS OVERRINGS                          ($_____ )      │
│      NET SALES                                $_____        │
│                                                                  │
│      CASH PAID OUTS                                              │
│                                                                  │
│      _____   $_____                      │
│      _____   $_____                      │
│      _____   $_____                      │
│      _____   $_____                      │
│      _____   $_____                      │
│      _____   $_____                      │
│      _____   $_____                      │
│      _____   $_____                      │
│      LESS TOTAL CASH PAID OUTS               ($_____ )      │
│      NET CASH                                 $_____        │
│                                                                  │
│      CASH DEPOSIT TO BANK                     $_____        │
│      CASH (OVER/SHORT)                        $_____        │
│      TAX RESERVE                              $_____        │
│                                                                  │
└────────────────────────────────────────────────────────────────┘
```

Our daily cash report.

THE DAILIES

The daily cash report—our "journal"—consists of the gross amount of cash and checks that we take in for the day, less any cash register over-rings and any purchases that we might have paid out of the till. They are all on the tape. For example, we pay all our dairy bills in cash every day. We pay our produce in cash every day. Then we review the gross, minus the over-rings and purchases, and come up with net cash for the day. By counting the money in the till for the day we can compare the two to see if we're over or under, which is how to keep track of the daily cash flow.

By comparing everything on the tape we can also see the number of over-rings and where they show up on the tape. Our counter staff keeps track of over-rings for the day and writes down things like, "I had to return $5.50 because the customer changed his mind on a sandwich." We don't want a $60 over-ring without an explanation. If someone rang in $60 wrong, we want to know who does it. If they do it over and over again, we need to talk about it.

Even the limited bookkeeping we do tends to be an unwelcome extra on top of everything else. When you get busy with the daily routine of running the bakery, the simplest approach is to do only the daily cash reports and get back a complete monthly report from outside. It's easiest to track daily income and expenses, take care of the bill paying and payroll, and then send out the monthly receipts and payroll generated on the computer. Your accountant or bookkeeper can then break down all the month's figures as percentages —the percentage that goes to payroll, to cost of goods, for insurance, and so on.

Pay attention to the industry ratios the accountant furnishes for comparing with your percentages. It's a quick way to judge how well the bakery is doing. The industry averages let you review your percentages at the end of the month to see if something is wrong. For example, your costs may be too high or someone might be stealing supplies. You would run a cost check and look for back-door losses.

TAXES AND TAX PLANNING

Another reason to see your bookkeeper/accountant before opening is to learn everything you can about advance tax planning. You have to identify self-employment tax, payroll withholding tax, unemployment tax, sales tax, quarterly estimated income tax, and more. The timing of many tax bills is based on a minimum level of business. For example, the federal deposit for payroll tax is due quarterly if you have less than $5,000 payroll a month. It is due monthly on the 15th if you have more payroll than $5,000 a month. Those are the kind of dates you should be aware of, and they exist for taxes at all levels of government from a score of different agencies on each level. That's what your bookkeeper or accountant should take care of for you. Our first accountant was almost a mother figure. If payroll taxes were due on the 15th, she'd call up on the 14th, Did you pay your payroll tax? She'd call up on the 15th, Did you pay your payroll tax? You could have those dates on a calendar, although they are sure to depress you. Your accountant also keeps track of any tax estimates and any payments or reports you need to submit.

As a retailer you have to collect and send in sales taxes from customers, and as an employer forward payroll taxes for employees. Many business people set up a separate tax account and keep their hands off it. The last line of our cash flow form reads Tax Reserve or Tax Collected for the day. If it's $35, we'll make a separate $35 deposit into the tax account. We do the same for payroll. Our gross payroll for one month may be $8,000. By the time we take out everybody's deductions we actually pay out $6,206. Payroll taxes account for the other $1,794. If we write a check for $1,794 and put it in a tax account each month, then on the 15th when we have to pay the payroll tax the money will be there.

Leaving that money in the business's general account is an invitation to start spending it. We all like to think we're disciplined enough to manage without spending funds withheld for taxes; but, if that $1,794 of tax money gets into the general account, we will use it when the cash flow is tight and bills are due or overdue. Then we'll worry about how to pay our taxes. Do not ever get behind on payroll taxes! Even if you go out of business and declare bankruptcy, they will not disappear but will follow you for the rest of your life.

There's one more thing. If our payroll withholding tax is $1,794 for the month, as an employer we have to match it and pay the government $3,588 on the 15th of each month. Your policy must be to deposit the whole $3,588 into the tax account. The accountant can then come up with how much you owe as your share of the payroll tax in addition to what you've withheld from the payroll. It's the best reminder that you don't just pay $10 an hour to get a $10-an-hour employee. Each employee costs $10 an hour plus the percentage of payroll taxes, workers' compensation, retirement benefits, medical insurance, paid vacation, sick leave, and whatever other benefits you provide. What you have to anticipate is $15- to $20-an-hour employees. Be careful about thinking you can afford an employee at $10 an hour, who is in fact a $20-an-hour employee. That's something else to discuss with your bookkeeper or accountant before you start up or at least before you start hiring.

You have to get a sales tax permit or license and collect sales tax on the items that are supposed to be taxed. Some states may require an advance deposit or surety bond against taxes to be collected. Either you have taxable items programmed into your cash register or you educate your help on what is and is not to be taxed. In California the Franchise Tax Board has brochures on what is taxed in each industry. Sales tax is especially complicated for a café or deli and it changes all the time. One year cookies are taxed, the next year they are off the list. Bread is not taxable. If somebody buys a danish for a dollar and takes it out the door, there is no sales tax. If you heat the same danish in the microwave, it's taxable because it's heated. To-go food items are usually not taxable unless they are a hot-food item. Carbonated soft drinks are taxable. Non-carbonated soft drinks are not. You can have a Gatorade sitting next to a bottle of Pepsi; neither has great nutritional value, but because one has

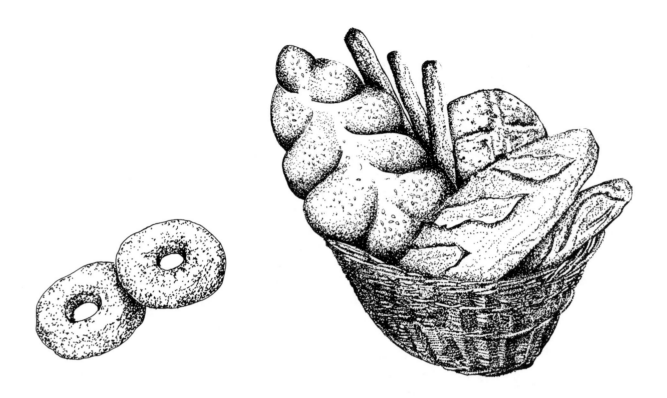

bubbles it will be taxed while the other is not taxed. That's this year, of course.

Document everything you've paid. Keep all the invoices and your check stubs. Keep the records as if you are preparing for an IRS audit. Set up a system to organize every kind of record. We keep everything: Our essential paperwork is our workers' compensation papers, our insurance papers, perhaps any purchasing agreements regarding the purchase of the building or other contracts, of which there aren't very many. We try to keep a copy of any document that involved the transfer of a large amount of money with the lawyer or at the bank. Your accountant or bookkeeper should know how long to keep different documents.

You should reconcile your checkbook with the bank's statement and make any corrections right away. Usually you have to inform your bank within two weeks to correct an error.

BUDGETS

You need a budget to keep expenses under control. Some items will fluctuate whether or not you set up a budget, but you can exercise more control with a budget. Take advertising: You'll be approached by numerous broadcast and print media salespeople. Once you learn which media work best for the business, budget for it. Then, when advertising salespeople call, you can demonstrate that you have so much money for advertising and it is already allocated

DONUTS

"A tribe of prehistoric Indians is believed to have been the originators of the doughnut. Excavations recently made in the Southwestern part of the United States revealed among other relics petrified fried cakes with holes in them. Of course, nobody can know what mixture was used by the ones who baked these cakes, but we are told that in appearance they closely resemble the doughnut as we know it today."
—THE WISE ENCYCLOPEDIA OF COOKING (1949)

Notwithstanding this rousing yarn, a donut with a hole in it is a relative newcomer to bakery shelves. It's true that fried breads were central to some tribes' fall ceremonies, but the Native-American connection is otherwise doubtful. Today's donuts are a modern version of a fried cake—the "olykolck"—which early Dutch settlers brought to the New World. It's a pastry that probably originated when the last scraps from a batch of dough were sweetened or filled with jam then fried as a treat for children or for a quick breakfast.

The holes in donuts did not arrive—or depart—until the middle of the 19th Century. The source of that archaeological note also claims that a sea captain who loved donuts though they gave him indigestion experimented with the cakes and finally punched a hole from their centers with a little can. The toroidal fix, no matter who made it, did promote better baking and more digestible cakes.

Donut dough must be handled gently, with very little flour rolled in, and the donuts fried quickly in at least three inches of fat or oil then turned as soon as they rise to the surface. Steam from the cooking dough keeps oil out of the donut. Too hot an oil breaks down into acrolein, which irritates the body's membrane tissues. It not only causes greasy donuts and indigestion, but early spoilage as well.

---

to the most productive media. The same is true of donations. Every donation is for a good cause. If you budget, say, $100 retail of baked goods for donations a month and an organization asks after you've given your quota, explain your policy. If you haven't used it up, explain how much is left and what you can give.

Payroll — If you budget payroll by aiming for a percentage of the bakery's gross within the industry averages—say 22 percent—and, on average, you gross $1,000 every day, then you can allocate about $220 a day to payroll. If on average you pay $12.50 an hour, including benefits, that lets you hire 17.6 employee hours within that $220 daily cap. In chapter 17 on business plans we discuss establishing staff budgets by estimating how many employees you'll need to make and sell your projected daily product. The approaches have to mesh, as we said before, but don't get hooked on the numbers. Watch how it works in real life. I worked for a place that kept a complete daily log of total payroll hours. It's an excellent idea, at least when you start out and maybe periodically thereafter. You don't need an elaborate system; a few sheets of paper will do. It's also a good idea to send your employees home on a slow day, because for every 15 minutes or half-hour in which an employee hangs around with nothing to do you lose money. If you can save one hour's payroll a day by sending one $12.50-an-hour person home an hour early, it's six hours saved at the end of the week. That's $75, which is over $300 a month, or better than $3,600 on the annual bottom line. It adds up; and that's from just one hour a day.

Despite the rules of payroll management, timeliness is critical for hiring and training. Ordinarily you wouldn't hire employees until needed; but you have to be ready for the busy season with qualified employees, even if it means paying to train them during the slow time. That way you'll have knowledgeable people during October, November, and December, your three peak months. If you wait until then to train new hires, they'll have a hard time learning. Everyone will be too busy to teach them. So be sure to anticipate and budget for your staff needs by checking your schedule a month or two in advance.

Talk Is Not Cheap — In a bakery like ours, which is a fairly social institution front and back, we get interrupted all day long. But it's a part of the business that lends atmosphere and appeal. People come back in the kitchen and hang around, and they drink a cup of coffee once in a while. You have to learn to work while you're talking. If you stop every time you're interrupted, the work grinds to a halt and costs plenty. You have to teach people to work and talk at the same time—unless they're cutting something. You don't want them to chop onions and talk to somebody: They'll cut their hand off. If talk begins to outrun the work in your bakery, you'll have to stop it altogether or make a firm policy restricting it.

Time Is Money, Which is Not Everything — There are arguments for and against saving time and labor in a bakery. Some devices pay for themselves over time even if their initial cost seems high. But some product is better made by hand, and those time-saving devices will lower the product's quality. For example, a dough rounder saves time but often pushes too much of the air out of the bread. It may be fine in a wholesale environment where uniformity counts, but in a small shop, when each of the loaves looks a little different, hand rounding adds character. With a rounder you get a uniform round loaf. We, on the other hand, can produce round or rectangular or square loaves—each one a little different—by hand. Besides, it's good exercise.

Utilities — As the boss you will have to hammer your help about turning off the lights when they leave the storage room—just the way your mom used to: Turn off the light! It's also important to keep your refrigerator condensers and vanes clean and dust free. Our electrical bill in just one shop is about $1,300 a month. If you can cut that by $100 a month with clean refrigeration, it's a big saving over the year.

Don't Over-Insure — As the eternal optimist, I always take a high deductible on our insurance. I assume that nothing is going to

Being creative is one thing, but I'm not a business person. Anyone who dreams about opening a bakery should have a strong grounding in that. You need to have your financial figures down and keep on top of it. I don't, because I don't have time. A girl comes in once a week and plugs our numbers into the computer for me, and I have an accountant who harangues me for not doing all these costs. But I just look at him and say I work six days a week. On my seventh day I do some of the bookkeeping but I don't have time for the figuring. If I ever got the computer to where I could just plug the figures in, it'll happen.

—Jacquie Lee
The Garden Bakery

happen—usually it doesn't—so we keep the deductible as high as possible. This amounts to balancing money saved on the premium for a number of years against the cost of a claim if it ever happens. It's a gamble. Gambling is what your insurance company does, and with a high deductible that's what you would do.

Arrange to make a single insurance payment. You could get dizzy paying 15 insurance bills from 15 different companies. To make payment easier find a good company that will "umbrella" all your insurance by shopping around for a good fee-based broker-age—not a salesperson—to get this kind of coverage.

Earlier we recommended shopping for the best workers' compensation insurance coverage if you can. You should also estimate your quarterly payroll accurately, otherwise, if you have a bigger than expected payroll, you'll get a surprise at the end of the quarter. If you estimated $100,000 in payroll for the quarter, for a worker's comp bill of $4,000, but the payroll runs $150,000, you suddenly owe $6,000. Nothing may have happened for a compensation claim, of course, but you had 50 percent more payroll so now you owe $2,000 more premium. You don't want to estimate a $150,000 payroll only to owe $100,000, either. You get the money back, but with a loss in interest and in the things you could have done with the money. What you couldn't do with the money is called "lost opportunity cost." So try to save money by estimating payroll carefully.

Buy Less, Be Happy — Scrutinize every purchase you are tempted to make. The world is full of wonderful gadgets and aids and advice. I've been caught up in the "I have to have that neat little management or reference book" syndrome and buy things like *The 10-Minute Tycoon*. The acquisitive urge seems to come over us in waves; but hold back. If business has been just fine without the latest wonder book, it will still do fine. The same goes for tools and equipment. Look at everything very skeptically. If buying it will save you money, go ahead and get it. If it is guaranteed to save you money but doesn't, send it back. Simplify the way you do things and the business will work better and cheaper.

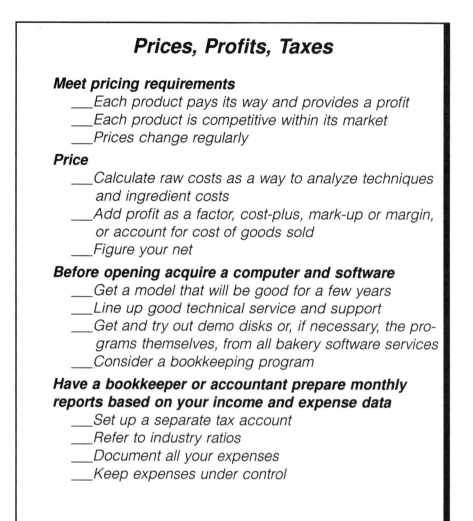

Prices, Profits, Taxes

Meet pricing requirements
___Each product pays its way and provides a profit
___Each product is competitive within its market
___Prices change regularly

Price
___Calculate raw costs as a way to analyze techniques and ingredient costs
___Add profit as a factor, cost-plus, mark-up or margin, or account for cost of goods sold
___Figure your net

Before opening acquire a computer and software
___Get a model that will be good for a few years
___Line up good technical service and support
___Get and try out demo disks or, if necessary, the programs themselves, from all bakery software services
___Consider a bookkeeping program

Have a bookkeeper or accountant prepare monthly reports based on your income and expense data
___Set up a separate tax account
___Refer to industry ratios
___Document all your expenses
___Keep expenses under control

FOLLOWING THROUGH

Enterprise (en´ter-prize)
n.s. [entreprise, Fr.]
An undertaking of hazard;
an arduous attempt.

—*Samuel Johnson*
A DICTIONARY OF THE ENGLISH
LANGUAGE

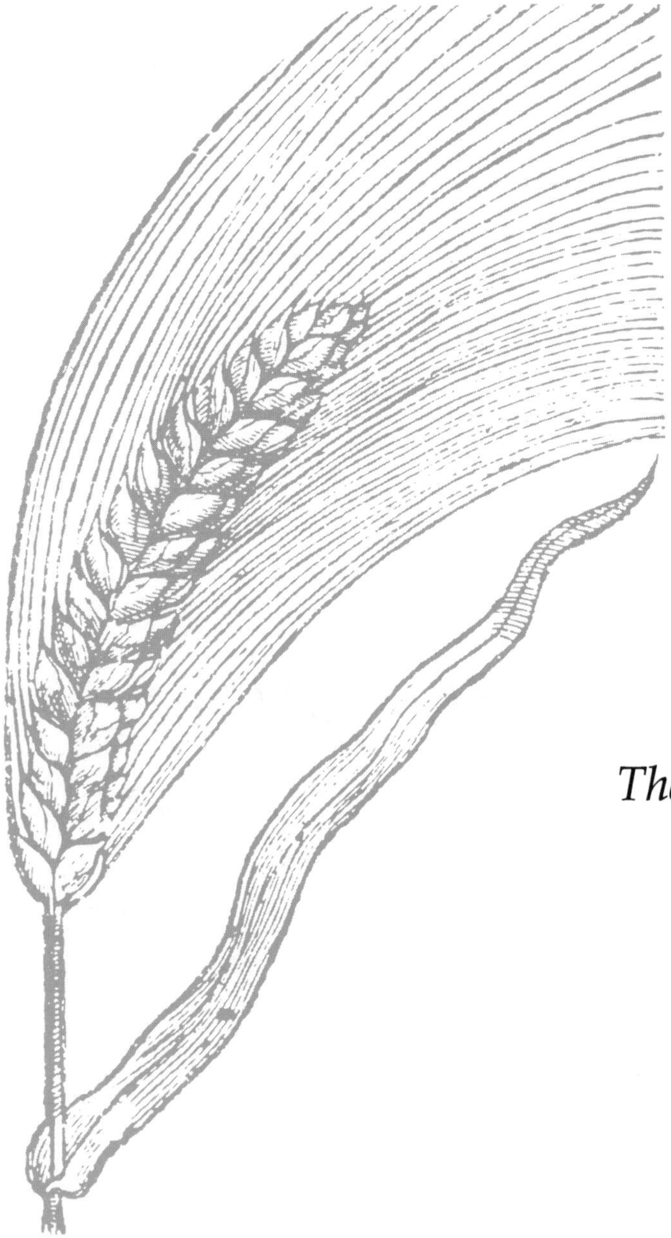

16

HANDLING PROBLEMS AND DISASTERS

T HIS CHAPTER is what used to, and may still, be called a "downer." Somewhere in the book, however, after telling you all the great things about running a bakery, we had to consider all the bad events that can occur, not only for a baker but for anyone. Life is full of hazards, and enterprise involves risk. Before you set up— even before you formulate a business plan—you should have an inkling of all the disasters that lie in wait, so that you can anticipate and, we hope, avoid them.

EMERGENCIES

People Emergencies — It's a good idea for a baker who runs a café to know cardio-pulmonary resuscitation (CPR) and the Heimlich maneuver. Choking is a risk in any business that serves food. Sometimes the fire department or local emergency medical treatment service holds CPR and first aid classes. If so, take your whole staff to them and learn how to do it. Also, you and your staff are working with machinery and sharp knives; so don't forget to have a first aid kit and keep it freshly supplied. In most states the law requires you to keep police, fire and life-support-service phone numbers posted in large print right next to the telephone. You should also put it where you hang all your employee information posters.

Building Emergencies — The fire codes in all states and localities require you to have a certain number of fire extinguishers within so many feet of each other in the building. You should get them checked and refilled once a year. You can plan for fires. In addition to having extinguishers, your main defense is to prevent panic and clear the building. Think about how to do it quickly and efficiently. Other emergencies like earthquakes and floods probably defy rational planning. If you can't exit the building fast in an earthquake the experts advise diving under a sturdy table or workbench. As for floods, it's not like we keep sand bags in back, and I doubt that stacking all our flour sacks in front of the building would do much good, either. This is the kind of havoc you make sure to get insurance for if you can.

Power Failure — Power failures are not uncommon in our neck of the woods. Most business places don't have back-up generators, and when the power fails in a bakery it can be devastating—especially if you're in the middle of making all your doughs. You never know where in the day you will be when it goes out. If you've already baked off everything, there is no problem. If you are in the middle of things, you either have to bake them as-is, or get them in a freezer and hope they chill enough so you can revive them later on. Otherwise you have to throw them away. So, if you have an electric oven or even a gas-fired one that rotates electrically, get everything in it, even if it's not ready. Some old rotaters have hand cranks for emergencies. Keep the oven door shut to keep all of the heat in. Keep all of your refrigerators shut. Then turn off the power to those units, because you don't want them to surge when the power comes on again. A power surge can ruin your systems, especially those with electronic controls. Have flashlights available and know where they are. Also keep a supply of candles. We have old gas stoves and have been able to stay open when the rest of the town is out of electricity. That's an advantage with antiquated, low-tech equipment. We'll make campfire coffee on the stove top and do what it takes to keep the front doors open. But we'll keep the oven and refrigerator doors closed, and bake off all we can.

You should have an extra key to your cash register drawer, because usually when the electricity goes out you can't open the cash

This may be heresy to some, but there's a dissenting view of our popular inclination toward whole-grain breads. In the last 30 years, white bread's market share has slipped by well over a third, due mainly to the continuing shift to "natural" foods. Wheat's germ and bran, after all, contain a quarter of its protein and most of its fiber, oil, and B vitamins. Never mind that we lack the enzymes to digest and absorb them all.

Ours is a fairly recent backlash from a historic preference for lighter breads. White flour, for not much reason, was long considered "purer" than whole-grain flour. Also, with a lower per-bushel yield because of extra refining, it was more expensive, hence, a status symbol. But there may be sound reasons for preferring refined grains.

Around 400 B.C., Hippocrates said in his REGI-MEN, "Bread made of [wheat] without separating the bran dries and passes; when cleaned from the bran it nourishes more but is less laxative." E.g., dark bread is more laxative, white more nutritious. This view went unchallenged until the late 19th Century when Sylvester Graham disagreed, and the shift began. It gained new respectability when in the Fall 1974 JOURNAL OF THE AMERICAN MEDICAL ASSOCIATION a group of British surgeons bolstered Graham's view. They argued that

dietary fiber, including whole-wheat (Graham) flour, could reduce the risk of diverticulosis, appendicitis, gallstones, varicose veins, hemorrhoids, colon and rectal cancer, and atherosclerosis. Since then, despite some interesting correlations, medicine has found no clear causal link between fiber intake and diverticulosis, appendicitis, or atherosclerosis. The main dietary cause of bowel cancer seems to be too much meat and animal fat. The medical community today is far from united on what fiber does—or even what it is.

Wheat bran and germ lower flour's storage and gluten qualities. There's also evidence that bran cuts its food value by blocking absorption of some nutrients. Science writer Harold McGee noted in his ON FOOD AND COOKING that wheat bran has a phytic acid that disrupts human calcium intake. During World War II, when Dublin was put on whole-grain bread, excess bran combined with low calcium and vitamin D intake caused a rickets outbreak that struck half the city's children. And the whole-wheat eating poor of Egypt and Iran appear to metabolize less iron and zinc. So "unrefined" may not necessarily mean healthful. While we who eat balanced and adequate diets can freely enjoy white or whole-grain breads, people on marginal diets probably should not eat "naturally."

drawer. Having a "manual" cash drawer with a bank of $100 in it for a back-up is a good idea because it doesn't interfere with your register sales. If you do decide to stay open, you can sell out of the back-up drawer and also make change for people who were already in line and made purchases. You would just write the items sold down on tabs and tally them up later. A little money on the side can be part of your power-failure supplies along with flashlights and candles.

THEFT AND BACK-DOOR LOSSES

Before we had a safe in our bakery we set aside a special hiding place for our money. Many businesses probably do it. If the owner isn't around at closing time, the staff is usually instructed to take the day's cash out of the till and squirrel it away in the hiding place. Our problem occurred because one of our help's boyfriend's friends was a thief and was hanging around when she hid the cash one evening. The friend and a buddy came back one night soon after and went right through the front window to the refrigerator where we were hiding the cash. I'll hazard a guess that every baker is inclined, like me, to hide things in the refrigerator. A thief could probably score every one of us by rifling our cold storage.

Now we have a safe and systems and procedures for where the money goes. The money goes into the safe through a slot, but you have to know the combination to get it out. Even with a safe, however, you should never have too much money on the premises. Make your deposits often and let the bank worry about theft; it has insurance and security for that kind of thing.

Also when you take the money out of the till each night, leave the cash drawer open, because if a thief does get into your store and can't figure out how to open the cash register, he'll break it open. Leaving the drawer ajar will show that there's no money in it. We've never considered getting security alarms. It depends, of course, on where you live, but also a bakery doesn't have much to take other than money. Anyone who wants to steal a loaf of bread probably needs it pretty badly, and a thief is not likely to walk out with a showcase. If you had a large place that kept 300 or 400 pounds of turkey or beef on hand, then there might be more cause for concern. Otherwise, at least in a neighborhood like ours, it's hard to justify the cost of a security system for a bakery.

Retail bakers should learn how short-change operators work and how to recognize counterfeit money. A discussion with your local police department will help. You should get one of those new currency pens that work on the new big bills. Talk to the police or your banker about these pens, which, if run over a $100 bill, leave the real bills alone but blacken a counterfeit. A self-service place is also often at the mercy of the customer who thinks that the extra refill cup of coffee, for which you charge 25¢, is free. Or, when a bowl of soup costs $3.00 while $4.00 buys all you can eat, everybody pays $3.00 but always goes back for more. It's a tough situation. You can't walk up to somebody having lunch with a friend and say, "You know, you owe me another dollar." They'll never come back. So you try to put signs up to make people aware. You do something to stir their conscience.

Our food never walks out our back door, because we don't have one; it goes out the front. For example, recently I went into the improvement-center store at 6:30 when we close, and our two counter people were leaving. Each had a big bag of baked goods they claimed was Plowshares product, day-old things we give to charity and which the staff can have within reason. I know what we baked two days ago, and what's for Plowshares and what is not. So

I told Alan [Scott] that we wanted to do pizzas also, so he shaped our brick oven so that it would keep the fire going and do pizzas, too. Unfortunately, we had to stop doing them. I loved our pizzas and it was a very hard decision. . . . Much as you may fall in love with a recipe or dish, you have to make level-headed business decisions. We actually had lower costs and better profits not doing pizzas than we did making them. Maybe we'll try it again someday, but I think we were fighting a location problem. We're not on Lansing or Main Street. We don't have people just strolling by and saying, oh, look, let's grab a pizza. People really had to know that we were here and doing this. Things change, and if it looks like at some point in the future the market might be there again, we'll give them another try.
—CHRISTOPHER KUMP
CAFE BEAUJOLAIS, THE BRICKERY

I said, "Open them up for me." Sure enough, there were fresh-baked bread and scones in each bag. You want to trust people and you want them to like you, but if you see a bag going out the door, you as an owner with a livelihood to protect have to decide to be a jerk at that point. You will hesitate; but the time comes when your only choice is to say, Hey! What's in the bag? and hope you won't have to do it again. Now we have chains and locks on the refrigerators at the home-improvement center store. All the security you need is a little chain with a lock to which your manager has the key. You only need enough to keep an honest person honest and make a thief think twice. Besides, this is where we keep our turkeys and hams that cost $30 or $40 apiece, so a little security is not unreasonable.

One way to stay alert to losses of this kind is to see whether food costs exceed the normal rates. Tell your bookkeeper to put a note on the paperwork if food costs begin to get out of line. That's another advantage of knowing industry ratios. Even when you first open your business you can get an idea of what your food costs will be and you can calculate them from there.

As an owner you will also learn to watch the cash register to see the numbers get hit. If something really dubious seems to be going on, you walk up and grab the tape. Say a friend of the counter person got a *latte* and a scone, which should go for $3.00 and you see that it's a 50¢ sale on the tape. The friend just got a $2.50 break. The friend tells your counter help, "Ah, thanks a lot kid—you're the greatest." And you just went a little into the red. You wouldn't have known that unless you went back to the office and read the tape. You will never catch all the tricks, either. They come along faster than you can spot them.

The only way to run a business is to assume everybody is honest, but when it's clear that someone is not, you can't waffle. Making idle threats in the face of dishonesty sends a bad message to everyone in the store. When somebody rips off the business, even if it's your key employee, you've got to act decisively. You can't actually accuse a person of stealing, however, because there is seldom hard evidence. The Fair Labor Standards Commission would be all over you like a steamroller asking, Do you have proof that this person stole? Do you have it on tape? . . . You won't, of course; so you just explain to the employee that it doesn't look like we will be able to work together anymore. As a general practice, in fact, any employer should telephone the nearest Fair Labor Standards Commission office early and often just to understand what the laws require. Check the government listings in your telephone book. You can listen to recordings on different overtime rules, break rules, lunch hour rules, termination rules and so on, and save yourself plenty of trouble—and expense. There are companies that will sell you reference booklets on all the compliance guidelines, but you can get the information free from the commission. As mentioned, many state

After the soft brittle shells
are blown off roasted cacao
beans, the bean fragments
or "nibs" are stone-ground.
The heat of grinding liquifies
the cocoa butter (54% of the
bean) and the rich, dark
liquid goes into tubs called
"conches" where for several
days it is aerated and
ground finer. Then the refined liquor is poured into
moulds to cool and become
unsweetened chocolate.

(Illus.: *The Fanny Farmer
Cookbook*, Little Brown
1918.)

chambers of commerce offer inexpensive or free publications on various management topics, including employee relations.

BUSINESS SLUMPS

For the first time now—it's been about six years—the Courthouse
bakery has regular busy and slow seasons. For the first three or four
years a good new business's sales and activity in general will
normally follow a straight-line curve up. Eventually it matures and
activity levels off and begins to have peaks and valleys. A bakery's
busy season is in October, November, and December with colder
weather, holidays, and a shift in eating habits. The slump season, at

least for us in Ukiah, is during the 105-degree weather of July, August, and part of September. These cycles look like they'll continue, so summer is a time to cut staff and offer vacations. It's also a time when product is likeliest to stale fast or go bad because of the heat, so it's good idea to reduce inventory to a limited supply.

This is also the time to crank up your marketing efforts. Offer cents-off coupons and two-for-one sales just to build up the foot traffic. You may not see the result in the cash receipts, because you're giving some of it away, but it does help the psyche to keep busy. It also gets people into the habit of coming in, which is important year around, not only in the slump season or when you are attracting newcomers in the community.

BIG TROUBLE

If major employers in town close shop, or a freeway diverts traffic from the business district, or some other major economic shift occurs, everyone in town will feel it. Unfortunately, for a business there is only a limited set of responses available in these situations. One is to cut back, sometimes to the bare minimum.

For example, a bakery could cut out lunches. Lunches bring in the most traffic but are the least profitable part of the business. They take the most help, preparation, food cost, overhead, and everything else. While a lunch trade does boost the sale of baked goods, it's intended to create a level of activity that might be unattainable in a leaner economy. If your business became solely a bakery with hours from 6:00 in the morning till 2:00 in the afternoon, you would cut back on all the payroll and other costs associated with your more expensive trade. If you did the baking and had two salespeople, you might even make more money than with 26 on the staff. More likely your return on the dollar would be proportionally higher although fewer dollars would come in. If you wound up with excess space you could sublease or try a complementary product line. Those would be extreme responses, of course, and they might not be available to businesses whose high fixed costs required a certain income level to pay the bills.

Whether you can avoid economic disaster by cashing out or moving to where opportunities are better depends on how timely you decide to do it. If you don't act in time when you see a decline coming, there may be no way to hold on or move out. It is a major mistake to wait and use up all your resources in an impossible market. And the longer you delay, the fewer your choices are.

In a small city 30 miles south of us the highway used to go right through downtown. People complained about it, but businesses thrived. Three years ago a new freeway bypass opened and downtown died, taking many of those businesses with it. The smart business person in that town would have looked ahead and seen that in two years or 18 months there would not be any traffic going by the front door, and that the time to sell and move to a better location was right away. Chances are that those who waited lacked time to find a good new place and could no longer afford to relocate if they did. The lesson here is to keep an eye on the planning commission, on the city council, on the county board of supervisors, and to start noticing trends.

Cashing out even in the best of circumstances requires a showing of strong financials. That's tough to do, because for the entire time that you're in business you are trying for tax purposes not to show too big a profit. You don't evade taxes but you want to write off all you're allowed to for expenses, new equipment, and depreciation. When you want to sell, buyers will look at your past records and think the business hasn't made any money in the past five years. You need to show where the money went, how it was used, and that it is available. When selling the business, do not just hand over your records to anyone. It's best to meet with an interested buyer and let them work with you for a day or two to get an idea how the business runs. Nothing puts the records in perspective better than letting a buyer run the cash register and see how many people come through the door in a day. Even then, if anybody wants to see your financials, make it clear that they are for serious buyers only.

WORST COMES TO WORST

If business actually declines and dies, you can only salvage what's left. The easiest way to cash out is to sell your equipment at an auction, but you would probably get the least amount for it that way. You are not auctioning off a fancy car with a guaranteed bid of $20,000. If only one bidder shows up, your equipment will go for the first calling number. When my dad retired and sold his bakery in Bishop he got 3¢ on the dollar. First try to approach people with whom you've done business, assuming you don't owe them money. Ask if they know anybody who is looking for a refrigerator, an oven, a mixer, or whatever. If you do owe them money and want to pay it back with the hope of saving your credit record, you might offer your equipment in lieu of payment. Not many will take it, but it's worth a try. This is the reverse of looking for equipment yourself. You could also talk to salespeople, who have a very good network and know who needs equipment.

You should get as much advice from outside sources as you can. You don't necessarily have to take it, but it's often just what you need. Remember the older, retired bakers mentioned earlier. If you can't find any, don't forget about the assistance the SBA offers through its Service Corps of Retired Executives (SCORE). Often it can fix you up with somebody who has been through exactly what you are struggling with.

If all else fails, you'll have to consult with a lawyer or accountant and consider the protection of the bankruptcy court. The Bankruptcy

At first we decided, and I think rightfully so, that we couldn't handle a retail outlet. Especially here in the wintertime without the tourists. And we don't want to move; we love it here. But also we didn't have enough energy to put into it. People told us one of the partners is going to have to be here all the time, and we are just spread too thin. My daughters have been down to Berkeley and seen how some of the bakeries there like Acme do in a high-population area. People just line up and come in. That's fine, but in Boonville when the people line up and come in that's two of them. The demographics are different.
—*BRUCE HERING*
BRUCE BREAD

Code provides for two kinds of protection. One is relief by a straight discharge of all your debts. The other is a reorganization, or reduction and payoff, of your debts. They can be either business debts, personal debts, or both. It is not the kind of subject we are qualified to give advice on, and you will definitely have to see a professional, if it comes to that.

We could have ended on a cheerier, if less realistic, note by ignoring all the tough things that can happen to a business. Unpleasant as these last few paragraphs are, however, they are worthwhile if they convince you to write a careful business plan—which is the best way to anticipate what might happen and prepare to deal with it. That is the subject of the next and final chapter.

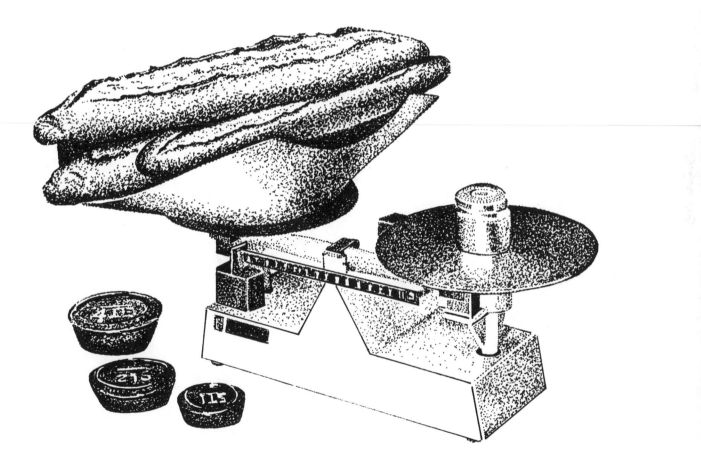

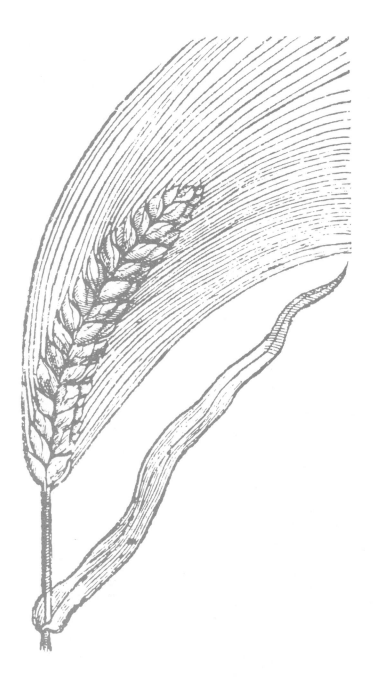

17

BUSINESS PLANS

SINCE you probably won't have enough of your own money to open a bakery, you'll most likely have to get a loan. And to do that you'll almost certainly need a business plan, which is the only way for lenders to see what a good deal you're offering. It's also the best way for you to find and fix any flaws in the project before you commit any resources to it. That, briefly, is why you draft a business plan: to weigh your bakery's prospects and to attract potential lenders.

Don't be afraid of the business plan. As the best way to test your assumptions, it makes you think carefully about how much money you need to get the business going, how much you need to run it and live on, what your goals are, and how you will reach them. It makes you identify your primary competitors and how you can compete with them or exploit a market niche they don't serve. It lets you run best- and worst-case models and show that your bakery can really happen. To do it at all you need a good understanding of the local market and what your share of it can be.

CONFRONTING THE TASK

There are three phases to drafting a plan. First, you have to learn the market the way we suggested in Chapter 7 by reading the statistical guides, talking to community and business leaders, and looking at the competition to figure out where your bakery will fit in. You write down all this information as you go and put it in a notebook, or on cards or slips of paper, so you can match up different facts and organize them. Second, once you have all that written information, you review it and think hard about what all the details and the large patterns mean. Third, you write up the plan and look for con-

traditions and holes in your facts or reasoning. Don't be easy on yourself. You want to find the problems now—not later when you have sunk your savings into the business and opened up. Planning will be one of the most rewarding investments of time and effort you can make over the entire course of your new enterprise.

But there's something else. . . . Drafting a business plan is a big job. Let's be honest—it can be drudgery. And writing it has nothing to do with your talents or experience as a baker. Many people who need business plans are so intimidated by the job they try to avoid doing it; so a whole industry has sprung up like that for drafting résumés to help draft business plans. All of them offer similar services, but like every industry, a few providers are excellent, the rest are poor. One excellent resource is David H. Bangs' *Business Planning Guide*. It probably has the best discussion in print on arranging all your thoughts about the business into a concise, careful report. Also consider *The Restaurant Planning Guide*, by Peter Rainsford and David Bangs. It covers all aspects of the restaurant business, with a strong emphasis on financial data. It also shows how to turn a business plan into a financial proposal for a bank loan or equity investment. There is a brief guide in *Entrepreneur* magazine's *Small Business Advisor*. If you check the Yellow Pages under "Business Consultants" you will sometimes find firms that develop business plans. As with all such professional services, it pays to shop and to get references from prior customers. Consultants cost money, however, and you can learn more by doing it yourself. You may be able to swing it if you follow Bangs' book and call in professional help when you need it for things like the financial tables and calculations.

In California everyone has access to a governmental service called a Small Business Development Center (SBDC) or Community Development Commission (CDC). They usually operate under county government auspices but sometimes are associated with community colleges. These agencies typically employ people who can teach you to write a business plan. Sometimes they will sit down and help develop your information into a usable document. To locate such a service in your area, look in the local government telephone listings for the SBA and see if your public library has the latest Directory of U.S. Microenterprise Programs. The directory is published by the Self-Employment Learning Project of the Aspen Institute, 1333 New Hampshire Ave., NW, Suite 1070, Washington, DC 20036 (telephone (202) 833-7434; fax (202) 467-0790). The SBA also offers business plan advice through SCORE, and you can ask about more information and publications, many of them free, by telephoning 1-800-827-5722.

THE BUSINESS PLAN

Briefly, a business plan gives basic data like your name, address, telephone number, and the location and name of the business. Then it explains what the business will do and states its purpose, it summarizes its objectives, it tells how it will work, and it forecasts its chances of success in its proposed market.

That is the last and perhaps the only brief remark you will see or hear about business plans. The good news is that, for as detailed as these plans can be, they all cover a limited amount of information. There is no approved formula for a business plan but we offer one way to organize it below. You can go down the list, answer all the questions in full, and eventually you have your plan. You will also have a better idea than ever about where your work and effort can take you. That's a very valuable advantage. You can break the plan down into six or seven parts: (1) the business definition; (2) your proposed business; (3) the market; (4) a competitive analysis; (5) development plans; (6) operations; and (7) financial projections.

Business Definition — The business plan itself is like a big term paper with a cover, title page, and table of contents. After the introductory pages you begin with a "business definition." You could also call it the "executive summary," "mission statement," or "statement of purpose." It's where you outline what the business will be. To keep it short and to the point, save it until last, after you have worked out all the details in the later parts. It is a lead paragraph. It goes up front for a good sales pitch. It should describe the business, the product, and the market *exactly*. It should emphasize the important financial points, the capital you need to start and to expand, and how you plan to do it.

The business definition also includes a short description of the industry—whether it is wholesale or retail, what are its normal sales plans and support systems, and that it is the food service industry. You also assess the industry's prospects, which I think at the moment are excellent. Then come back and tell reader how your bakery will stand out. Use numbers. Tell about your competitive edge, how you will make money, and why the business will be profitable. This is also where you should list whatever professional assistance and advice you received to prepare the plan.

You might also invest a few dollars to make the plan look as good as possible by hiring someone skilled in editing and desktop publishing to review the text and grammar, add tables and graphics, design the pages, and set it in type. In short, it should look professional. Your plan will have to succeed on the facts rather than looks alone, but the more compelling and attractive you can make it, the likelier it is that a lender or venture capitalist will read and endorse it.

Your Proposed Business—Give the business's address and describe its location in terms of the neighborhood and customer access, and your nearness to competitors, suppliers, and transportation. Describe the building, equipment, and furnishings. Tell about all the products and services you will offer, and discuss any trademarks and proprietary features. Tell if the business is a sole proprietorship, a partnership, limited partnership, or corporation. List your staff and include an organization chart if necessary, noting who does what. Lay out your pay structure. Describe everyone's experience and skills, and tell what happens if somebody leaves. List and give the qualifications of your professional support team—your lawyer, accountant, ad agency, and advisors.

The Market—Describing the market and your business's place in it requires very painstaking, even cold-blooded, analysis. A market breaks down into a total potential market, a total feasible market, then your target market and, within that, the actual market segments you expect to reach, such as geographic, social, or product-oriented subgroups. Explain how you expect to get them. Tell about your projected peak business hours, who your customers will be, and what their consumption habits are. This is all subjective, but try to back it up with as solid figures and facts as you can. For example, if you plan on some wholesale business, you can begin by approaching likely customers right away if you have product to demonstrate. That will give you a good sense of how receptive your potential market is. Think about industry growth based on population changes and shifting tastes. Remember, the information is for your benefit as well as for persuading lenders.

Competitive Analysis—This is where you compare your business with the competition. Identify all your current and potential competition. Describe it from the customer's point of view and group your competitors by how they appeal to the pocketbook. Analyze where each firm succeeds and where it misses; how it motivates customers; what are its apparent major problems and strengths; and what keeps other firms from setting up. Then tell how you will develop assets and skills your competitors lack. One handy reference guide recommends making up a "competitive strength" grid. You list assets and skills along one axis and put the company names along the other. Put your bakery in the first or last company space and show where it fits in. Then tabulate the skill and asset mix to show how your bakery's qualities will get and keep a market share. A bakery's competitive strength depends mainly on its products but also on distribution, pricing, promotion, and advertising.

The supermarket in this center used to have doors on the side. When they remodelled they moved the doors to face front toward the parking lot. Till then people, especially the elderly, would park in front of us and come in to get their breads and pastries, then use the side door to shop for groceries. But the front doors shifted parking away from us. Now I have to work to get people in here. After the supermarket moved that door we stopped selling as much French bread as before. I had sold it for 99¢, the same price as the supermarket's; so I lowered the price to 75¢. Every day I sell out now. I make 24¢-a-loaf less profit but I'm not just giving all that bread away to Food Bank.

—MURIEL GLAVE
THE LANDMARK BAKERY

THE ACADEMY-TRAINED BAKER

Just before my last employer closed down completely, our local Private Industry Council (PIC) came in to help us draft résumés and look for jobs. As a banker and accountant, I had no prospects of local employment and no luck when I tried to relocate. Elodia Lopez at PIC asked me, "Have you ever thought about going to baking school?" I had noted a hobby of making candies and desserts on my information sheet. I said, "Yes, but I've never been able to afford it; it's very expensive." She said, "Well let's see what we can do." We needed three culinary schools for PIC to approve the application. After comparing we found San Francisco's to be the most suitable.

The California Culinary Academy in San Francisco is in a beautiful four-story German baroque style building. It has two restaurants and a retail bakery, which are very profitable. People eat downstairs in the restaurant, and upstairs the students cook and have a view of the restaurant. The main restaurant, is very formal—with reservations, linen, and crystal—but you can just walk into the other one, the Sonoma Grill, for lunch or dinner.

I was 48 years old. When I went to take the tour I asked admissions if I was going to be the oldest student enrolled. "No," the woman said, "we've got some here who are in their 60s." One, she said, worked in computers all his life then left to enroll in the cooking chef program. A 19-year-old from Los Angeles had been going to school to study law. One student came from Taiwan, another from Korea.

Donald Pittman
Graduate of the
California Culinary Academy

Besides submitting two letters of reference, I had to write a 500-word essay on why I thought I'd be a good candidate for the academy. To show real commitment, applicants have to send in a $500 nonrefundable deposit with their application. The school is serious about education. Before approving an application it gives a written test with a lot of grammar and math. In my class it expelled several students who had missed one day a week for four or five weeks. If you get kicked out after a certain number of weeks, you don't get any of your money back. Tuition for the baking and pastry chef program is $15,000, to which you have to add San Francisco living expenses. It cost me just over $20,000.

You can choose either the year-and-a-half cooking chef program or the baking and pastry chef program, which runs for seven months, seven hours a day. Classes start when the enrollment fills. We started in December, and there was a class three months ahead of us. Nearly 800 cooking and pastry chef students were in attendance while I was there. There are about 20 chef instructors and a number of part time instructors. The school also has a two-year class for people who work during the week but can attend all day Sunday. Its 10 to 12 kitchens are just like commercial bakeries with butcher block and steel tables, usually with two students per table. Everything is restaurant grade, with the ovens around the walls and all our equipment nearby. The school had just outgrown its main building and installed a new kitchen a block up the street.

Most of the faculty have extensive backgrounds in their specialties and are at the peak of their profession. One chef attended Cordon Bleu in France. The bread baking chef had owned Brother Juniper's Bakery in Santa Rosa, until he sold it to begin teaching. He had recently taken first place at the World Bread

Baking contest in New York City. Another had been the head pastry chef at the Fairmont Hotel in San Francisco for eight years and then decided to teach.

Classes for the first three and a half months ran from 2:30 till 10:00 p.m., and in the last three and a half from 7 a.m. till 2:30 p.m., to give us a taste of night and morning shifts. We did production work all week and took an exam every Friday. In the middle of the seven months we had three weeks of classroom instruction in human resources, sanitation, and nutrition. Each covered 500 pages a week in four nights, with exams on Friday night. We received a certificate if we scored high enough in those subjects.

We baked for the two restaurants and the bakery then had to go home and study. I studied on the average of two to three hours a night. We studied things like the history of cakes—all kinds of cakes. We also learned about the ingredients, what they are composed of, and how they react with each other. I have three thick binders of the recipes we used. There was a lot of homework.

Each day we had deadlines for getting our products ready for the two restaurants and bakery. It was a hectic, almost commercial environment, because they are very busy restaurants. The chef graded the product before it went out the door and often would say, "I don't like that, take it back and do thus and so with it." We not only baked, we worked for the school by setting up the dessert tables in the Sonoma Grill. It would have been working for free if we hadn't been paying for the privilege.

I had seven weeks of cakes and cake decorating. Our final exam was to design, cook, and decorate a wedding cake in one week. We had to start baking by Wednesday, assemble it on Thursday, and come in early Friday to finish it. Our final exam in another class consisted of a number of plated desserts. We had two hours to find recipes, name the desserts, make up a menu as if we were in a restaurant, price it, bake all the desserts, and then plate and present them. The chef instructor then tasted and graded them. The program was sometimes pretty stressful, but the knowledge and the diploma have been worth it.

The academy teaches baking on a different level. When I came back to work at Schat's, Zach wanted to know if he and his staff could look over my shoulder. The school's placement program is excellent, too, but I'll learn about setting up on my own from Zach.

—Donald Pittman

Editor's Note: We were lucky enough to be able to include the first-hand experiences of a graduate of one of the nation's outstanding culinary schools. CCA is one of numerous institutions in North America and throughout the world that teach how to become an accomplished baker. We list a few of them in the Appendix. You can consult your local public or academic library to find more in your area.

Explain in detail how you will position your bakery relative to its competition. That means describing your products' attributes, the customer needs you will fulfill, and your products' originality. Set out a pricing strategy that will cover costs, will show your awareness of the market, and will preserve order in marketplace. (You don't want to introduce "ruinous competition.") Tell how you will move product from the mixing bench to the end user: Will you use direct retail sales, wholesale, retail distributors, mail order? Outline your promotional strategy—your publicity, advertising, packaging, public relations, and personal sales techniques—and include an advertising budget. Let the reader see the business's entire retail and wholesale life.

Development Plans — Now you describe your products' qualities, and chart how the company will develop. In the first part of this section you describe your production process and note any of its advantages. This is where you show the reader you know your stuff. You would also tell about your products and product mix, how they mesh with the market, and how you plan to develop the products further to improve their market share. These development goals should arise from your earlier analysis of the market and competition. You need to *quantify* the goals with time lines based on real events such as new products, better equipment, an outdoor dining area, or the like. Top it off with a development budget for reaching each goal.

The other part of development plans refers to your organizational goals for the bakery. That means how you will learn any business and technical skills necessary to expand your product or service lines. After you set out the goals and skills, write out detailed procedural tasks and job assignments at each stage. You have to link these tasks and assignments to associated expenses such as raw materials, labor costs, overhead, general and administrative costs, marketing and sales costs, professional services, capital equipment, and anything else you need along the way. You may have to use temporary figures at this point until you nail down the estimates later in the Operations section. Be sure to tie goal-setting to facts and don't let your imagination run away with the process. Finally, to keep things balanced, identify and address all the risks involved.

Operations — This seemingly innocuous section title—Operations—refers to how a number of tables measure the business. The tables are: a cost of goods table, an operating expense table, and a capital requirements table. The going starts to get heavy about here, but you or your professional assistance will have to do it. The tables for Operations tie everything together and will be the foundation of your Financial Projections section.

A Cost of Goods table includes materials, labor and overhead, as in our pricing chapter, and it helps forecast profitability for your

There are about 3,200 billion living yeast cells per pound of fresh yeast. No two of them are exactly alike. Among other things, yeast improves bread's keeping qualities. Yeast doughs are called *almas*, or souls, in Mexico because the yeast seems to enspirit them. The introduction of commercial yeast meant also that not every bread dough had to be sour.

(Illus.: *The Fanny Farmer Cookbook*, Little Brown, 1918.)

cash flow statement, income statement, and balance sheet. The cost of goods table, if based on the raw-cost analyses we talked about, can be the most complicated you do. Costs multiplied by projected units sold for the year (remember that?) prepares you to make financial projections.

Operating expenses take account of the business's organizational structure, and its expense and capital requirements. Generally it covers marketing and sales (including customer relations and service), production, and how you organize and run the business. In

SOURDOUGH

Sourdough breads are as local as wines, and nearly as hard to manage and perfect. Results are often unpredictable. Rising times can vary and a dough may fail for no apparent reason—although often it means the starter has died. Then you can only throw away the dough and perhaps the starter, and begin again.

Flour and water left out in the open will sour on their own. In medieval times wooden baking troughs never got totally clean, and accumulated yeasts in the wood grain leavened the next batch of dough. An approved way to start a sourdough today has been to introduce the wild yeasts on grape skins into a new dough mix. Grapes are tied in cheesecloth and submerged in fresh dough. Yeasts adhere to the skins of any plant matter, however, not just grapes. Christopher Kump of Cafe Beaujolais in Mendocino says he chopped up a few pears from his orchard and wrapped them in cheesecloth to create the house starter. The results are very satisfactory.

Starter develops faster in warm, humid conditions, 75-80°F. It should inhabit the warmest room in the house, usually the kitchen, covered with a thin damp dish towel. The towel will attract wild yeasts in the air and encourage them to multiply.

Keep the towel damp over several days while beginning a starter. If a starter is not used and replenished about every three days with a batter of fresh flour and water, increasing acidity will slow then stop fermentation. If you're worried about your starter jar getting contaminated, pour the starter into a bowl to replenish it and scald the jar or run it through the dishwasher.

Established sourdough cultures will travel but won't emigrate. Away from home the yeasts languish, and local yeasts replace them. A San Francisco sourdough starter in Yuma, Arizona, will soon become a Yuma starter. Freshening a sourdough batch with flour and water hastens the replacement of special sourdough yeasts with local varieties.

A starter that smells bad, not sour, or has mouldy patches has weakened if not died. Signs of life are surface bubbles and a yeasty or purely sour smell. The mixture should turn grey as it ferments. Don't add salt to a starter, as salt inhibits yeast, although later in the baking process salt can control tartness. Use unbleached flour, because the bleach residue seems to hinder starter's development and may even give it a chlorine taste, as may chlorinated water.

---

order to work up the figures, you have to list tasks and who will perform them. Then you describe each task and how much each will cost in order to make money for the business. For example, if you project your volume of business and how many customers each employee can serve, you'll know how many employees you need. With the number of employees needed, you can project labor costs (and see if it falls within the 25% limit). You would base all the other variable costs on volume of business in the same way.

This is also how to determine how many units each piece of equipment must handle. That way you can work out your capital requirements, such as how much money you need to buy equipment and what depreciation to assign to it. You do it this way because these capital requirements are tied to projected sales, which you discussed earlier in the plan.

By now you begin to see why your earlier projections are important, and how the plan is linked together to make a tight working model of the business. That's a terrific help but it can also be deceptive. As Dwight D. Eisenhower said just before D-Day, "Planning is everything; but, once the bullets start flying, plans are nothing." That's why you shouldn't treat the plan as chiseled in granite. It's a guess, as good a guess as you can make, but still only conjectural.

After your bakery has been open awhile go back to the plan and look at it. You should do that at regular intervals—ideally every month or quarterly at least—and adjust your projections. If you have to revise it, do so and look at it again. Does it show what the business is really doing? What works and what does not? Will the business still fly? Are you doing better than expected? If disaster is roaring down the track at you, you will want to know that right away. Then you either derail the disaster or get out of the way—even if it means bailing out. But since you have a plan you will be on top of the business and can make the right decision in time. Besides, once you have gone to all the trouble of drafting a business plan, you shouldn't just throw it away.

Financial Projections — About here you will probably need professional assistance to set up an income statement, cash flow statement, and balance sheet.

The income statement sets out how much money the business will make. Revenue minus expenses will show a profit or loss, You may have to take a loss until break-even. You set up the income statement on monthly basis for the first year, and quarterly for later years. It shows income, cost of goods, gross profit margin, operating expenses, total expenses, net profit, depreciation, net profit before interest payments, net profit before taxes, taxes, profit after taxes.

Your cash flow statement—monthly for the first year and quarterly over the rest of the plan—tells how much cash you'll need to meet the business's obligations. You have to know where the cash is coming from and that it will be there when you need it. This statement shows cash sales, receivables, and other income, for total income. Expenses will include materials, labor, overhead, marketing and sales costs, administration, loan payments, and taxes.

The balance sheet shows the business's assets and liabilities, and your equity in it—that is, the business's net worth. If you are already in business or bought a going concern, the balance sheet should include previous years' balance sheets. That's where you show how much you expect to increase cash flow and profits.

Total assets comprise current and other assets. Current assets are cash, accounts receivable, and inventory. "Other" assets are capital and plant (book value less depreciation), investments you can't convert to cash, and whatever else is not current. Add up liabilities the same way: Current liabilities include accounts payable, accrued liabilities, and taxes due; long term liabilities are such things as bonds payable, mortgage, and notes payable. Your equity is the difference between your total assets and total liabilities.

Would I go into baking again? Yeah, it's rewarding, seeing the product of your labor there—when we have a good day and everything comes out really nice. It doesn't happen all the time. This is a handmade product. It does come out different every day. Like today: This kind of weather's good bread weather.

—ELLEN HERING
BRUCE BREAD

The financial statements will let you analyze the time to break-even, and the business ratios will tell you if the bakery can operate within industry averages. It's comforting to have a sense of where the bakery will stand relative to those numbers before you start. Once you set them up, it is very helpful to be able to track them as you go.

A lender will probably require you to include two or three years' prior income tax returns, a personal financial statement or balance sheet, any articles of incorporation or partnership agreements, copies of leases, and any other document that would help predict the venture's success.

THE MARKETING PLAN

When we decided to open our branch at the improvement center we used a fairly informal plan to show our banker that we were serious and to explain exactly what we intended to do. At this stage you call your working blueprint a "marketing plan," because, rather than proposing a new business, it tells how an established business plans to expand its market. At first, with only a new idea, you can't be sure exactly how everything will fall into place; but writing the idea down and filling in the details sets it up on paper. Basically, for example, we projected a café serving baked goods delivered from the original location for sale at the same price in a store seating 25 people, where an expected 1100 customers would walk through the improvement center doors each day, and where fixed costs were known quantities. Like a business plan, a marketing plan lets you figure out on paper whether the germ of your great idea will grow and bear fruit.

FINAL THOUGHTS

A business plan can be an enormous job, but it is *not* theoretical and definitely not a waste of time. It's a way to help you think about the future and make real choices economically—and safely—in advance. As you plan, ask yourself if you are being realistic and if you can do or learn to do each task as it arises. Ask if you are looking at your market coldly and objectively enough. Ask what kind of contingency plans you would set up at every step if an idea doesn't work as projected. How will you cover yourself when you have to get over-extended in order to expand? How would you handle a major disaster, even one your insurance covers? Who would you turn to or keep on tap for consultation?

Continually modified, a business plan can reflect all the knowledge and experience you acquire along the way. It can be a vehicle to put your business and working life into perspective. And, if you do the job right, it can be a tool to serve you for many years, all the way to winding up the business. Winding up is just as important as starting up. Unless you're sure you'll have an ongoing family business, you'll probably sell the bakery eventually. And bringing that off, with style and a good return, calls for doing all you can as a baker and entrepreneur to make that goodwill you add to the price a real and marketable asset. If it is, you'll know you've had a rewarding career as a baker who created and owned a great little bakery.

Business Plans

___Learn the market, using
   ___Statistical guides
   ___Direct observation
   ___Interviews
___Write down and analyze each fact learned
___Start to write the plan, looking for problems and cont-tradictions
___Consider using written guides, and help from government agencies and professional services
___Build the contents of the plan:
   ___Describe the business's basic facts, name, address, management team, etc.
   ___Evaluate the whole market and its subparts
   ___Analyze competition and where your bakery fits in
   ___Lay out marketing and development plans for the bakery, and consider risk
   ___Draft operations tables
   ___Do financial projections and analysis for five years: cash flow, assets & liabilities, income & expenses
   ___Attach any supplements lenders require
   ___Summarize the plan's critical facts for the beginning section
___Consider taking the plan to a desktop publisher for final polish if you will use it for financing

APPENDIXES

A TIME-LINE FOR BAKERY START-UP
("From Gleam in Your Eye to Grand Opening")

Date

_____ Review the criteria for where to set up your bakery and choose from potential localities

_____ Determine what your selected market needs and how you can satisfy it profitably

_____ Work up a business plan, company name, logo, market identity

_____ Having calculated start-up costs in the business plan, locate and compare sources of finance, then get the money

_____ Look for suitable commercial space within your chosen market and negotiate a real estate lease or purchase; or consider buying an existing bakery

_____ Begin to acquire equipment and put it in temporary storage if necessary

_____ Begin the licensing, permit, and construction process.

_____ Find a bookkeeper or accountant, and other necessary professionals

_____ Locate, evaluate, and select suppliers

_____ Create and start to carry out a marketing plan

_____ Draft personnel policies, then advertise for, hire, and train staff (even if it's only one helper).

_____ Get set for the grand opening: Stock up, advertise, bake and

_____ Go!

B. START-UP COSTS LIST

Make your own copy of this list and add new costs as you plan your bakery. Line up all the items down the left side of the sheet and put costs to the right. Use category subtotals and a grand total. Then increase your estimate by at least 25% to allow for surprises.

Equipment

Oven
Proof box
Freezer
Refrigerator
Mixers
Benches
Racks
Storage bins
Pots, pans, utensils
Dishwasher
Three-drop sink
Lighting
Showcases
   Standard
   Refrigerated
Steam table
Display hardware
Cash register
Computer and printer
Computer software
Coffee/espresso machines
Microwave oven
Cold-drink case
Dishes, cups, glassware, service
Tables/chairs
Service tables
Outdoor tables/chairs/umbrellas
Office furniture
Trash containers

Building improvements and construction costs

Signage and façade
Awning
Electrical
Plumbing
Sewerage
HVAC
Locks and security

Interior walls and built-ins
Wall and floor treatments
Lighting, ceiling fans, etc.
Exterior construction
Landscaping
Telephone installation
Utilities deposits
Pre-opening sanitation and trash
   removal

Permits/Licenses

Fictitious/assumed business name
Business license
Public/environmental health depart-
   ment clearance
Construction permit

Marketing costs

Graphic design
Business cards, stationery, packag-
   ing, menus
Media ads
Handbills, coupons
Opening extras and events

Supplies

This will vary with each business. Other than flour, sugar, salt, and yeast, the cost of supplies must be worked out from your starting menu. Don't forget cleaning supplies, linens, and paper goods.

Professional services

Advertising agency
Architect/designer
Building contractor
Bookkeeping
Legal
Insurance

JOB DESCRIPTION FOR COUNTER PERSONNEL

Each counter person is to uphold the highest customer service standard as well as to have product knowledge.

WE'RE HERE TO SELL.

Sample bread out daily, especially at lunch time for people who are standing in line. It helps ease those hunger pangs and gives a taste of our delicious specialty breads.

People like new ideas and change. Make their experience here interesting by telling them about a product they may not know about. Tell the customer about specials and low prices.

We'd like to try to limit donations. If there is lots of bread left late in the afternoon, put it on sale with one of our pre-made sale signs. Then advertise: "Did you see our great bread sale? Buy one at the regular price and get the second for 99¢?"

Always remember to be friendly and to go the extra mile. Correct orders that are not top quality. For example, when items are not prepared to the customer's wishes, fix the order speedily and without fuss.

REMEMBER ALWAYS TO:
1. Smile
2. Greet the customer early, at least acknowledge his or her presence if you are busy
3. Use the customer's name if you know it (Look at order forms.)
4. Promote a product

Always focus your attention on the customer; please attend to customer needs first, interrupting another task if necessary. When the phone rings, tell the caller you will be right back, place him or her on hold, and finish waiting on the customer. Try to make the experience as enjoyable as possible for the customer, but don't forget the caller.

We expect counter personnel to have a product knowledge based on the menu and price list that's posted on the blackboard. Please take a menu home and study it carefully. It is important to know a product's content to fit a customer's needs, i.e., for diabetics.

SKILLS

Counter personnel need a working knowledge of the cash register and all its functions pertaining to sales. Counter personnel are not authorized to make cash pay-outs.

Counter personnel need to be familiar with the functions of the espresso machine and the characteristics of the specialty coffees we offer on our menu.

HOUSEKEEPING

Everyone is responsible for keeping the bakery in an orderly, clean and safe condition. Please make sure the display cases look exceptionally well organized.

We promise you will never have a dull moment here; but if you find one, you don't have to stand around getting bored. There is always something to clean, like tables, the top of the refrigerator, the coffee and tea station, inside the cabinets, etc., etc., etc.

Please share the duties described in the closing list. Everyone will take turns cleaning, bussing tables, washing and drying dishes, stocking, etc.

After washing dishes, please remember to drain the water. Nobody likes to stick his or hands in dirty dish water. And remember to share the sink with the kitchen help. They have to wash their dishes as they go. And we all have to get out of each other's way in a hurry.

MISCELLANEOUS

All food, including lunches, is 50% off during a shift. On non-working days lunches (but not baked goods) are 50% off for the employee but not for whoever accompanies the employee.

All juices, Cokes, V-8s, etc, will cost an employee 50¢. There is no charge for tea, coffee, or hot chocolate. You may eat before or after your shift and during a management-designated break during the shift.

Don't eat or drink behind the counter. When you sample bakery items in order to tell customers about them, please do it behind the divider wall, out of customer view.

Except for emergencies do not make personal phone calls during work. They interfere with customer service. Make personal calls on your own time only. Return calls that come in while you're working during your break or have your callers try to reach you then.

Let's keep gossip to a minimum. It lowers morale. If you have a genuine concern please tell your supervisor so we can see how to resolve the problem.

Information changes constantly, so take time to scan the bulletin board when you arrive for your shift.
During summer vacation times there are lots of extra hours to work if you want them. Let us know how many you want. And be sure to notify us about when *you* plan to go on vacation.

Staff are not allowed behind the counter except during their shift. We can't make exceptions, even if it's your shift and you know the other staff person.

It is great working with you. I notice and appreciate your dedication. You're doing fine. We're all learning and growing. Our motto: WHATEVER IT TAKES! We can't be the best without you.
Thank you.

CUSTOMER SERVICE STANDARDS

We ask that all employees consider this policy seriously. Great customer service is the hallmark of our bakery. We are committed to improving customer service, and all of us must follow these guidelines.

1. The customer is always right. Do not argue with a customer ever!
2. When a customer walks through the door greet him or her in the following manner every time!
   "Hi, how are you today? What can I get for you?" (If the customer needs a few moments make some suggestions.)
3. Remember to take one customer at a time, no matter how long the lines are, and give each one the quality service each deserves. When delivering food to customers seated at tables, make sure it has been prepared properly. If it hasn't, bring it to the cooks' attention. Make sure the customers are happy before you leave the table, and ask if they require anything else. You will have done an outstanding job. It reflects positively on you, on the bakery, and on every one of us, and it gives the bakery a reputation for outstanding food and service.
4. Once you serve the customer the farewell is as follows:
   Thank you, enjoy your ____, have a great day." When you thank a customer, mean it. Make the customer feel good about their purchase. We appreciate a customers' business. We wouldn't be here without it.
5. Answer the phone like this:
   "_____ bakery café, this is ____. May I help you?" When another call comes in or you have to look something up, say, "May I put you on hold while I check?" Then, "Thanks for holding." Close with "Have a great day."
6. Use paper tissues when handling all product, especially the bread.
7. All hair should be pulled back. Don't comb your hair with your hands in the customer's presence.
8. All employees will wear the bakery's shirt while working. Other dress: No jeans with holes or cut-offs. No open-toed shoes. No pants worn below the waist with boxer shorts sticking out. Every employee will be issued a company apron to wear while at the counter. If you lose it or don't return it when your employment ends, you'll have to pay for it. Right now aprons run $15.00.
9. If you sneeze, wash your hands immediately before continuing to serve customers.
10. **Lunchtime!**
    a. Always make sure each order is marked appropriately.
    b. Make sure you have everything when delivering food.
    c. On arriving at the table give the customers your full attention and ask if you can get them anything else. If they ask for water or if they didn't know where to get soup, do them a favor and get it for them. If someone at the table did not get food, ask their name and what they ordered, and tell them you will be right back with it.
    d. If we mess up an order, don't worry about whose fault it is, just take care of the problem immediately. No yelling among ourselves.
    e. If you notice someone waiting for a to-go order, ask his or her name and find out how the order is coming along.
    f. Always provide a clean table and silverware.
    g. During the lunch ask how everyone is and do cookie runs.

h. When people get up to leave, tell them thanks and to have a good day.

i If a customer wants lunch after we've closed down the lunch line, tell them kindly about our 11 to 3 weekday and 11 to 4 weekend lunch hours. Then offer soup, pizza, a quiche á la carte, or a ready-made sandwich from the cold case if they're available.

11. Whenever a customer places a special order there may be a reason why we can't get it out on time. If so, warn of the problem and try to find a way to get the order out as fast as possible. Your supervisors or I can help you with this.

12. If you have a problem customer, one you cannot make happy, turn the situation over to one of the managers. If a manager is unavailable, get the customer's phone number and tell them will take care of it. Always apologize first, then reassure.

13. If a customer has a complaint, make a note of it after you've taken care of it. We need to keep track of complaints so that we can improve our service.

14. Finally, to be completely professional, you'll have to leave your personal problems at home. If you have a problem and think I can help out, my door is always open. Treat all baked goods honestly and give the customer 100% of your attention. Don't use rude or loud language in front of a customer. If a problem arises, don't embarrass the customer with it. Just call your supervisor calmly for help.

15. Help keep a clean, sanitary environment.

PROGRESSIVE DISCIPLINARY POLICY

The bakery reserves the right to terminate any employee at any time. Employees have the right to quit at any time.

We, the management, will take progressive action to correct problems as they arise. To maintain a good working relationship we will try to counsel employees about conduct in an open discussion. We want the discussion to be courteous and businesslike, and we'll suggest how to work together effectively.

If we can't solve problems, we will have to conduct a documented conversation about misconduct. Employees will be told what happens if their conduct does not improve, and they will get a written note. If conduct does not improve, the next step will be a written warning. After a period of time, we will hold a follow-up discussion to assess progress. A lack of improvement at that point could result in suspension or termination with a written note of our decision.

To summarize:
1. First time - discussion with note.
2. Second time - written notice and loss of a shift.
3. Third time - goodbye if no improvement. You will be terminated.

I have read and understand how everything covered above is to be done.

Signed: _____ Date: _____

D. EQUIPMENT, CONSULTANTS, SUPPLIERS

We explained where to find equipment and tools in the book, but here are two examples of an item we did not cover in detail that you may want to investigate.

Brick and stone bake ovens

EARTHSTONE WOOD-FIRE OVENS
1233 North Highland Avenue
Los Angeles, CA 90038
Telephone (800) 840-4915; fax (213) 962-6408
EARTHSTONE installs commercial and residential wood- or gas-fired "stone" ovens throughout the United States, Canada, Mexico, and abroad. Their modular and pre-assembled ovens of advanced refractory materials are U.L. listed and warranted for five years. Commercial installations appear to be mainly in restaurants. The California Culinary Academy and the New England Culinary Institute in Vermont have them.

Alan Scott
OVENCRAFTERS
5600 Marshall Road, RR2
Petaluma, CA 94952
Telephone (415) 663-9010
Scott, an Australian-born blacksmith, is a baker who now designs and builds domestic and commercial brick ovens. Ovencrafters' is accessible on the Internet; use your search engine to look for "brick bakeoven." Scott will publish a book on the subject with Dan Wing which promises to be the definitive reference on brick oven specifications, construction, and performance. Although Scott favors home bake ovens, Wing leans toward commercial installations. They may end up with two books. The projected book's title and publication date were unavailable at time of printing.

Major restaurant design, equipment, and supply companies also handle wood-fired pizza ovens. Look in big-city Yellow Pages, and even in middle-sized city Yellow Pages.

E. CULINARY AND BAKING SCHOOLS

California

California Culinary Academy, 625 Polk Street, San Francisco, CA 94102; (800) BAY CHEF; fax (415) 771-2194
Rated among U.S.-based culinary institutions as second only to New York's Culinary Institute of America (CIA) CCA was founded in 1977. It has over 700 students at any one time and offers a 16-month culinary arts course three times a year and a 30-week certificate course in baking and pastry arts. It is accredited by the Accrediting

Commission of Career Schools and Colleges (ACCSCT) and the American Culinary Education Institute (ACFEI). Ninety-three percent of students find employment within six months of graduation.

The Culinary Institute at Greystone, 2555 Main Street, St. Helena, CA 94574; (707) 967-1100 See The Culinary Institute of America, New York.

Colorado
Johnson & Wales, Vail, CO. See Rhode Island.

Florida
Florida Culinary Institute, 2400 Metrocentre Boulevard, West Palm Beach, FL 33407; (800) 826-9986.
Founded in 1982 by New England Institute of Technology, a vocational college in Rhode Island, it severed ties with NEIT in 1984. FCI offers associate degrees in culinary arts and international baking and pastry arts. Its student body is 450 and 95 percent of graduates find employment.

Johnson & Wales, North Miami, FL. See Rhode Island.

Illinois
The Cooking and Hospitality Institute of Chicago, Inc., 361 West Chestnut, Chicago, IL 60610; (312) 944-0882.
Established in 1983, CHIC offers a two-year associate degree in culinary arts and six-month programs in professional cooking, pastry, and restaurant management. CHIC is accredited by ACCSCT. It offers day and evening classes and operates the CHIC Café, which offers a three-course lunch for $12.00.

New York
Culinary Institute of America, 433 Albany Post Road, Hyde Park, NY 12538-1499; (800) 285-4627.
The first of its kind in the United States, CIA was founded in New Haven, Connecticut, in 1946. Its more than 100 instructors come from 20 countries. CIA offers associate degrees in culinary arts and pastry arts, as well as bachelor's degrees in culinary arts management and baking and pastry arts management. Each year CIA trains more than 2,000 undergraduates and offers continuing education to 4,000 professionals. A new class of undergraduates begins every three weeks. Accredited by ACCSCT, it also awards a certificate in baking and pastry arts. Eighty percent of CIA undergraduates receive some form of financial aid. Ninety-two percent are employed within six months of graduation, the remaining eight percent advancing to graduate or continuing education programs.

New York Restaurant School, 75 Varick Street, New York, NY 10013; (800) 654-CHEF; fax (212) 5644.

The New York Restaurant School started in 1981 as a division of the New School for Social Research and was independently licensed in 1987. It offers certificates in pastry arts and culinary skills, as well as associate degrees in culinary arts and restaurant management. Classes run around the clock, and students can attend full time or part time. NYRS is ACCSCT accredited, and 93 percent of students find jobs in their fields.

Peter Kump's New York Cooking School, 307 East 92nd Street, New York, NY 10128; (800) 522-4610; fax (212) 522-4610.

Peter Kump's New York Cooking School requires all applicants to have at least two years of college. Students can choose either culinary or pastry arts full-time (20 weeks) or part-time (26 weeks). Following course work students take six-week "externships," preferably in France. Selected students may take a one-year grand diploma course, comprising the culinary and pastry curricula, two externships, and seven more weeks of instruction.

Rhode Island

Johnson & Wales University. College of Culinary Arts, Providence, RI 02903; (800) 343-2565. Charleston, SC (800) 868-1522. Norfolk, VA (800) 277-2433. North Miami, FL (800) 232-2433. Vail, CO (303) 476-2993.

Founded in 1914, Johnson & Wales offers a two-year AAS degree in culinary arts at Providence, Charleston, Norfolk, and North Miami. It offers a degree in baking and pastry arts at all but the Norfolk campus. Norfolk offers a one-year certificate in baking and pastry arts.

South Carolina

Johnson & Wales, Charleston, SC. See Rhode Island.

Virginia

Johnson & Wales, Norfolk, VA. See Rhode Island.

Canada

Stratford Chefs School, 68 Nile Street, Stratford, ONT N5A 4C5, Canada; (519) 5679

This non-profit school is based on an apprenticeship model and its tuition is very reasonable for Canadian citizens. Tuition for non-citizens is competitive with U.S. schools like CIA and CCA. It is a small school, taking just 65 students at a time. All find jobs.

George Brown School of Hospitality, 300 Adelaide St. E, Toronto, Ont. M5A 1N1, Canada; (416) 867-223.

LOCAL BAKING SCHOOLS

Here is a partial list of local baking schools. Anyone who wants to take courses in baking, should see what is available at locally. While investigating the schools' training programs evaluate their requirements and review each school's accreditation, standards and affiliations, the basic and advanced degrees and certifications the instructors hold, and the degrees and certifications the schools offer.

Alaska

Alaska Vocational Technical Center, Box 615, Seward, AK 99664; (907) 224-3322.

University of Alaska, Culinary Arts Dept., 3750 Giest Rd., Fairbanks, AK 99701; (907) 474-5080.

Arizona

Metro Tech V.I.P., 1900 Thomas Rd., Phoenix, AZ 85015; (612) 271-2655.

California

Cerritos College, 11110 E. Alondra Blvd., Norwalk, CA 90650; (213) 860)-2451.

Laney College, 900 Fallon Ave., Oakland, CA 94607-4804; (510) 464-3407.

Tante Marie's Cooking School, Inc., 271 Francisco St., San Francisco, CA 94133; (415) 788-6699.

Florida

Robert Morgan Technical Institute, 18180 SW 122 Avenue, Miami, FL 33177; (305) 253-9920.

Kansas

American Institute of Baking, 1213 Bakers Way, Manhattan, KS 66502; (913) 537-4750.

Kansas State University, Dept. of Grain Science & Industry, Schellenberger Hall, Manhattan, KS 66502; (913) 532-6161.

Illinois

William Rainey Harper College, 1200 W. Algonquin Rd., Palatine, IL 60067; (312) 397-3000.

Indiana

Country Kitchen, 3225 Wells St., Ft. Wayne, IN 46808; (219) 482-4835.

Iowa

Iowa Western Community College, 2700 College Rd., Box 4c, Council Bluffs, IA 51502; (712) 325-3778.

Maryland

Baltimore's International Culinary Arts Institute, Harbor Campus, Baltimore, MD 21202-4066; (301) 752-4593, (800) 624-9926.

L'Academie de Cuisine, 5021 Wilson Lane, Bethesda, MD 20814; (301) 986-9490.

Massachusetts

The Cambridge School of Culinary Arts, 2020 Massachusetts, Avenue, Cambridge, MA 02140; (617) 353-4130.

Michigan

Schoolcraft Community College, 18600 Haggerty Road, Livonia, MI 48152; (313) 462-4400.

Minnesota

Duluth Technical Institute, 2102 Trinity Rd., Duluth, MN 55811; (218) 722-2801.

Dunwoody Institute, 818 Wayzata Blvd., Minneapolis, MN 55403; (612) 374-5800.

Mankato Technical Institute, 1920 Lee Blvd., North Mankato, MN 56001; (507) 625-3441.

New Hampshire

New Hampshire Vocational College, 2020 Riverside Dr., Berlin, NH 03570; (603) 752-1113.

New Jersey

Atlantic County Vocational, Rt. 40 Mays Landing, NJ 08330; (609) 625-2249.

Union County Vocational Technical Schools, 1776 Rairtan Rd., Scotch Plains, NJ 07076; (201) 889-2000.

New Mexico

Albuquerque Technical Vocational Institute, 525 Buena Vista SE, Albuquerque, NM 87106; (505) 848-1442.

New York

Adirondack Community College, Bay Road, Glen Falls, NY 12804; (518) 793-4491.

Chocolate Gallery, 135 W. 50th St., New York, NY 10020; (212) 582-3510.

International Pastry Arts Center, 525 Executive Blvd., Elmsford, NY 10523; (914) 347-3737.

Mohawk Community College, Rome Campus, Upper Floyd Ave., Rome, NY 13440; (315) 339-3470.

Paul Smith's College of Arts and Sciences, Routes 86 and 30, P.O. Box 265, Paul Smith's, NY 12970-0265; (800) 421-2605.

Ohio

Owens Technical College, C.S. #10,000 Oregon Rd., Toledo, OH 46399; (419) 666-0588.

Oklahoma

Oklahoma State University, Okmulgee Branch, 4th & Mission, Okmulgee, OK 74447; (918) 756-6211.

Pennsylvania

Bucks County Technical School, Wister Rd., Fairless Hills, PA 19630; (213) 949-1700.

The Restaurant School, 2129 Walnut St., Philadelphia, PA 19103; (215) 561-3446.

Tennessee

Memphis Country Academy, Inc., 1252 Peabody Avenue, Memphis, TN 38104; (901) 722-8892.

Texas

St. Phillips College, 2111 Nevada Street, San Antonio, TX 78203; (512) 531-3315.

Vermont

New England Culinary Institute, 250 Main St., Montpelier, VT 05602; (802) 223-6324.

Washington

Anderson School Restaurant/Hospitality Program, 18603 Bothell Way NE, Bothell, WA 98011; (206) 485-0244.

Bellingham Technical College, 3028 Lindbergh Ave., Bellingham, WA 92225.

Clark College, 1800 E. McLoughlin Blvd., Vancouver, WA 98663; (206) 699-0156.

Seattle Central Community College, 1701 Broadway, Seattle, WA 98122; (206) 587-5424.

South Seattle Community College, 1819 N. Greene St., Spokane, WA 99207-5399; (509) 536-7284.

Wisconsin

Wisconsin Indianhead Technical College, 2100 Beaser Ave., Ashland, WI 54806; (715) 682-4591.

Lakeshore Technical College, 1290 North Avenue, Cleveland, WI 53015; (414) 458-4183.

F. SELECTED BAKING FRANCHISES

Blue Chip Cookies, 100 First Street, Suite 2030, San Francisco, CA 94105, telephone (415) 546-3840; fax (415) 546-9717. Contact Matt Nadler, president. A gourmet cookie chain whose franchisees prepare its cookies from scratch. It sells 20 different varieties of cookies and brownies, fruitbars, cinnamon rolls, muffins, coffee cake, carrot cake, and a line of fat-free cookies. It also markets beverages, including espresso, and ice cream and yogurt. It has been in business since 1983 and franchising since 1986. There are 32 franchises in 11 states, and 8 company-owned stores. The franchise fee is $29,500 and capital requirements are from $117,000 to $190,000. The company assists in site location and construction, lease negotiation, and third-party and SBA financing. It offers a training program in product preparation, business operating procedures, and marketing. On-going support is by corporate operational visits and field assistance.

Breadsmith, Inc., 3510 N. Oakland Avenue, Sherwood, WI 55211; e-mail, bread@franchise.com. Contact, Marc Cayle. A traditional European bread retail bakery in which customers can watch the baking process. Award winner at the National Restaurant Show bread-baking contest. There are 39 units franchised in 16 states. Breadsmith has been in business since 1994 and has been franchising since 1994. Franchise fee is $25,000 and capital requirements run from $20,000 to $250,000. The company requires no prior experience and offers two weeks of hands-on training to master the company's baking system. It provides on-going support in staffing and management techniques.

Dunkin' Donuts, Inc., 14 Pacella Park Drive, Randolph, MA 02368, telephone (800) 777-9983. This is a retail coffee chain that sells muffins, bagels, donuts and other bakery products. There are 4,139 franchised units in 43 states and 20 countries. The company began in 1950 and started franchising in 1955. The franchise fee is $40,000, and capital requirements are $200,000 in liquid funds, with a net worth minimum of $400,000. The five-week training and support at the Dunkin' Donuts University in Braintree, MA, covers product preparation, profit skills. The company provides pre- and post-opening assistance. Dunkin' Donuts has recently associated with Baskin-Robbins Ice Cream and expanded into non-traditional locations such as airports, universities, and hospitals. *Entrepreneur* magazine rated it among the top 10 franchisors.

Great Harvest Bread Co., 23 South Idaho St., Dillon MT 59725. Franchise sales telephone (800) 442-0424. Retail bakeries using premium whole wheat flour stone ground fresh daily on premises. Franchise established 1970. Fee $20,000. Royalty 6% of monthly gross, plus 2% for advertising budget. Total investment about $75,000.

Mrs. Fields Cookies, 462 West Bearcat Drive, Salt Lake City, UT 84115. Contact: Keith Gerson, Vice President Franchising and Licensing; telephone (801) 463-2194; fax (801) 463-2176; website, www/mrsfields.com. Company now has three divisions, the original firm, Big Apple Bagels, and Seattle's Best Coffee. In spring 1997 the company inaugurated bakery-café outlets, centered around its croissants and bagels, for sit-down noon-to-evening meals. Franchise fee $25,000. Capital requirements for a new outlet vary depending on micro-market and regional costs. Experience in major malls has fixed capital-requirement ranges from $175,000 to $239,100. Capital to purchase existing store, based on actual sales volume and cash flow, can be much lower or higher ($42,825 to $414,100). Company seeks management or retail small-business experience—preferably but not necessarily in food service. To assure highest quality control the company wants the "intrapreneur" who will work hard within company guidelines. Two weeks' training; ongoing support.

Here's a random sample of other franchises:

Atlanta Bread Co. International, Inc., 115 Davis Cir., Marietta, GA 30060.

Big Sky Bread Company, 455 Delta Ave., No. 204, Cincinnati, OH 45226

Cheri Brook & Company, 9645 E. Colonial Drive, Orlando, FL 32817.

Coffee Treat, 19 Yarn Road, Etobicoke, Ont. M7B 6J6, Canada.

Coffee Way, 123 Rexdale Blvd., Rexdale, Ont. M9W 1P3, Canada.

Saint Cinnamon Bake Shop, 7181 Woodbine Ave., Suite 222, Markham, Ont. L3R 1A3, Canada.

Wetzel's Pretzels, 65 North Raymond Ave., Suite 310 Pasadena, CA 91103.

G. FURTHER READING

GENERAL BUSINESS BOOKS

Bangs, David H., Jr. *Business Planning Guide* (Dover, NH, 6th rev. Ed., 1992, Upstart Publishing Co.).

Cities of the United States: A Compilation of Current Information on Economic, Cultural, Geographical, and Social Conditions (Detroit, MI, 1994, Gale Research, Inc.).

Clifford, Denis, and Ralph Warner. *The Partnership Book* (Berkeley, CA 1991, Nolo Press).

Cohen, William A. *Building a Mail Order Business: A Complete Manual for Success* (New York, 4th ed., 1996, Wiley & Sons).

Goldstein, Arnold S. *The Complete Guide to Buying and Selling a Business* (New York, 1983, Wiley & Sons).

Holmes, Roy H. *Common Sense Management & Motivation for the Real World* (Lancaster, PA 1993, Starburst Publishers).

Kamoroff, Bernard Bear. *Small Time Operator: How to Start Your Own Small Business, Keep Your Books, Pay Your Taxes and Stay Out of Trouble* (Laytonville, CA, 5th ed., 1997, Bell Springs Publishing).

Levinson, Jay Conrad. *Guerrilla Advertising: Cost-Effective Techniques for Small-Business Success* (Boston, 1994, Houghton Mifflin).

_____ *Guerrilla Marketing: Secrets for Making Big Profits from Your Small Business* (Boston, MA, 2nd Ed. 1993, Houghton Mifflin).

_____ *Guerrilla Marketing Attack: New Strategies, Tactics & Weapons for Winning Big Profits from Your Small Business* (Boston, MA, 1989, Houghton Mifflin).

Rainsford, Peter, and David H. Bangs, Jr. *The Restaurant Planning Guide* (Dover, NH, 1992, Upstart Publishing Company).

Savageau, David, and Geoffrey Loftus. *Places Rated Almanac* (New York, 5th ed., 1997, Simon & Schuster-Macmillan).

Simon, Julian, et al. *How to Start and Operate a Mail Order Business* (New York, 5th ed., 1993, McGraw-Hill).

Steingold, Fred S. *Legal Guide for Starting and Running a Small Business* (Berkeley, CA, 1992, Nolo Press).

U.S. Department of Commerce, Bureau of the Census. *Statistical Abstract of the United States* (Washington, DC, 1992, U.S. Government Printing Office).

Wylie, Peter, and Mardy Grothe. *Problem Employees: How to Improve Their Performance* (Dover, NH, 2d ed., 1991, Upstart Publishing Co.).

BAKERY AND FOOD SERVICE BOOKS

Alford, Jeffrey, and Naomi Duguid. *Flatbreads and Flavors: A Baker's Atlas* (New York, 1995, Morrow). Pizza, fougasse, tortillas, matzoh, bannock—flatbreads worldwide with local dishes.

Bacon, Richard M. *The Forgotten Art of Building and Using a Brick Bake Oven* (Dublin, NH, 1977, Yankee, Inc.). A discussion of small New England home ovens of the 17th and 18th Centuries. Construction techniques and methods. Illustrated. Out of print and hard to find.

Bailey, Adrian. *The Blessings of Bread* (New York, 1975, Paddington Press). Wheat, flour, and bread through the ages. Good recipes.

Clayton, Bernard, Jr. *Bernard Clayton's New Complete Book of Breads* (New York, Rev. ed., 1995, Fireside Books). Encyclopedic, a classic.

Collister, Linda, and Anthony Blake. *The Bread Book* (New York, 1993, Sedgewick Press). Originally published in Great Britain, this is a good survey of contemporary uses of traditional European baking.

David, Elizabeth. *English Bread and Yeast Cookery*, (Newton, MA, new American ed., 1994, Biscuit Books, Inc.). An exhaustive history of the craft from a noncommercial British perspective.

Field, Carol. *The Italian Baker* (New York, 1985, Harper & Rowe). Baking in the Italian style, with plenty of recipes.

Fields, Debbi, and Alan Furst. *"One Smart Cookie:" How a Housewife's Chocolate Chip Recipe Turned into a Multimillion-Dollar Business* (New York, 1987, Simon & Schuster). A young woman who started with no business experience but a good product, plenty of determination, and a banker who believed. It is the real thing and definitely worth reading.

Fox, Margaret, and John Bear. *Cafe Beaujolais*, (Berkeley, CA, 1984, Ten Speed Press). Life on California's Mendocino Coast in a successful small restaurant with a production bakery serving a mail-order business.

Leader, Daniel, and Judith Blahnik. *Bread Alone* (New York, 1993, William Morrow). Back to baking's roots for old-fashioned breads baked the old-fashioned way.

Malgieri, Nick. *How to Bake* (New York, 1995, Harper Collins). A good baker from a strong baking background considers the craft and gives recipes.

McGee, Harold. *On Food and Cooking: The Science and Lore of the Kitchen* (New York, 1984, Scribner & Sons). The most accessible and probably best scientific guide to everything about the lore and chemistry of nutrition, foodstuffs, and cooking.

Ortiz, Joe. *The Village Baker* (Berkeley, CA, 1993, Ten Speed Press). One owner of the exemplary Gayle's Bakery & Rosticceria reveals his exploration and perpetuation of old world bread-baking traditions. Buy your own copy, read it, keep it!

Reinhart, Br. Peter. *Brother Juniper's Bread Book: Slow Rise as Method and Metaphor* (New York, 1990, Addison-Wesley). The founding and rise of a stellar Sonoma County, California, bakery, and its approach to the craft.

Silverton, Nancy. *Nancy Silverton's Breads from the La Brea Bakery: Recipes for the Connoisseur* (New York, 1996, Villard Books [Random House]). Another good discussion of traditional bread-baking technique, with excellent recipes.

PERIODICALS

Baker's Journal ($15 [Can.] per year), 106 Lakeshore Rd. East, Ste 209, Mississauga, Ont. L5G 1E3, Canada. National business publication serving the Canadian baking industry.

Bakery Production and Marketing ($14 per year, free to qualified bakery personnel) 1350 East Touhy Ave., P.O. Box 5080, Des Plaines, IL 60017-5080. Nonmember subscriptions: 8773 South Ridgeline Boulevard, Highlands Ranch, CO 80126-2329; (800) 662-7776. $99.90 per year.

Modern Baking ($60 per year; free to qualified personnel), Meehan Publishing Co., 2700 River Road, Des Plaines, IL 60018.

A FEW SOURCES FOR BOOKS ON BAKING ARE:

Nach Waxman's Kitchen Arts and Letters Bookstore, 1435 Lexington Ave., New York, NY 10128

C.H.I.P.S., 1307 Golden Bear Lane, Kingwood, TX 77339

J.B. Prince Co., 29 West 38th St., New York, NY 10018

And don't forget *www.amazon.com* on the Internet

H. ASSOCIATIONS

Allied Trades of the Baking Industry (ATBI)
4510 West 89th Street
Prairie Village, KS 66207
Telephone (913) 341-0765; Fax (913) 341-3625

Founded in 1920, ATBI has about 1,000 members. Individual dues are $25 and corporate dues $250. It is for salespeople from allied trades servicing the baking industry. It promotes the industry through corporate service to national, state, and local bakery associations, encourages mutual understanding and goodwill between the baking industry and the allied trades. It publishes the *Allied Tradesman*, every two years, a handbook of information on baking schools and scholarships.

American Institute of Baking (AIB)
1213 Bakers Way
Manhattan, KS 66502
Telephone (913) 537-4750; Fax (913) 537-1493
Web Page: www.bakery-net.com/rdocs/aib.html

Founded in 1919, the AIB now has 689 members and a staff of 120, with a budget of about $9 million. Corporate dues are $300. The AIB conducts basic and applied baking research and has an education center for hands-on training. Its website provides an international baking magazine resource and a buyers' guide. It has a museum and educational and scientific advisory committees. It publishes the *American Institute of Baking - Technical Bulletin* (monthly at $30 per year) and *Baker's Way*, a monthly newsletter free to members.

Bread Bakers' Guild of America, Inc. (BBGA)
Executive Director, Gregory Mistell
P.O. Box 22254
Pittsburgh, PA 15222
Telephone (412)322-8275; Fax (412) 322-3412
Web Page: www.bbga.org

Founded 1993, the BBGA has a staff of three and 1,300 members and is growing rapidly; 250 new members joined in the first six months of 1997. Annual budget is approximately $300,000. The scale of dues ranges from $35 to $65 for individuals, and company dues from $75 for a new bakery on up. The Guild publishes a quarterly newsletter and has one educational event a year, consisting of seminars and panel discussions, which coincides with the Retailers Bakery Association (RBA) convention. In addition to regional educational and networking programs, the Guild sponsors Baking Team USA to compete in the world bread-baking competition in France. The next international competition, for which the Guild will sponsor preliminary regional competitions, is in 1999. It also funds two international trips a year, sending American bakers to schools in France and Germany.

Retailers Bakery Association (RBA)
14239 Park Center Drive
Laurel MD 20207
Telephone (301) 725-2149; Fax (301) 725-2187
Web Page: www.dunwoody.tec.mn.us/fact.html

Founded in 1918 the RBA now has about 3,500 members and a staff of 17, with a budget of about $2.2 million. There are 41 local groups. For independent and in-store bakeries and bakery-delicatessens (2,500), allied companies (780), and other (220). It provides information, management, production, merchandising, and special events services. It maintains a library of 200 books on retail baking. Publications are the *Allied Directory*, an annual listing member firms servicing the baking industry, information on products, equipment, ingredients, or services offered. It is free to members. It also publishes a newsletter, *RBA Insight*, 11 times a year, and *Retail Bakers of America—Government Bulletin*, periodically. Free to members.

The RBA holds its annual convention for three days each spring, with hundreds of exhibitors displaying the latest trends and equipment in baking, local events and tours, and a few dozen valuable programs on bakery management and production.

I. SOFTWARE

Baker's Choice. Computer Services Co., 2602 West Silver Spring Drive, Milwaukee, WI 53209-4220; telephone (414) 461-6006, fax, (414) 461-6912. Baker's Choice software. $199. Product and formula costing, product planning; nutrition analysis add-on.

Datapax Bakery & Food Processing System. Datapax, Inc., 5125 North 16th Street, Suite A210, Phoenix, AZ 85016; (602) 274-13121; fax, (602) 274-1476. High-end product and formula management, ac--counting, and production control program. Basic module free. Additional modules for above a thousand to a few thousand dollars.

SweetWARE stockCoster and *nutraCoster*. SweetWARE, 1906B Alameda Avenue, Alameda, CA 94501; (510)814-8800; fax (510) 814-8844; order number, (800) 526-7900. Formula costing and inventory module and nutritional analysis and printing module, $149 and $99. 45-day free trial.

INDEX

n

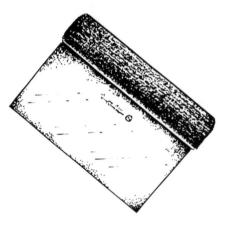

Copy this page to order from

ACTON CIRCLE—

***The Baker's Trade: A Recipe for Creating the Successful Small Bakery,* by Zachary Y. Schat.** Everything you need to know to start and manage a successful small retail or wholesale bakery. 275 pages, 8½x11", index, bibliog., $24.95.

***Bookkeeping and Tax Preparation: Start and Build a Prosperous Bookkeeping, Tax, and Financial Services Business,* by Gordon P. Lewis.** The techniques and information you need to build your flair for figures into a highly profitable, well-rounded business. 179 pages, 7x10", index, bibliog., forms, $18.95.

***Lawn Care & Gardening: A Down-to-Earth Guide to the Business,* by Kevin Rossi.** Everything about soils, fertilizers, grasses, plants, pests, tools, techniques, and the good business practices that make a landscaping business pay. Full-size reproducible forms. 220 pages, 8½x11", illus., index, bibliog., $21.95.

***The Poison Ivy, Oak & Sumac Book: A Short Natural History and Cautionary Account,* by Thomas E. Anderson.** For the first time, color photographs of each North American species of this noxious family of plants in different seasons. Full of little-known historical, medical, and botanical facts. 138 pages, 6x9", illus., index, anno. bibliog., $14.95.

Send your check or money order to
      Acton Circle Publishing Co.
      P.O. Box 1564
      Ukiah, CA 95482

Enclosed is $_____ for _____ copy(ies) of

_____ $_____

and $_____ for _____ copy(ies) of

_____ $_____

Shipping/Handling ($1.50 1st book; $0.75 others)* $_____
CA residents add 7.25% sales tax $_____

      Total $_____

Name_____
Street_____Apt._____
City_____State_____ZIP_____

* Or Postal First Class, $3.00 per book.
  You may return any book for a full refund, no questions asked.

Copy this page to order